PENGUIN  CLASSICS

GENERAL EDITOR, POETRY: CHRISTOPHER RICKS

SELECTED POEMS: JOHN MILTON

JOHN MILTON was born in 1608, the son of a scrivener (a notary and moneylender). He was educated by private tutors and attended St Paul's School and Christ's College, Cambridge. He left Cambridge in 1632 and spent the next six years in scholarly retirement. *A Masque* and *Lycidas* belong to this period. Following his Italian journey (1638–9), he took up the cause of Presbyterianism in a series of hard-hitting anti-prelatical pamphlets (1641–2). His divorce pamphlets (1643–5), written after his first wife had temporarily deserted him, earned him much notoriety and contributed to his breach with the Presbyterians. In 1649 he took up the cause of the new Commonwealth. As Secretary for Foreign Tongues to the Council of State, he defended the English Revolution both in English and Latin – and sacrificed his eyesight in the process. He risked his life by publishing *The Ready and Easy Way to Establish a Free Commonwealth* on the eve of the Restoration (1660). His great poems were published after this political defeat. A ten-book version of *Paradise Lost* appeared in 1667, and *Paradise Regained* and *Samson Agonistes* were published together in 1671. An expanded version of his shorter poems (first published in 1646) was brought out in 1673, and the twelve-book *Paradise Lost* appeared in 1674, the year of his death.

JOHN LEONARD has taught at the universities of Cambridge, Ottawa and Western Ontario. He has published widely on Milton, and his book *Naming in Paradise* (1990) was a co-winner of the Milton Society's James Holly Hanford Award. He is a Professor of English at the University of Western Ontario, where he has taught since 1987.

Samson Agonistes   214

Acknowledgements

In preparing this edition I have received valuable help and guidance from many learned colleagues, as well as from graduate and undergraduate students at the University of Western Ontario. I owe a special debt of gratitude to Gordon Campbell, John Carey, John Creaser, Roy Flannagan, Alastair Fowler, William Kerrigan, Christopher Ricks, John Rumrich and Gordon Teskey, both for their own work as editors and for their advice on numerous points of detail. I have also received generous assistance from Christopher Brown, Gardner Campbell, Ann Coiro, Dennis Danielson, Stephen Fallon, Richard Green, Lynne Greenberg, John Hale, Margaret Kidnie, Paul Klemp, Douglas Kneale, Al Labriola, the late Jeremy Maule, Diane McColley, the late Earl Miner, John Mulryan, Jane Robertson, Alan Rudrum, Dick Shroyer and Archie Young. Any errors are my responsibility alone. My work has been assisted by a grant from the Social Sciences and Humanities Research Council of Canada. To the Council I extend my sincerest thanks.

Chronology

1608 9 *December*: John Milton born in Bread Street, Cheapside, London, eldest son of John Milton, scrivener and musician.

1615 24 *November*: Brother Christopher born.

1620 (?) Enters St Paul's School, London.

1625 12 *February*: Matriculates at Christ's College, Cambridge.

27 *March*: Charles I becomes king.

1626 Probably rusticated (suspended) from Cambridge for part of the Lent term.

1629 *March*: BA degree.

December: 'On the Morning of Christ's Nativity' composed.

1632 *On Shakespeare* published in second Shakespeare folio.

July: MA degree.

1632–4 Life of scholarly retirement at family home in Hammersmith.

1634 29 *September*: A Masque (*Comus*) performed at Ludlow Castle.

1635–8 Life of scholarly retirement at family home in Horton, Bucks.

1637 *A Masque* published.

3 *April*: Mother dies.

30 *June*: John Bastwick, Henry Burton and William Prynne lose their ears for writing anti-prelatical pamphlets. They are confined in prison ships on the Irish Sea throughout the autumn.

10 August: Milton's classmate Edward King drowns in the Irish Sea.

November: 'Lycidas' written.

1638–9 Travels in Italy.

1638 'Lycidas' published in a volume of elegies for Edward King.

August: Charles Diodati, Milton's closest friend, dies.

1639 *March*: First Bishops' War with Scotland.

1639–40 Settles in London, where he takes pupils, including his nephews Edward and John Phillips.

1640 *3 November*: Charles convenes Long Parliament.

1641 Rebellion in Ireland. Publication of Milton's first anti-prelatical tracts: *Of Reformation*, *Of Prelatical Episcopacy*, *Animadversions upon the Remonstrant's Defence*.

1642 *May–June*: Marries Mary Powell, who leaves him a month or two later.

22 August: Civil War begins. More anti-prelatical pamphlets: *The Reason of Church Government*, *Apology for Smectymnuus*.

October?: Sends for Mary without success.

1643 *1 August*: *Doctrine and Discipline of Divorce* (first edition).

1644 *2 February*: *Doctrine and Discipline of Divorce* (second edition). Thomas Young, Milton's old tutor, warns Parliament against advocates of 'digamy'. Herbert Palmer denounces Milton in a sermon before Parliament. Further attacks from the Stationers' Company, from Prynne and other Presbyterians.

5 June: *Of Education*.

6 August: *Judgement of Martin Bucer Concerning Divorce*.

24 November: *Areopagitica*.

28 December: Milton summoned before the House of Lords, but soon dismissed.

1645 *4 March*: Publication of more divorce tracts, *Tetrachordon* and *Colasterion*.

14 June: New Model Army victorious at Naseby.

July or August: Wife returns.

1646 *2 January*: *Poems of Mr John Milton* published (dated 1645).

29 July: Daughter Anne born.

1647 *13 March*: Father dies.

1648 *25 October*: Daughter Mary born.

6 December: Colonel Pride purges Parliament, paving the way for trial of Charles I.

1649 *30 January*: Charles I executed.

13 February: *The Tenure of Kings and Magistrates*.

15 March: Council of State appoints Milton Secretary for Foreign Tongues.

11 May: Salmasius's *Defensio Regia* appears in England.

16 May: *Observations on the Articles of Peace*.

6 October: *Eikonoklastes* (Milton's answer to *Eikon Basilike*).

1651 *24 February*: *Pro Populo Anglicano Defensio* (Milton's answer to Salmasius).

16 March: Son John born.

1652 *February*: Becomes totally blind.

2 May: Daughter Deborah born. First wife dies three days later.

June: Son John dies.

1653 *20 April*: Cromwell forcibly dissolves Rump Parliament.

3 September: Salmasius dies.

12 December: Cromwell becomes Lord Protector.

1654 *30 May*: *Defensio Secunda*.

1655 *8 August*: *Defensio Pro Se*.

1656 *12 November*: Marries Katherine Woodcock.

1657 *19 October*: Daughter Katherine born (she dies six months later).

1658 *3 February*: Second wife dies.

3 September: Cromwell dies.

1659 *16 February*: *A Treatise of Civil Power* registered.

24 May: Richard Cromwell abdicates.

August: *Considerations Touching the Likeliest Means to Remove Hirelings out of the Church* published.

1660 *21 February*: Long Parliament restored.

3 March: *The Ready and Easy Way to Establish a Free Commonwealth* published.

April: *Brief Notes upon a Late Sermon* published.

29 May: Charles II enters London in triumph. Milton now in hiding.

29 August: Act of Indemnity. Milton not excluded, but his books are burned by the hangman soon after.

October?: Milton arrested and imprisoned until December.

1662 Sir Henry Vane executed. Milton's sonnet to Vane published.

1663 *24 February*: Marries Elizabeth Minshull.

1665 *June?*: Takes house in Chalfont St Giles to escape the plague.

1666 *2–6 September*: Great Fire of London.

1667 *August?*: *Paradise Lost* published in a ten-book version.

1670 *The History of Britain* published.

1671 *Paradise Regained* and *Samson Agonistes* published.

1673 *Of True Religion* published. Revised and enlarged edition of *Poems* (1645) published.

1674 Second (twelve-book) edition of *Paradise Lost*. Milton dies on or about 8 November.

Introduction

MILTON'S LIFE AND TIMES

John Milton lived through one of the most tumultuous periods of English history, a period comprising the Civil War, the trial and execution of Charles I, the constitutional experiments of the Commonwealth and Protectorate, and the eventual Restoration of the monarchy under Charles II. Milton never took up arms in this conflict, but he contributed many pugnacious pamphlets, and he was willing to risk his life when, on the eve of the Restoration in 1660, he dared to speak out in a last desperate plea for the freedom the English people had fought so hard to attain and which they were about to throw away.

Milton had not always held radical views. He was born on 9 December 1608, in London, into a prosperous Puritan family. His father was a scrivener, a profession that combined the functions of moneylender, investment broker and notary. Milton was born in the family home in Bread Street, Cheapside. He was John and Sarah Milton's eldest son. John Milton senior was a cultured man, a musician and a composer, so Milton the poet grew up in a house that cherished music. The love of music was to stay with him all his life: in old age, when he suffered from gout, he would play the organ and sing to relieve his pain.

The young Milton was provided with the very best education. He was taught by private tutors at home, and at some time between 1615 and 1620 his father sent him to St Paul's School, one of the best schools in England. It abutted St Paul's Cathedral, so the boys were likely to have heard the poet John Donne preach there after he was appointed Dean of St Paul's in 1621. Milton learned Greek, Latin and Hebrew at school, and his private tutors gave him further instruction in these languages, as well as in French and Italian. He was admitted to Christ's College, Cambridge, in 1625, when he was seventeen, but his university career did not start propitiously. The biographer John Aubrey (1626–97) tells us that Milton fell out with his first tutor, William Chappell, who whipped him, after which he was briefly 'rusticated' (suspended) from the university. Readmitted, he was assigned a new tutor, Nathaniel Tovey, and his academic career flourished. While at Cambridge, the young Milton wrote two Latin epitaphs on bishops, those stalwart pillars of the seventeenth-century establishment. Some have inferred from this that he was at home in and with the Church of England. This conclusion is lent some support by the early poem 'Il Penseroso', which contains a warm description of Anglican worship, and by the fact that Milton, like other graduating students, had to sign a written declaration acknowledging the doctrines of the Church of England and the supremacy of the king. But we should not assume that Milton was untouched by religious or political dissent in these early years. In his Latin poem 'Elegia Quarta', written in about 1627 when he was not quite twenty, he sternly criticizes the Anglican Church for driving Puritan ministers into exile.

Milton's parents had intended him to be a minister in the Anglican Church and his entire education had been a preparation for this. He had shared the same aspiration, but his disillusionment with the Church of England was such that he could not bring himself to take holy orders when he left Cambridge in 1632. Instead, he spent the next six years in scholarly retirement, living off his father, then (still at his father's expense) he rounded out his education with a Grand Tour of Italy (1638–9). 'He who would take Orders,' Milton wrote in *The Reason of Church Government* (1642), 'must subscribe slave'.[1] Milton had most likely held reservations about the Anglican Church since his early youth, but ecclesiastical controversy had become more heated in the 1630s. Charles I ruled without Parliament between 1629 and 1640, a period that his enemies called the 'Eleven Year Tyranny'. This was not a safe time in which to voice criticism of the Crown or the Church. William Laud, appointed Archbishop of Canterbury in 1633, introduced innovations that smacked of Catholicism to the resentful Puritans. He also used the hated Court of Star Chamber to enforce conformity. Some outspoken pamphleteers had their ears cut off for speaking ill of bishops. We should remember this when reading the anti-ecclesiastical passages in 'Lycidas', which was written just a few weeks after the most notorious of these mutilations – the cropping of the ears of John Bastwick, Henry Burton and William Prynne on 30 June 1637. Laud's attempts to impose uniformity of worship precipitated the slide into civil war.

Milton had planned to cross to Sicily and Greece after his Italian tour, but the outbreak of hostilities at home caused him to abandon this plan – or so he claimed fifteen years later in his Latin *Defensio Secunda* (1654), written to justify the king's execution. 'The sad tidings of civil war from England', he then wrote, 'summoned me back. For I thought it base that I should travel abroad at my ease for the cultivation of my mind, while my fellow-citizens at home were fighting for liberty.'[2] Milton has sometimes been mocked for the pretentiousness of this claim. Samuel Johnson (an arch-Tory who denigrated Milton as 'an acrimonious and surly republican') wrote in 1779: 'Let not our veneration for Milton forbid us to look with some degree of merriment on great promises and small performance, on the man who hastens home because his countrymen are contending for their liberty, and when he reaches the scene of action, vapours away his patriotism in a private boarding-school.' Johnson has a point. One might have expected Milton to have played a more active role on his return to England. Instead, he turned to teaching and took in a few private pupils, including his own nephews.

But he was not politically idle during these years. He entered the fray in 1641, when he threw in his lot with the Presbyterians, who were seeking extensive church reform. Milton has sometimes been criticized for voicing his opinions only when it was safe to do so, after Charles had been forced to convene the Long Parliament in November 1640. It is true that Milton's first anti-prelatical pamphlet, *Of Reformation*, did not appear until May 1641, but this was the culmination of several years of intense study.

Civil war broke out in England on 22 August 1642. In May or June of that year the thirty-three-year-old Milton had travelled from London to Oxfordshire to collect a debt for his father. He returned a month later without the money, but with a wife, having married Mary Powell, the debtor's daughter. At seventeen, she was half Milton's age. The marriage was not happy (at least not in its beginning) and after about a month Mary asked permission to return to her father's house for the remaining part of the summer. Milton permitted her to go, on condition that she return by Michaelmas (29 September). Meanwhile, war broke out. Mary's family were Royalists, while Milton was ardently supportive of Parliament. This divide did not bode well for the couple's happiness, and Mary did not return as agreed. Milton sent several letters imploring her to return, but all went unanswered. He then sent a messenger, who was rudely dismissed. In the following year Milton created a scandal by publishing his most notorious pamphlet to date, *The Doctrine and Discipline of Divorce*. His basic argument in this work is that divorce should be permitted on grounds of incompatibility. This seems innocuous to many people today, but it created a scandal in 1643. The Presbyterians, Milton's erstwhile allies against the bishops, were horrified and Milton soon fell out with them, never to be reconciled (though his wife eventually returned to him in 1645).

The rift between Milton and the Presbyterians grew even wider after the execution of King Charles on 30 January 1649. The Presbyterians had begun the war fighting against the king, but their aim had never been regicide. Oliver Cromwell and the more radical Parliamentarian army officers had to purge Parliament of its moderate members before the trial and execution could proceed. Milton approved of these acts, and defended them in *The Tenure of Kings and Magistrates* (1649), published just two weeks after the king's death. In this tract he vilifies the Presbyterians as backsliders. Appointed Secretary for Foreign Tongues by the Council of State, he went on to

defend the new regime both at home and abroad, in English
and Latin, winning both fame and notoriety in his pamphlet
war with the Protestant French scholar Salmasius, who had
espoused the cause of the Stuart monarchy. During these years
Milton's eyesight deteriorated to the point that he became
totally blind in 1652. His wife Mary died a few weeks after he
lost his sight, leaving him with three daughters (one newborn)
and an infant son, who died a few weeks later. In November
1656 Milton married his second wife, Katherine Woodcock,
whom he dearly loved, but she died in February 1658, closely
followed by her infant daughter. Most critics have thought
that Milton wrote his great sonnet, 'Methought I saw my late
espousèd saint', in response to his loss of Katherine. The sonnet
describes a dream in which Milton's wife returns to him after
death. She wears a veil – presumably because her blind husband
had never seen her face. Just as she is about to embrace him
– and lift her veil – he awakes to blindness and disillusion:
'I waked, she fled, and day brought back my night' (14).

Disillusion was to torment Milton in his later years. The
Restoration of the monarchy in 1660 was a particularly bitter
blow: at one stroke, it shattered all of his hopes for England
and undid everything he had worked for in the past twenty
years. He had put politics before poetry for most of this time.
So far as we know, he wrote no original poems (except for a
few sonnets) between 1637, when he wrote 'Lycidas', and about
1658, when he began to work in earnest on *Paradise Lost*. He
did not abandon his poetic ambitions during these years; he
delayed fulfilling his vocation while he attended to what he
believed were more pressing matters. On the very eve of the
Restoration he was willing to risk his life (and his unfinished
masterpiece) by publishing *The Ready and Easy Way to Estab-
lish a Free Commonwealth* – his passionate plea to his fellow
countrymen not to throw away their hard-won liberty. The plea
fell on deaf ears and Milton came close to suffering a traitor's
death. Several of his friends and erstwhile colleagues were
hanged, disembowelled and quartered. Even the dead were not
safe: in 1661 the corpses of Oliver Cromwell and two others
who had judged Charles I were exhumed from their graves and

beheaded in a grisly public spectacle. It is likely that Milton
alludes to these events in *Samson Agonistes*, when the Chorus
(ostensibly referring to Old Testament heroes, but with an
eye on recent English history) complains that God too often
abandons his loyal servants, leaving them

> to the hostile sword
> Of heathen and profane, their carcasses
> To dogs and fowls a prey, or else captíved:
> Or to th' unjust tribunals, under change of times,
> And condemnation of the ingrateful multitude. (692–96)

Milton went into hiding while the (now Royalist) House of
Commons discussed the question of which of the king's former
enemies should die. He was arrested and imprisoned, and copies
of his books were burned by the public hangman. We do not
know how he managed to escape with his life. He doubtless
owed much to the intervention of influential friends, such as
the poet Andrew Marvell (1621–78), MP for Hull and Milton's
former assistant as Latin Secretary to Cromwell's Council of
State. Milton's blindness might also have helped to save him,
for Royalist propagandists could (and did) triumphantly point
to it as a sign that he had been punished by God. This argument
meant that he was more useful to the Royalist cause alive than
dead.

Milton married his third wife, Elizabeth Minshull, in 1663,
by which time relations with his three surviving daughters (all
by Mary Powell) had become strained. If these final years of
Milton's life were characterized by political disappointment
and domestic unhappiness, they were also the time in which
his lifelong poetical ambitions at last bore fruit. He published
Paradise Lost in 1667, and *Paradise Regained* and *Samson
Agonistes* in 1671. A revised edition of his shorter poems (many
of which had been published in an earlier edition, dated 1645)
appeared in 1673. In 1674 he published the second edition of
Paradise Lost. Where the original 1667 version had consisted
of ten books, for this second edition Milton split the original
Books VII and X into two, thus creating a twelve-book epic on

the model of Virgil's *Aeneid*. He died in November 1674 in his
house in Bunhill Fields. His friend Cyriack Skinner relates that
'hee dy'd in a fitt of the Gout, but with so little pain or Emotion,
that the time of his expiring was not perceiv'd by those in the
room'.[3]

THE POEMS

Milton wrote his first great poem, 'On the Morning of Christ's
Nativity', in the early hours of Christmas Day 1629, when he
was twenty-one. He clearly thought it a significant landmark in
his poetic career, for he placed it first in both his 1645 and
1673 *Poems*. It is now commonly referred to as 'the Nativity
Ode', but Milton never called it that, and the familiar title is in
some ways misleading. The poem does refer to itself as a 'humble
ode' (24), but the ensuing twenty-seven stanzas (the bulk of the
poem) are designated 'The Hymn'. Odes differ from hymns in
that the former are addressed to men, the latter to gods, or God.
Since Jesus is both man and God, we have as much reason to
call the poem 'the Nativity Hymn' as 'the Nativity Ode'. The
ambiguity – ode or hymn – goes to the heart of the mystery of the
Incarnation, which is a significant part of the poem's subject.

The final third of 'The Hymn' describes the banishment of the
pagan gods. Following a tradition dating from early Christian
times, Milton identifies pagan deities with devils. Some of these
(such as Moloch, with his cult of child-sacrifice) are unappeal-
ing and we may suppose that Milton was glad to see them go,
but a note of regret is audible when he describes the banishment
of Apollo from Delphi (176–8) or the exile of the 'yellow-
skirted fays' from their 'moon-loved maze' (235–6). The sense
of loss is most poignant in stanza XX:

> The lonely mountains o'er,
> And the resounding shore,
>   A voice of weeping heard, and loud lament;
> From haunted spring, and dale
> Edged with poplar pale,

> The parting Genius is with sighing sent,
> With flow'r-inwoven tresses torn
> The nymphs in twilight shade of tangled thickets
>   mourn. (181–8)

Editors since the eighteenth century have detected in this 'voice of weeping' an echo of Herod's slaughter of the innocents: 'In Rama was there a voice heard, lamentation, and weeping' (Matt. 2:18). Are we to infer that the banished devils are innocent? This may be going too far, but the cries of grief are incongruous in a supposedly joyful Christian hymn. The inevitable result of this incongruity is moral ambivalence.

Such ambivalence is present not only at the end of the poem; it is also found earlier, when the angels sing. Their music is so beautiful that it briefly raises the hope that nothing else is necessary to restore lost Paradise. As so often in Milton, however, hope is dashed with a 'But':

> But wisest Fate says no,
> This must not yet be so,
>   The babe lies yet in smiling infancy,
> That on the bitter cross
> Must redeem our loss. (149–53)

The question 'Why?' inevitably presents itself. Why should God permit suffering if he can restore lost Paradise with music? Moments like this have led some readers to wonder whether Milton had mixed feelings about Christianity and the paganism that it supplanted. Readers must decide for themselves where Milton's deepest sympathies lie in his first great English poem. Whatever we decide, it is clear that 'On the Morning of Christ's Nativity' anticipates the probing questions of *Paradise Lost*.

Milton's poems often express, or at least explore, a division of loyalties. This is most evident in 'L'Allegro' and 'Il Penseroso', the companion poems written early in Milton's career, probably in the 1630s. The titles respectively mean 'the cheerful man' and 'the contemplative man'. There are many exact parallels and oppositions between the two poems, beginning with the ten-line preludes in which Mirth rejects Melancholy ('L'Allegro', 1–10) and Melancholy rejects Mirth ('Il Penseroso', 1–10). Critical opinion is divided as to whether the poems are crafted so as to present two carefully balanced alternatives, neither of which prevails, or whether 'Il Penseroso' emerges triumphant. Much depends on whether the Melancholy rejected by 'L'Allegro' is the same as that welcomed by 'Il Penseroso'. The joys hailed by 'L'Allegro' closely resemble the joys that 'Il Penseroso' calls 'deluding' (1), but it is less certain whether the two poems are talking about the same kind of melancholy. The melancholy rejected by 'L'Allegro' is that of the Greek physician Galen. Milton's contemporary, Robert Burton (1577–1640), author of *The Anatomy of Melancholy* (1621), had associated this kind of melancholy with madness and depression. The Melancholy of 'Il Penseroso', however, is that of Aristotelian medicine, which the Florentine Platonist Marsilio Ficino (1433–99) had associated with poetic and prophetic inspiration. Ficino's melancholy would appeal to a poet of Milton's high seriousness. 'Il Penseroso' enjoys two further advantages over 'L'Allegro': it is given more words (176 lines as opposed to 152), and it is given the last word. Milton was nevertheless a poet of the senses who in his prose tract *Of Education* (1644) averred that poetry should be 'simple, sensuous and passionate'. His poems often seek to control sensuousness, but they do not reject it outright.

In *A Masque Presented at Ludlow Castle* we see the first appearance of what will be the major theme of Milton's mature poems – the theme of temptation. *A Masque* was written to celebrate the formal inauguration of John Egerton, Earl of Bridgewater, as President of Wales and the Marches. It was performed before the Earl and his guests at Ludlow Castle in Shropshire on 29 September 1634. The roles of the Lady and her two brothers were played by the Earl's daughter Alice, aged fifteen, and her brothers John, Viscount Brackley, aged eleven, and Lord Thomas Egerton, aged nine. Henry Lawes, the children's music tutor, composed the music for the songs and played the role of Attendant Spirit. Lawes was Milton's friend, so it was probably he who invited Milton to write the text.

A Masque has been known since the late seventeenth century as *Comus*, though Milton himself did not give it that title. Both the familiar and the authentic titles are problematic. The familiar title *Comus* gives too central and exalted a status to the villain. But *A Masque* is also something of a misnomer, for the work is not a representative Stuart masque. In traditional court masques, music and spectacle predominate over plot and character. Milton's masque places unprecedented importance on dramatic dialogue and so is perhaps better described as a pastoral drama. It nevertheless includes some traditional masque elements. Following Jonson, Milton includes an 'anti-masque' in the revels of Comus and his bestial followers. He also retains the processional quality of a court masque in his story of the children's journey to Ludlow. Court masques were intended to compliment their royal or aristocratic audiences, who would often be included in the action, sometimes as the recipients of a direct eulogy, sometimes as participants in a concluding dance. The climax of Milton's masque is the presentation of the three children to their father, who would have been conspicuously seated in the audience. The children resemble conventional aristocratic masquers in that they play idealized versions of themselves.

The story is simple, though its meaning and significance have been much debated. Comus is a pagan god invented by Milton: the son of Bacchus, god of wine, and Circe, the immortal sorceress who turns Odysseus's men into swine in Homer's *Odyssey*. Like his mother, Comus waylays unsuspecting travellers and tempts them to drink his magic liquor. The faces of those who do drink are magically transformed to those of beasts. The Lady, having become separated from her brothers in a wood, meets the disguised Comus, who offers to lead her to safety. Instead he leads her to his palace, where he throws off his disguise and offers her his cup. In a long and eloquent speech he urges the Lady to partake of the earth's riches and (in particular) to 'be not cozened / With that same vaunted name Virginity' (737–8). The Lady speaks earnestly in virginity's defence, and Comus is temporarily discomfited. The Lady's brothers then rush in and drive Comus from the stage – but neglect to seize his wand. The Lady is left silent and immobilized on Comus's magic chair. The Attendant Spirit then invokes Sabrina, goddess of the river Severn, who releases the Lady, though all three children remain silent when the Attendant Spirit presents them to their parents.

This story is obviously allegorical, but its significance is unclear. Just what is meant by 'Virginity'? Some have inferred that the youthful Milton had taken a vow of lifelong sexual abstinence when he wrote the masque, but in Puritan usage 'virginity' could include married chastity, so it is not certain that the Lady intends to remain unmarried for her whole life. Her immobility and silence after Comus's exit have provoked much debate. Is she frozen by Comus's magic or her own? Freudian commentators have suggested that she is frozen by her own repressed desires, but Comus had threatened to freeze her if she did not drink (659–62) and the fact that she is frozen suggests that he has acted on his threat. The Attendant Spirit says that she is immobilized by 'the clasping charm' and 'the numbing spell' (853). The 'clasping charm', imposed by Comus's chair, prevents the Lady from rising to her feet, but it does not completely immobilize her or prevent her from speaking. The more potent 'numbing spell' freezes the Lady like 'a statue' (661). Comus presumably casts 'the numbing spell' by waving his wand just before the brothers drive him offstage – but there is no explicit stage direction to this effect, so readers are free to imagine that the Lady is frozen by some other force. One of the key decisions a director must make in a modern stage production is whether or not to have Comus wave his wand before exiting.

A persuasive tempter, Comus has charmed many critics. He speaks some of the loveliest lines in the poem, and many have felt that he wins his argument with the Lady. Critics in the mid-twentieth century often dismissed both the Lady and Milton as nay-saying prigs. In recent years, however, the Lady has been defended by feminist commentators, some of whom have likened her to a victim of sexual assault. Comus's temptation of the Lady is certainly different from Satan's temptation of Eve. Unlike Eve, the Lady is not free to walk away from her tempter. It may be significant that the words 'tempt', 'tempter' and 'temptation' never appear in *A Masque*, though they are common in *Paradise Lost*, *Paradise Regained* and *Samson Agonistes*.

'Lycidas', the greatest of Milton's short poems, is a pastoral elegy, a form established in the third century BC when Theocritus composed his lament for Daphnis (*Idyll* 1). The most famous English examples before Milton were Edmund Spenser's *Astrophel* (1595, a lament for Sir Philip Sidney) and Spenser's November eclogue in *The Shepheardes Calender* (1579). 'Lycidas' includes many of the traditional features of pastoral elegy, such as the procession of mourners and the lament of nature, but it omits the refrain which was prominent in ancient examples of the form.

The immediate occasion of 'Lycidas' was the premature death of Edward King, a former classmate of Milton's at Cambridge, who drowned in the Irish Sea on 10 August 1637. His body was never recovered. The poem was first published in a commemorative volume of Latin, Greek and English obsequies, *Justa Edouardo King naufrago* (1638). 'Lycidas' was placed last of the English poems, perhaps in recognition of its superior quality. Milton was probably not close to Edward King, whose political and religious opinions differed from his own; but 'Lycidas' is not only about King. Milton's further subject is the meaning and purpose of human life when mortality can cut it short at any moment. Like Milton, King had poetic ambitions and a vocation to serve the Church. His premature death prompted Milton to reflect upon his own lofty ambitions and unfulfilled promise. What would Milton's own life amount to if he too were cut off in his prime?

> Alas! What boots it with uncessant care
> To tend the homely slighted shepherd's trade,
> And strictly meditate the thankless Muse? (64–6)

The 'shepherd's trade' signifies both the writing of poetry and the service of God as a clergyman. This latter sense was of course alien to pagan pastoral, but Christian poets were able to combine classical decorum with biblical metaphors of good and bad shepherds so as to turn pastoral into a vehicle for anti-ecclesiastical satire. Petrarch, Mantuan and Spenser had used pastoral eclogues in this way, and Milton does too, most notably in St Peter's 'digression' excoriating false ministers in the Church of England (113–31). The Laudian censorship was still strong in 1637, so Milton had to word his criticisms carefully. The headnote in which he congratulates himself for foretelling 'the ruin of our corrupted clergy then in their height' was added only in 1645 after the Laudian Church had collapsed.

Milton began *Paradise Lost* in about 1658 and finished it in about 1663, but the poem's roots lie deep in his youth. His lifelong ambition had been to write an epic, and he had also wanted to re-create the story of the Fall of Man. His original intent had been to write an epic on an ancient British subject, and to present the story of the Fall as a tragedy. Several brief drafts for such a tragedy, probably dating from the early 1640s, survive in a manuscript at Trinity College, Cambridge. At some later date Milton decided that the subject he had intended for a tragedy was better suited to an epic. He was 'long choosing, and beginning late' (IX, 26), but he eventually matched the right subject with the right genre. War, the traditional epic subject, did not suit his poetic temperament or his exalted notions of moral heroism. *Paradise Lost* includes some fighting (Book VI describes the War in Heaven), but its main action is very simple: two people eat an apple in a garden. This would have seemed absurd to Virgil. Even the Christian poet Torquato Tasso (1544–95) had chosen a military subject (the First Crusade) for his epic *Gerusalemme Liberata* (*Jerusalem Delivered*) (1580). Rejecting this long tradition, Milton writes a wholly new kind of epic – one that aims to redefine heroic values.

Paradise Lost is paradoxically more dramatic for not being confined to the limits of a drama. The drafts in the Trinity Manuscript follow the classic limitation to a single place and time. The epic form gave Milton a licence to cover vast tracts of space and time. Spatially, the action ranges over the whole earth, throughout the universe, and beyond our universe to Heaven, Chaos and Hell. The action extends back in time to depict events before the creation of our universe, and forward to the Final Judgement and beyond. This cosmic sweep would have been impossible in a drama. Had Milton stuck with his plan to present the Fall on stage he would have faced another insuperable obstacle. Adam and Eve could not have appeared naked. Milton would have had either to garb them in flesh-coloured robes or keep them offstage until after the Fall. The epic form allowed him to portray Adam and Eve before, during and after their Fall, and to make 'naked majesty' (IV, 290) a major theme of his poem. This was a bold decision and we should not take it for granted.

Milton's decision to portray Adam and Eve before the Fall gave him great freedom but it also presented difficulties. One of these was how to present (or even imagine) a state of innocence. Many first-time readers of *Paradise Lost* expect innocence to be identical with inexperience. If we approach the poem with that assumption we will misread a number of key episodes. Chief among these are the newly created Eve's attraction to her own reflection in a lake (IV, 449–91), her dream of eating the apple (V, 28–94), unfallen Adam's passion for Eve (VIII, 521–611), and Adam and Eve's argument about working separately (IX, 205–384). Each of these episodes (two of which are included in the present edition) teases us with the possibility that Adam and Eve are somehow 'fallen before the Fall'. The easy inference is either that Milton has botched his job (sinlessness being difficult to portray) or that he is unconsciously impugning God by implying that he created Adam and Eve with a fatal flaw. But easy inferences are dangerous, especially in *Paradise Lost*, which repeatedly challenges us to refine our first impressions. Milton's God did not place Adam and Eve in Paradise with the intention of keeping them there for ever. They are on probation. God's intent is that they should work their way up to Heaven by a slow process of trial. The crucial point is that Adam and Eve are free to make mistakes, and it is part of God's design that they should grow by learning from these. The only fatal error is to eat the apple God told them not to eat. The point about such episodes as Eve's attraction to her own reflection, therefore, is not that they lead inevitably to the

Fall, but that they provide Adam and Eve with an opportunity
to learn and grow.

Milton's declared purpose in *Paradise Lost* is to 'justify the
ways of God to men' (I, 26). God's justice was a major concern
for Milton, who chose for his greatest poems subjects that
called God's justice into question. We have seen an instance of
this in *Lycidas*, with its urgent questions as to why a good
God would permit his servants to suffer premature death. The
question of God's justice will recur in the tragedy *Samson
Agonistes*, where the chorus affirm: 'Just are the ways of God, /
And justifiable to men' (293–4). But does Milton succeed in
justifying the Christian God? Many have thought that he fails,
and many have thought that he was presumptuous even to try.

Milton sets himself a hard task in *Paradise Lost* – one that
some Christians wish he had left well alone. He sets out to
convince his readers that it is beautiful and just that they and
all of humankind should die (and most people suffer torment
in Hell for all eternity) because two people ate an apple in
Mesopotamia some thousands of years ago. For Milton, the
question of God's justice is compellingly urgent, not just an
academic issue of literary criticism. A sense of moral urgency
also characterizes the best of Milton's critics, whether they be
Christian apologists, like C. S. Lewis, or foes of Christianity,
like Percy Bysshe Shelley in the nineteenth century and William
Empson in the twentieth. Empson famously quipped that 'the
reason why the poem is so good is that it makes God so bad'.[4]
Empson, like Shelley before him, thought Christianity a wicked
religion, and its God 'the wickedest thing yet invented by the
black heart of man' (p. 251). If Empson is right about Christian-
ity, Milton might deserve our gratitude for failing to justify the
Christian God – even though Milton himself would not have
been grateful for Empson's backhanded praise.

Many readers have had misgivings about Milton's depiction
of Satan and God. William Blake, in *The Marriage of Heaven
and Hell* (c. 1790–93), coined the most famous and provocative
aphorism about Milton's Satan: 'The reason Milton wrote in
fetters when he wrote of Angels & God, and at liberty when of
Devils & Hell, is because he was a true poet & of the Devils

party without knowing it'. Blake's precise meaning is a matter of some dispute, but his brief comment has become a rallying call for those who suspect that Milton's deepest sympathies in *Paradise Lost* lie with Satan. This suspicion is not (as critics of God's party often claim) merely silly. *Paradise Lost* is, among other things, a poem about a civil war. As such, it inevitably invites us to think of the English Civil War, which occupied so much of Milton's time and energy. The difficulty is that Milton's declared loyalties in the poem are the opposite of what we might expect, given his politics. Milton had championed the revolutionary cause in England, applauding the new republic for having the courage to depose and execute a tyrant. In his poem he takes the side of 'Heav'n's awful Monarch' (IV, 960). Readers have long wrestled with the question of why an anti-monarchist and defender of regicide would have chosen a subject that obliged him to defend monarchy. C. S. Lewis addresses, and swiftly dismisses, this question in his influential book *A Preface to 'Paradise Lost'* (1942). Arguing from the principle that 'the goodness, happiness, and dignity of every being consists in obeying its natural superior and ruling its natural inferiors', Lewis contends that there is no contradiction between Milton's poem and his politics, since God is Milton's 'natural superior', while Charles Stuart is not.[5] Charles was merely playing God; God *is* God.[5] Milton is therefore consistent in arguing that we should obey God and disobey Charles. Within its own terms, this is a satisfying answer, but it fails to engage with the sheer emotive power of Satan's revolutionary rhetoric.

Milton's Satan is certainly charismatic. His manly beauty and commanding presence are a surprise to readers who expect to see the familiar monstrous figure with horns and cloven feet. Milton's Satan is a ruined Archangel, shining still, though with 'faded splendour wan' (IV, 870). His resplendent glory is arguably even more appealing for being partly extinguished:

> he above the rest
> In shape and gesture proudly eminent
> Stood like a tow'r; his form had yet not lost

> All her original brightness, nor appeared
> Less than Archangel ruined, and th' excess
> Of glory obscured: as when the sun new ris'n
> Looks through the horizontal misty air
> Shorn of his beams, or from behind the moon
> In dim eclipse disastrous twilight sheds
> On half the nations, and with fear of change
> Perplexes monarchs. (I, 589–99)

Milton's Satan is not the Prince of Darkness but the Prince of Twilight. William Wordsworth (1770–1850) did not share the moral admiration for Satan felt by many other Romantic poets, but even he was bewitched by these lines. William Hazlitt (1778–1830) recalls that Wordsworth would read the lines 'till he felt a certain faintness come over his mind from a sense of beauty and grandeur'.[6]

It is not just Satan's physical appearance that seduces many readers. He also moves us with his finer sensibilities. The sight of his loyal followers in Hell moves him to tears, 'Tears such as angels weep' (I, 620). His first impulse on seeing Adam and Eve in Paradise is to love them (IV, 363), and he almost abandons his quest to destroy humankind when he is temporarily enraptured by the sight of Eve's innocent beauty (IX, 459f.). It is possible to dismiss such moments as instances of Satanic hypocrisy, but to do that is to cheapen the poem. Satan may harden his heart, but at least he has a heart to harden. Milton's Satan is one of the great tragic figures in English literature, and we do Milton as well as Satan an injustice if we do not acknowledge this.

Satan's appeal does not rest solely on heroics. Some of his most probing questions occur not in his great public orations, but in the seemingly casual asides that arise unprompted from his lips, often in soliloquy. Shortly after arriving in Paradise, the disguised Satan approaches Adam and Eve in order to overhear their conversation. When he hears Adam recount the terms of the prohibition, his immediate and spontaneous response takes the reader by surprise:

> all is not theirs it seems:
> One fatal Tree there stands of Knowledge called,
> Forbidden them to taste: knowledge forbidd'n?
> Suspicious, reasonless. Why should their Lord
> Envy them that? Can it be sin to know,
> Can it be death? (IV, 513–18)

It would be rash to assume that Satan here has humankind's best interests at heart. He at once goes on to express glee at the opportunity God's prohibition gives him ('O fair foundation laid whereon to build / Their ruin!'). But this does not remove all the ethical difficulties. Satan may be a wicked opportunist, but he is also genuinely incredulous on hearing of the prohibition. He had believed that God was low, but he had never dreamed he would sink to *this*. Satan's motives are not pure, but his spontaneous response to the prohibition raises probing questions about God. It is part of the enduring value of *Paradise Lost* that it does not shrink from asking tough questions. 'The sacred Milton', wrote Shelley in his Preface to *Prometheus Unbound* (1819), 'was, let it ever be remembered, a republican, and a bold inquirer into morals and religion.'[7] Shelley offers a one-sided view of *Paradise Lost*, but he was right to see Milton as a bold inquirer.

Paradise Regained and *Samson Agonistes* were published together in one volume in 1671. Thomas Ellwood, a friend and pupil of Milton's in the early 1660s, claims to have played some part in the engendering of *Paradise Regained*. Milton lent Ellwood the completed manuscript of *Paradise Lost*, which Ellwood read and returned, commenting: 'Thou hast said much here of *Paradise lost*; but what hast thou to say of *Paradise found*?' Milton did not reply, 'but sate some time in a Muse'. Some time later he presented Ellwood with the completed *Paradise Regained*, saying: 'This is owing to you; for you put it into my head by the question you put to me at Chalfont; which before I had not thought of.'[8] Milton's nephew, Edward Phillips, confirms that Milton began *Paradise Regained* only after the publication of *Paradise Lost*. Phillips also tells us that the first readers of *Paradise Regained* considered it 'much inferiour' to *Paradise Lost*. Most subsequent readers have agreed with this verdict, but Milton himself 'could not hear with patience any such thing when related to him'.[9]

The plot of *Paradise Regained* is based upon the Gospels account of Christ's temptation in the wilderness. By resisting temptation, Jesus, the Second Adam, stands where Adam fell. Jesus's 'firm obedience' (*Paradise Regained*, I, 4) contrasts with 'man's first disobedience' (*Paradise Lost*, I, 1). This sounds straightforward, but the poem has provoked a wide divergence of critical opinions, even on the most basic interpretative questions. It is not clear just how (or even whether) Jesus's withstanding of temptation regains Paradise for Adam and Eve's descendants. Most Christians have thought the Crucifixion more important than the temptation in the wilderness, but Milton in his mature poems never portrays the Crucifixion, and barely even mentions it. Are we to conclude that he thought it unimportant? Some have made this inference, but it may be rash to do so. At the end of *Paradise Regained*, a chorus of hymning angels congratulates the Son of God and exhorts him to 'begin to save mankind' (IV, 635). The significant word 'begin' implies that Jesus's mission is not yet complete. But it is not clear, in that case, why the poem is called *Paradise Regained*.

In presenting Jesus's temptation, Milton combines different elements from the Gospels of Matthew and Luke. He follows Matthew in placing all of the temptations after Jesus's forty-day fast (in Luke, the temptations themselves last forty days). But he follows Luke, not Matthew, in the order of the temptations. In Matthew, Jesus's first temptation is to turn stones into bread, his second to cast himself down from the temple, and his third to worship Satan in exchange for the kingdoms of the world. Following Luke, Milton reverses the second and third temptations so that the temptation on the pinnacle becomes the climactic episode. Biblical commentators had long discussed the question of just what Satan was trying to accomplish by tempting Christ. One view was that he was trying to discover Christ's true identity, and that the temptations were intended to make him acknowledge his divinity. It is possible to attribute such a motive to Satan in *Paradise Regained*. Satan remembers the 'first-begot' (I, 89) who drove him out of Heaven, but he is tortured with anxiety as to the identity and significance of this new Son of God. Jesus too is unsure of who he is – though it is possible that memory comes flooding back to him at the climax of the poem when he tells Satan on the pinnacle to 'Tempt not the Lord thy God' (IV, 561). Jesus's curt imperative is a quotation from Deuteronomy 6:16 such as any pious man might utter, but it also invites the deeper meaning 'Do not tempt *me*, your God'.

Jesus's stern rejection of Athenian philosophy and poetry (IV, 286–364) has dismayed many readers, not least because Milton had devoted so much of his own life to the study of the classics. Milton has been chided for his bad literary taste in making Jesus declare that Greek literature is 'unworthy to compare / With Sion's songs' (IV, 346–7). In fairness to Milton, however, we should remember that his verdict was based on a knowledge of both literatures in the original languages. Few if any literary critics can claim such knowledge today. Jesus's rejection of Greek culture is in any case not unequivocal. Satan offers the kingdoms, and asks for Jesus's worship, *before* he turns from Rome to Athens (IV, 155–69). The implication is that Athens is not in Satan's gift in the way that Parthia and Rome are.

Samson Agonistes is usually seen as Milton's last poem, though there is no firm evidence as to the date of composition. A closet drama modelled on Greek tragedy, it was never intended for the stage. Critics differ as to whether the prevailing spirit is Hellenic, Hebraic or Christian. It combines elements of all three. Following Greek practice, Milton limits the action to one day, the last of Samson's life. At the beginning of the action, Samson is a broken man, blinded and imprisoned by the Philistines, and tortured with guilt at having betrayed the secret of his strength to Dalila in one fatal moment of weakness. Here Samson's crime differs from those of most Greek tragic protagonists. Samson has not incurred divine envy by aspiring too high; he has fallen by relaxing his vigilance. This notion of transgression is Hebraic rather than Greek. The Christian elements in Milton's tragedy are harder to recognize, and not all readers agree that they are there, but the majority view is that the drama traces Samson's progress towards spiritual regeneration.

The word *Agonistes* in the title is Greek and means 'champion' or 'contestant in the games'. It refers to Samson's display of strength in Dagon's temple and so (in the manner of such titles as *Prometheus Bound* or *Oedipus at Colonus*) indicates which episode in the hero's life the drama will present. Edward Phillips compiled a dictionary, *The New World of English Words* (1658), in which he defines 'agonize' as 'play the champion'. The chorus in *Samson Agonistes* several times refers to Samson as God's 'champion' (556, 705, 1152, 1751). *Agon* is also a Greek term for a set-piece in a tragedy (usually a distinct scene) where two hostile characters confront each other with opposing speeches of about equal length. Samson's confrontations with Dalila and Harapha are 'agones' in this sense. In Christian usage the word implied a spiritual struggle. Jesus's 'agony' at Luke 22:44 is called an *agonia* in the Greek. The name 'Samson' was defined by Phillips as meaning 'there the second time', and this (false) etymology may have suggested Milton's idea of a second encounter with Dalila (which is not found in Judges).

In his prefatory comment 'Of that Sort of Dramatic Poem which is Called Tragedy', Milton names the Greek tragedians Aeschylus, Sophocles and Euripides as his models. He also offers a detailed discussion of catharsis ('purgation'), a much-disputed term that Aristotle had applied to tragedy in his *Poetics*. Following Italian Renaissance critics, Milton understands catharsis in terms of homoeopathic medicine ('like cures like'). According to this view, tragedy does not (as Plato had argued) improperly feed negative passions. Rather, it cleanses and releases them by first raising them, then reducing them 'to just measure'. The final line of *Samson Agonistes* – 'And calm of mind all passion spent' – confirms that Milton's aim is to leave his reader in a state of peace and inner harmony.

It is a moot point whether *Samson Agonistes* achieves this aim. An insuperable obstacle for many readers is Samson's final slaughter of the Philistines. The scale of the destruction is so appalling that many readers find catharsis impossible. Some have excoriated both Samson and Milton for their savagery; others have persuaded themselves that Samson is Milton's villain rather than his hero. Several critics, including William Empson in 1961, have likened Samson to a suicidal terrorist. John Carey, writing in the *Times Literary Supplement* a year after the terrorist attacks of 11 September 2001, has gone so far as to ask whether *Samson Agonistes* might be 'an incitement to terrorism'. Carey's letter provoked a flurry of angry responses in the weeks that followed, and the debate about Samson's destruction of the Philistines is not likely to go away any time soon. One of the most hotly debated questions is whether Samson acts in accordance with God's will when he pulls down Dagon's temple. Samson agrees to go to the temple only after he has received the spontaneous prompting of 'Some rousing motions' (1382). Do these mysterious 'motions' come from God or are they rooted in Samson's own vengeful malice? The spontaneity of Samson's 'motions' tells against Carey's analogy with terrorism. As Samson exits with the Philistine officer, he senses that God has called him to perform 'some great act' (1389), but he does not yet have a clearly formulated plan. His is not the calculating malice of a suicide bomber.

Critics on both sides of the argument about Samson have tended to use the word 'terrorist' in a way that implies that terror has no place in tragedy. This is odd, since terror is one of the two emotions that Aristotle had deemed most appropriate to the genre. As Milton writes in his preface 'On That Sort of Dramatic Poem Which is Called Tragedy', tragedy is 'said by Aristotle to be of power by raising pity and fear, or terror, to purge the mind of those and suchlike passions, that is to temper and reduce them to just measure with a kind of delight, stirred up by reading or seeing those passions well imitated'. One might argue that *Samson Agonistes* is deficient in pity or delight, but it is strange to complain that a tragedy has too much terror. Milton certainly takes pains to stir up terror in *Samson Agonistes*. 'O what noise! / Mercy of Heav'n what hideous noise was that?' cries Manoa on hearing the temple

crash to the ground (1508-9). Terror is also clearly audible in
the voice of the Messenger who brings news of the destruction.
Since the Messenger is a Hebrew, one might expect him to
express grim satisfaction (as the Chorus do), but instead he
expresses horror. The Chorus have not *seen* the destruction.
The Messenger has, but wishes he had not:

> O whither shall I run, or which way fly
> The sight of this so horrid spectacle
> Which erst my eyes beheld and yet behold?
> For dire imagination still pursues me. (1541-4)

As Carey rightly notes, the Messenger wants only to rid his
mind of what he has seen.

One of the advantages of the tragic genre is that it can excite
pity and terror even at the spectacle of an enemy's ruin. This
was well understood by the Greeks, who were capable of being
moved by the suffering of their enemies. Euripides presented
The Trojan Women just a few months after his fellow Athenians
had killed or enslaved the entire population of the island of
Melos in 416 BC. Milton shows something like Euripides' mag-
nanimity in allowing his readers to be moved by the horror of
the Philistines' destruction. A lesser poet would have offered
only propaganda. Milton also follows the Greek example in
allowing his 'bad' characters to voice strong arguments – the
strongest he can give them. Milton's Dalila, like Aeschylus'
Clytemnestra, Sophocles' Creon, and Euripides' Medea, speaks
with passion and conviction, and she has persuaded many
critics of her sincerity and even the justice of her cause. This is
entirely in the spirit of Greek tragedy and is much to Milton's
credit. Readers must decide for themselves whether *Samson
Agonistes* is successful in raising and purging pity and terror.
Some might feel that Milton has more success in raising than
in purging these passions, but that is an objection that can be
made about many tragedies, ancient or modern. How many of
the world's great tragedies really do leave us in 'calm of mind,
all passion spent'? Some of the world's greatest philosophers,
including Aristotle, Hegel, Schopenhauer and Nietzsche, have

wrestled with the difficult question of how tragedy can give pleasure when the things it depicts are those we try to avoid in real life.

Milton is a poet who demands moral engagement, but readers often find it difficult to make confident moral judgements. In part, this is because the great theme of all his major poems is temptation. If this theme is to command our interest, it is both inevitable and desirable that the poems should express and create a division of loyalties. W. B. Yeats famously wrote: 'We make out of the quarrel with others, rhetoric, but of the quarrel with ourselves, poetry.'[10] John Milton in his lifetime had many quarrels with others, but it is his quarrels with himself that give his poems their enduring life and potency.

NOTES

1. *The Complete Prose Works of John Milton*, edited by Don M. Wolfe et al., 8 vols (New Haven: Yale University Press, 1953–82), vol. 1, p. 823.

2. *Complete Prose Works*, vol. 4, pp. 618–19, translated (from the Latin) by Donald C. Mackenzie.

3. Helen Darbishire (ed.), *The Early Lives of Milton* (London: Constable, 1932), p. 33. Darbishire attributes this anonymous *Life* to Milton's other nephew, John Phillips, but it is now generally attributed to Cyriack Skinner.

4. William Empson, *Milton's God* (London: Chatto and Windus, 1961), revised edition 1965, p. 13.

5. C. S. Lewis, *A Preface to 'Paradise Lost'* (London: Oxford University Press, 1942), p. 73.

6. Joseph Wittreich, *The Romantics on Milton* (Cleveland: Case Western Reserve University Press, 1970), p. 119.

7. Ibid., p. 532.

8. Thomas Ellwood, *The History of the Life of Thomas Ellwood* (London: J. Sowle, 1714), pp. 233–4.

9. Edward Phillips, *The Life of Mr John Milton* (1694), in Darbishire, *Early Lives*, p. 76.

10. W. B. Yeats, 'Anima Hominis', in *Essays* (London: Macmillan, 1924), p. 492.

Further Reading

EDITIONS OF MILTON

Carey, John (ed.), *Milton: Complete Shorter Poems*, 2nd edn (London: Longman, 1997).

Flannagan, Roy (ed.), *The Riverside Milton* (New York: Houghton Mifflin, 1998).

Fowler, Alastair (ed.), *Milton: Paradise Lost*, 2nd edn (London: Longman, 1998).

Leonard, John (ed.), *John Milton: the Complete Poems* (London: Penguin, 1998).

Wolfe, Don M. (Gen. ed.), *The Complete Prose Works of John Milton*, 8 vols (New Haven: Yale University Press, 1953–82).

BIOGRAPHIES

Darbishire, Helen (ed.), *The Early Lives of Milton* (London: Constable, 1932).

Lewalski, Barbara K., *The Life of John Milton: a Critical Biography* (Oxford: Basil Blackwell, 2000).

Masson, David, *The Life of John Milton: Narrated in Connexion with the Political, Ecclesiastical, and Literary History of His Time*, 7 vols (London: Macmillan, 1859–94).

Parker, William Riley, *Milton: a Biography*, 2 vols, revised version edited by Gordon Campbell (Oxford: Clarendon Press, 1996).

CRITICAL STUDIES

Brown, Cedric, *John Milton's Aristocratic Entertainments* (Cambridge: Cambridge University Press, 1985).

Burden, Dennis, *The Logical Epic: a Study of the Argument of 'Paradise Lost'* (London: Routledge and Kegan Paul, 1967).

Corns, Thomas N. (ed.), *A Companion to Milton* (Oxford: Blackwell Publishers, 2001).

Danielson, Dennis, *Milton's Good God* (Cambridge: Cambridge University Press, 1982).

Danielson, Dennis (ed.), *The Cambridge Companion to Milton*, 2nd edn (Cambridge: Cambridge University Press, 1999).

Empson, William, *Milton's God* (London: Chatto and Windus, 1961; revised edition, 1965).

Evans, J. Martin, *'Paradise Lost' and the Genesis Tradition* (Oxford: Clarendon Press, 1968).

Evans, J. Martin, *The Road from Horton: Looking Backwards in 'Lycidas'* (Victoria, BC: University of Victoria Press, 1983).

Evans, J. Martin, *Milton's Imperial Epic: 'Paradise Lost' and the Discourse of Colonialism* (Ithaca: Cornell University Press, 1996).

Fallon, Stephen M., *Milton among the Philosophers* (Ithaca: Cornell University Press, 1991).

Fish, Stanley Eugene, *Surprised by Sin: the Reader in 'Paradise Lost'* (London: Macmillan, 1967). Second edition with a new Preface (Cambridge, MA: Harvard University Press, 1997).

Forsyth, Neil, *The Satanic Epic* (Princeton: Princeton University Press, 2003).

Hill, Christopher, *Milton and the English Revolution* (London: Faber and Faber, 1977).

Kerrigan, William, *The Sacred Complex: on the Psychogenesis of 'Paradise Lost'* (Cambridge, MA: Harvard University Press, 1983).

Kolbrener, William, *Milton's Warring Angels: A Study of Critical Engagements* (Cambridge: Cambridge University Press, 1997).

Krouse, F. M., *Milton's Samson and the Christian Tradition* (Princeton: Princeton University Press, 1949).

Leonard, John, *Naming in Paradise: Milton and the Language of Adam and Eve* (Oxford: Clarendon Press, 1990).

Lewalski, Barbara K., *Milton's Brief Epic* (Providence: Brown University Press, 1966).

Lewalski, Barbara K., *'Paradise Lost' and the Rhetoric of Literary Forms* (Princeton: Princeton University Press, 1985).

Lewis, C. S., *A Preface to 'Paradise Lost'* (London: Oxford University Press, 1942).

Lieb, Michael, *Milton and the Culture of Violence* (Ithaca: Cornell University Press, 1994).

Loewenstein, David, *Milton and the Drama of History* (Cambridge: Cambridge University Press, 1990).

Martindale, Charles, *John Milton and the Transformation of Ancient Epic* (Totowa: Barnes & Noble, 1986).

McColley, Diane K., *Milton's Eve* (Urbana: University of Illinois Press, 1983).

Newlyn, Lucy, *'Paradise Lost' and the Romantic Reader* (Oxford: Clarendon Press, 1993).

Patterson, Annabel (ed.), *John Milton* (London: Longman, 1992).

Peter, John, *A Critique of 'Paradise Lost'* (New York: Columbia University Press, 1960).

Pope, Elizabeth, *'Paradise Regained': the Tradition and the Poem* (Baltimore: Johns Hopkins University Press, 1947).

Porter, William, *Reading the Classics and 'Paradise Lost'* (Lincoln, NB: Nebraska University Press, 1993).

Prince, F. T., *The Italian Element in Milton's Verse* (Oxford: Clarendon Press, 1954).

Quint, David, *Epic and Empire: Politics and Generic Form from Virgil to Milton* (Princeton: Princeton University Press, 1993).

Radzinowicz, Mary Ann, *Toward 'Samson Agonistes': the Growth of Milton's Mind* (Princeton: Princeton University Press, 1978).

Revard, Stella Purce, *The War in Heaven: 'Paradise Lost' and the Tradition of Satan's Rebellion* (Ithaca and London: Cornell University Press, 1980).

Ricks, Christopher, *Milton's Grand Style* (Oxford: Clarendon Press, 1963).

Rumrich, John P., *Milton Unbound: Controversy and Reinterpretation* (Cambridge: Cambridge University Press, 1996).

Rushdy, Ashraf A., *The Empty Garden* (Pittsburgh: University of Pittsburgh Press, 1992).

Schwartz, Regina M., *Remembering and Repeating: Biblical Creation in 'Paradise Lost'* (Cambridge: Cambridge University Press, 1988).

Summers, Joseph, *The Muse's Method: an Introduction to 'Paradise Lost'* (Cambridge, MA: Harvard University Press, 1962).

Tanner, John S., *Anxiety in Eden: a Kierkegaardian Reading of 'Paradise Lost'* (Oxford: Clarendon Press, 1993).

Turner, James Grantham, *One Flesh: Paradisal Marriage and Sexual Relations in the Age of Milton* (Oxford: Clarendon Press, 1987).

Waldock, A. J. A., *'Paradise Lost' and its Critics* (Cambridge: Cambridge University Press, 1947).

Wittreich, Joseph, *Shifting Contexts: Reinterpreting Samson Agonistes* (Pittsburgh: Duquesne University Press, 2002).

Wood, Derek N. C., *Exiled from Light: Divine Law, Morality, and Violence in Milton's 'Samson Agonistes'* (Toronto: University of Toronto Press, 2001).

A Note on the Text

The present text represents a partial modernization. Spelling has been modernized, italics removed, and most capitals reduced. Contractions have for the most part been preserved, for they provide a guide to Milton's prosody. I have modernized punctuation only when the original pointing might impede a modern reader. Most of my changes are from a comma to a semi-colon or full stop. An example is 'Lycidas', 128–31, which the editions of 1645 and 1673 point as follows:

> Besides what the grim Wolf with privy paw
> Daily devours apace, and nothing said,
> But that two-handed engine at the door,
> Stands ready to smite once, and smite no more.

The comma after 'said' is potentially confusing, for it gives the momentary signal that the 'two-handed engine' is something that the bad shepherds said. I have printed a full stop. In this instance I have the support of the 1638 edition, which also has a full stop. Occasionally I have modernized against all early texts.

Throughout the present edition I have added quotation marks where there is direct speech. This is a departure from the practice of the earliest editions of the poems, which do not use quotation marks. Several modern texts, including Alastair Fowler's two monumental Longman editions (1968 and 1998) and my own Penguin Classics edition (1998), also omit quotation marks and a good case can be made for not intruding them. Their absence from the text can create a momentary

uncertainty as to who is speaking, but this very uncertainty can
sometimes be the occasion of suggestive and even beautiful
ambiguities. Towards the end of Book IV of *Paradise Lost*,
Milton describes Adam and Eve praying as they retire to their
bower. This is how the lines appear in the second edition
(1674):

> Thus at thir shadie Lodge arriv'd, both stood,
> Both turnd, and under op'n Skie ador'd
> The God that made both Skie, Air, Earth and Heav'n
> Which they beheld, the Moons resplendent Globe
> And starrie Pole: Thou also mad'st the Night,
> Maker Omnipotent, and thou the Day,
> Which we in our appointed work imployd
> Have finishd happie in our mutual help
> And mutual love. (IV, 720–28)

Modernized editions (including this one) insert an opening quo-
tation mark before 'Thou' in line 724 to signal that what
follows is direct speech, spoken by Adam and Eve. In this
particular instance, such disambiguating punctuation exacts a
price, for it robs the text of an enhancing suggestion. For a
moment it had seemed that the prayer beginning 'Thou' was
spoken by Milton's own narrative voice, breaking irresistibly
into the narrative. Only when we come to 'we in our appointed
work' (726) do we realize that it is Adam and Eve who are
speaking. Milton's eighteenth-century critics had no doubt that
this effect was deliberate. Joseph Addison (*Spectator*, No. 321,
8 March 1712) thought that Milton was imitating a Homeric
technique that Longinus, an ancient literary critic of the first
century AD, had recommended for epic poets. Longinus had
praised the 'sudden transition' by which Homer 'himself passes
into' his speakers, and Addison credits Milton with the same
kind of 'sudden transition'. Modernized punctuation is a liabil-
ity in this instance because it signals the 'transition' prematurely
and so deprives it of its suddenness.

   It is with some reluctance, then, that I have decided to adopt
quotation marks in the present edition. Quotation marks come

at a price. The price is nevertheless worth paying when one considers those occasions where disambiguation helps the modern reader. One such moment occurs in the debate in Hell, when Belial summarizes (in order to discredit) the argument of the previous speaker, Moloch. Moloch had urged the devils to resume armed struggle against God, since the worst they have to fear is annihilation, and even that is preferable to Hell. Belial has two answers to this. First, he denies that God will annihilate his enemies, since annihilation would be a mercy, and then he drives the point home by seizing on Moloch's word 'worse'. I once again quote the 1674 text:

> Will he, so wise, let loose at once his ire,
> Belike through impotence, or unaware,
> To give his Enemies thir wish, and end
> Them in his anger, whom his anger saves
> To punish endless? wherefore cease we then?
> Say they who counsel Warr, we are decreed,
> Reserv'd and destin'd to Eternal woe;
> Whatever doing, what can we suffer more,
> What can we suffer worse? is this then worst,
> Thus sitting, thus consulting, thus in Arms?
>   (II, 155–64)

Here, as in Adam and Eve's prayer, it is hard to tell where one voice ends and the other begins, but in this instance nothing is gained, and much is lost, by blurring the boundaries. Belial is quoting Moloch in order to mock him. The cut and thrust of Belial's rhetoric – and its perfect timing – become clearer if one modernizes the punctuation, as follows:

> 'Wherefore cease we then?'
> Say they who counsel war, 'We are decreed,
> Reserved and destined to eternal woe;
> Whatever doing, what can we suffer more,
> What can we suffer worse?' Is this then worst,
> Thus sitting, thus consulting, thus in arms?

In this version it is clear that 'Wherefore cease we then?' ('Why stop fighting?') is Moloch's question, not Belial's, and (most importantly) that 'Is this then worst' is a rejoinder to Moloch's rhetorical question 'What can we suffer worse?' Without quotation marks, the crucial line 'What can we suffer worse? Is this then worst?' is likely to confuse the modern reader, who might erroneously infer that both questions come from the same speaker. With quotation marks, it is clear that Belial is trumping Moloch's question with one of his own – a question that he will proceed to elaborate and answer in the ensuing thirty lines, where he will painstakingly point out that quite a few things could be 'worse'. To withhold quotation marks at this moment would deprive Belial's rhetoric of its pointed acerbity. Clearly, there are advantages and disadvantages to both editorial practices, but my own view is that quotation marks earn their keep in an edition designed, as this one is, for the reader approaching Milton for the first time.

Attention should be drawn to a liberty I have taken in my use of capitals. The early editions usually capitalize 'Heaven', and they make no typographical distinction between God's empyreal Heaven and the stellar heavens of the created universe. I have used the upper case for God's Heaven and the lower case for the stellar heavens. The justification for this typographical distinction is that it can serve the modern reader as a helpful guide (see e.g. *Paradise Lost*, II. 1004–6). Modern-spelling editions invariably make such a distinction between 'God' and 'god', even though the early texts use the upper case for pagan gods as well as God.

In arranging the shorter poems I have followed the order that Milton himself adopted in his 1645 and 1673 *Poems* rather than try to arrange them by putative date of composition. For the most part I have preferred the 1645 text to that of 1673, but I have silently incorporated a few of the 1673 revisions that are widely accepted as authorial. As in my Penguin editions of the *Complete Poems* and *Paradise Lost*, I have been eclectic in choosing between the variants of the 1667 and 1674 editions of *Paradise Lost*. The present edition offers in their entirety four of the twelve books of *Paradise Lost*: Books I, II, IV and

IX. The first two books, which most nineteenth- and early twentieth-century critics considered the best in the poem, present Satan in Hell, planning revenge after his failed rebellion in Heaven. It was these books, more than any other, which convinced Romantics such as Byron and Shelley that Satan was the poem's real hero. Nineteenth-century readers often skipped the later books, or dismissed them as a disappointment after the poem's heroic beginning. It was only in the mid-twentieth century that Book IX, the book of the Fall, really came into its own. It is now widely regarded as the real heart of the poem – and most critics think that it contains Milton's best poetry. Book IV, which depicts Paradise before the Fall, has also risen in critical esteem, to become one of the poem's most loved books. I have chosen these four books for the present edition partly because they contain the essentials of the story, and partly because they typify the different poles of Milton's creative imagination. In making selections from *Paradise Regained*, I have concentrated on the key temptations. *Samson Agonistes* is here offered in its entirety. As the present edition prints only selections of *Paradise Lost*, I have omitted the 'arguments' or prose summaries that were prefaced to each book during the printing of the first edition, but I have kept the note on 'the Verse' that was added at the same time.

I should add a word of explanation about the numbering and titling of the sonnets. The present edition contains all of Milton's English sonnets (Sonnets II–VI, not included here, were written in Italian), but readers might still be puzzled by a discrepancy between the numbering followed here and that adopted by several other editions as well as innumerable anthologies. To give one obvious example, the sonnet beginning 'Methought I saw my late espousèd saint' (one of the most loved and widely anthologized of Milton's poems) is here identified as Sonnet XIX, even though the reader might be more familiar with it as Sonnet XXIII. The explanation lies in four uncollected English sonnets, which were not printed in Milton's *Poems, &c. upon Several Occasions* (1673). All four of these sonnets address political topics, and two of them (those addressed to Oliver Cromwell and Sir Henry Vane) praise men who in 1673 were reviled as traitors. It has been plausibly suggested that Milton excluded these poems from the 1673 volume because it would have been dangerous or impossible to publish them under his own name. Their absence from the 1673 *Poems* accounts for the numbering followed here, which accords with the printed editions of Milton's own lifetime. By identifying these four sonnets as 'uncollected', my aim is to draw attention to their political significance. This has become standard practice in recent editions, but the traditional numbering survives in current anthologies, hence the confusion. I have taken one other liberty with the sonnets – a liberty I did not take in my 1998 Penguin edition of Milton's *Complete Poems*. In the present edition I have included sub-titles to Sonnets VIII, XI and XIV even though no sub-titles are given to these poems in the editions printed in Milton's lifetime. In each case I have taken the sub-title from Milton's manuscript, now in Trinity College, Cambridge. I have printed the sub-titles to these poems in the belief that they offer useful information to the reader. I have decided not to print the sub-title to Sonnet X ('Daughter to that good Earl') because in this instance I think it likely that Milton wanted his reader to decipher the identities of daughter and earl, and to that end withheld the manuscript title 'To the Lady Margaret Ley'.

Selected Poems

from POEMS 1645

On the Morning of Christ's Nativity.
Composed 1629.

I

This is the month, and this the happy morn
Wherein the Son of Heav'n's eternal King,
Of wedded maid, and virgin mother born,
Our great redemption from above did bring;
For so the holy sages once did sing,
   That he our deadly forfeit should release,
And with his Father work us a perpetual peace.

II

That glorious form, that light unsufferable,
And that far-beaming blaze of majesty,
Wherewith he wont at Heav'n's high council-table,   10
To sit the midst of trinal unity,
He laid aside; and here with us to be,
   Forsook the courts of everlasting day,
And chose with us a darksome house of mortal clay.

III

Say Heav'nly Muse, shall not thy sacred vein
Afford a present to the infant God?
Hast thou no verse, no hymn, or solemn strain,
To welcome him to this his new abode,
Now while the heav'n by the sun's team untrod,

20   Hath took no print of the approaching light,
       And all the spangled host keep watch in squadrons
            bright?

IV

See how from far upon the eastern road
The star-led wizards haste with odours sweet:
O run, prevent them with thy humble ode,
And lay it lowly at his blessèd feet;
Have thou the honour first, thy Lord to greet,
     And join thy voice unto the angel choir,
From out his secret altar touched with hallowed fire.

The Hymn

I

It was the winter wild,
30   While the Heav'n-born-child,
          All meanly wrapped in the rude manger lies;
       Nature in awe to him
       Had doffed her gaudy trim,
          With her great Master so to sympathize:
       It was no season then for her
       To wanton with the sun her lusty paramour.

II

Only with speeches fair
She woos the gentle air
     To hide her guilty front with innocent snow,
40   And on her naked shame,
Pollute with sinful blame,
     The saintly veil of maiden white to throw,
Confounded, that her Maker's eyes
Should look so near upon her foul deformities.

III

But he her fears to cease,
Sent down the meek-eyed Peace;
   She crowned with olive green, came softly sliding
Down through the turning sphere
His ready harbinger,
   With turtle wing the amorous clouds dividing.   50
And waving wide her myrtle wand,
She strikes a universal peace through sea and land.

IV

No war, or battle's sound
Was heard the world around:
   The idle spear and shield were high up hung;
The hookèd chariot stood
Unstained with hostile blood,
   The trumpet spake not to the armèd throng,
And kings sat still with awful eye,
As if they surely knew their sov'reign Lord was by.   60

V

But peaceful was the night
Wherein the Prince of Light
   His reign of peace upon the earth began:
The winds, with wonder whist,
Smoothly the waters kissed,
   Whispering new joys to the mild Oceán,
Who now hath quite forgot to rave,
While birds of calm sit brooding on the charmèd
     wave.

VI

The stars with deep amaze
Stand fixed in steadfast gaze,
   Bending one way their precious influence,   70
And will not take their flight,

For all the morning light,
   Or Lucifer that often warned them thence;
But in their glimmering orbs did glow,
Until their Lord himself bespake, and bid them go.

VII

And though the shady gloom
Had given day her room,
   The sun himself withheld his wonted speed,
80   And hid his head for shame,
As his inferior flame,
   The new-enlightened world no more should need;
He saw a greater Sun appear
Than his bright throne, or burning axle-tree could
     bear.

VIII

The shepherds on the lawn,
Or ere the point of dawn,
   Sat simply chatting in a rustic row;
Full little thought they then,
That the mighty Pan
90   Was kindly come to live with them below;
Perhaps their loves, or else their sheep,
Was all that did their silly thoughts so busy keep.

IX

When such music sweet
Their hearts and ears did greet,
   As never was by mortal finger strook,
Divinely-warbled voice
Answering the stringèd noise,
   As all their souls in blissful rapture took:
The air such pleasure loath to lose,
With thousand echoes still prolongs each Heav'nly
100   close.

X

Nature that heard such sound
Beneath the hollow round
   Of Cynthia's seat, the airy region thrilling,
Now was almost won
To think her part was done,
   And that her reign had here its last fulfilling;
She knew such harmony alone
Could hold all Heav'n and earth in happier union.

XI

At last surrounds their sight
A globe of circular light,   110
   That with long beams the shame-faced night arrayed;
The helmèd Cherubim
And sworded Seraphim,
   Are seen in glittering ranks with wings displayed,
Harping in loud and solemn choir,
With unexpressive notes to Heav'n's new-born heir.

XII

Such music (as 'tis said)
Before was never made,
   But when of old the sons of morning sung,
While the Creator great   120
His constellations set,
   And the well-balanced world on hinges hung,
And cast the dark foundations deep,
And bid the welt'ring waves their oozy channel keep.

XIII

Ring out, ye crystal spheres,
Once bless our human ears,
   (If ye have power to touch our senses so)
And let your silver chime
Move in melodious time;
   And let the bass of heav'n's deep organ blow,   130
And with your ninefold harmony
Make up full consort to th' angelic symphony.

XIV

For if such holy song
Enwrap our fancy long,
   Time will run back and fetch the age of gold,
And speckled Vanity
Will sicken soon and die,
   And lep'rous Sin will melt from earthly mould,
And Hell itself will pass away,
140   And leave her dolorous mansions to the peering day.

XV

Yea, Truth and Justice then
Will down return to men,
   Orbed in a rainbow; and, like glories wearing,
Mercy will sit between,
Throned in celestial sheen,
   With radiant feet the tissued clouds down steering,
And Heav'n as at some festival,
Will open wide the gates of her high palace hall.

XVI

But wisest Fate says no,
150   This must not yet be so,
   The babe lies yet in smiling infancy,
That on the bitter cross
Must redeem our loss;
   So both himself and us to glorify:
Yet first to those ychained in sleep,
The wakeful trump of doom must thunder through the
   deep.

XVII

With such a horrid clang
As on Mount Sinai rang
   While the red fire, and smould'ring clouds out brake:
160   The agèd earth aghast
With terror of that blast,

Shall from the surface to the centre shake;
When at the world's last sessïon,
The dreadful Judge in middle air shall spread his
    throne.

XVIII

And then at last our bliss
Full and perfect is,
    But now begins; for from this happy day
Th' old Dragon under ground
In straiter limits bound,
    Not half so far casts his usurpèd sway,   170
And wroth to see his kingdom fail,
Swinges the scaly horror of his folded tail.

XIX

The oracles are dumb,
No voice or hideous hum
    Runs through the archèd roof in words deceiving.
Apollo from his shrine
Can no more divine,
    With hollow shriek the steep of Delphos leaving.
No nightly trance, or breathèd spell,
Inspires the pale-eyed priest from the prophetic cell.   180

XX

The lonely mountains o'er,
And the resounding shore,
    A voice of weeping heard, and loud lament;
From haunted spring, and dale
Edged with poplar pale,
    The parting Genius is with sighing sent,
With flow'r-inwoven tresses torn
The nymphs in twilight shade of tangled thickets
    mourn.

XXI

In consecrated earth,
190   And on the holy hearth,
      The lars and lemures moan with midnight plaint;
In urns, and altars round,
A drear and dying sound
      Affrights the flamens at their service quaint;
And the chill marble seems to sweat,
While each peculiar power forgoes his wonted seat.

XXII

Peor and Baälim
Forsake their temples dim,
      With that twice-battered god of Palestine,
200   And moonèd Ashtaroth,
Heav'n's queen and mother both,
      Now sits not girt with tapers' holy shine;
The Libyc Hammon shrinks his horn,
In vain the Tyrian maids their wounded Thammuz
      mourn.

XXIII

And sullen Moloch, fled,
Hath left in shadows dread,
      His burning idol all of blackest hue;
In vain with cymbals' ring,
They call the grisly king,
210   In dismal dance about the furnace blue;
The brutish gods of Nile as fast,
Isis and Orus, and the dog Anubis haste.

XXIV

Nor is Osiris seen
In Memphian grove, or green,
      Trampling the unshow'red grass with lowings loud:
Nor can he be at rest
Within his sacred chest,

Naught but profoundest Hell can be his shroud,
In vain with timbrelled anthems dark
The sable-stolèd sorcerers bear his worshipped ark.   220

XXV

He feels from Judah's land
The dreaded infant's hand,
   The rays of Bethlehem blind his dusky eyn;
Nor all the gods beside,
Longer dare abide,
   Not Typhon huge ending in snaky twine:
Our babe to show his Godhead true,
Can in his swaddling bands control the damnèd
   crew.

XXVI

So when the sun in bed,
Curtained with cloudy red,   230
   Pillows his chin upon an orient wave,
The flocking shadows pale,
Troop to th' infernal jail,
   Each fettered ghost slips to his several grave,
And the yellow-skirted fays,
Fly after the Night-steeds, leaving their moon-loved
   maze.

XXVII

But see the virgin blest,
Hath laid her babe to rest.
   Time is our tedious song should here have ending;
Heav'n's youngest teemèd star,   240
Hath fixed her polished car,
   Her sleeping Lord with handmaid lamp attending.
And all about the courtly stable,
Bright-harnessed angels sit in order serviceable.

On Time

Fly envious Time, till thou run out thy race,
Call on the lazy leaden-stepping hours,
Whose speed is but the heavy plummet's pace;
And glut thyself with what thy womb devours,
Which is no more than what is false and vain,
And merely mortal dross;
So little is our loss,
So little is thy gain.
For when as each thing bad thou hast entombed,
And last of all, thy greedy self consumed,
Then long eternity shall greet our bliss
With an individual kiss;
And joy shall overtake us as a flood,
When every thing that is sincerely good
And perfectly divine,
With Truth, and Peace, and Love shall ever shine
About the súpreme throne
Of him, t' whose happy-making sight alone,
When once our Heav'nly-guided soul shall climb,
Then all this earthy grossness quit,
Attired with stars, we shall for ever sit,
    Triúmphing over Death, and Chance, and thee O
    Time.

At a Solemn Music

Blest pair of Sirens, pledges of Heav'n's joy,
Sphere-borne harmonious sisters, Voice and Verse,
Wed your divine sounds, and mixed power employ
Dead things with inbreathed sense able to pierce,
And to our high-raised fantasy present
That undisturbèd song of pure concent,
Ay sung before the sapphire-coloured throne
To him that sits thereon

With saintly shout, and solemn jubilee,
Where the bright Seraphim in burning row   10
Their loud uplifted angel trumpets blow,
And the Cherubic host in thousand choirs
Touch their immortal harps of golden wires,
With those just spirits that wear victorious palms,
Hymns devout and holy psalms
Singing everlastingly;
That we on earth with undiscording voice
May rightly answer that melodious noise;
As once we did, till disproportioned sin
Jarred against Nature's chime, and with harsh din   20
Broke the fair music that all creatures made
To their great Lord, whose love their motion swayed
In perfect diapason, whilst they stood
In first obedience, and their state of good.
O may we soon again renew that song,
And keep in tune with Heav'n, till God ere long
To his celestial consort us unite,
To live with him, and sing in endless morn of light.

Song. On May Morning

Now the bright morning star, day's harbinger,
Comes dancing from the east, and leads with her
The flowery May, who from her green lap throws
The yellow cowslip, and the pale primrose.
   Hail bounteous May that dost inspire
   Mirth and youth, and warm desire!
   Woods and groves are of thy dressing,
   Hill and dale doth boast thy blessing.
Thus we salute thee with our early song,
And welcome thee, and wish thee long.   10

On Shakespeare. 1630

What needs my Shakespeare for his honoured bones
The labour of an age in pilèd stones,
Or that his hallowed relics should be hid
Under a star-ypointing pyramid?
Dear son of Memory, great heir of fame,
What need'st thou such weak witness of thy name?
Thou in our wonder and astonishment
Hast built thyself a live-long monument.
For whilst to th' shame of slow-endeavouring art,
Thy easy numbers flow, and that each heart
Hath from the leaves of thy unvalued book,
Those Delphic lines with deep impression took,
Then thou, our fancy of itself bereaving,
Dost make us marble with too much conceiving;
And so sepúlchred in such pomp dost lie,
That kings for such a tomb would wish to die.

On the University Carrier
*Who sickened in the time of his vacancy, being forbid
to go to London, by reason of the plague.*

Here lies old Hobson, Death hath broke his girt,
And here alas, hath laid him in the dirt;
Or else, the ways being foul, twenty to one
He's here stuck in a slough, and overthrown.
'Twas such a shifter, that if truth were known,
Death was half glad when he had got him down;
For he had any time this ten years full,
Dodged with him, betwixt Cambridge and the Bull.
And surely, Death could never have prevailed,
Had not his weekly course of carriage failed;
But lately finding him so long at home,
And thinking now his journey's end was come,

And that he had ta'en up his latest inn,
In the kind office of a chamberlain
Showed him his room where he must lodge that
    night,
Pulled off his boots, and took away the light:
If any ask for him, it shall be said,
'Hobson has supped, and's newly gone to bed'.

L'Allegro

Hence loathèd Melancholy,
    Of Cerberus and blackest Midnight born,
In Stygian cave forlorn
    'Mongst horrid shapes, and shrieks, and sights
        unholy,
Find out some uncouth cell,
    Where brooding Darkness spreads his jealous
        wings,
And the night-raven sings;
    There under ebon shades, and low-browed rocks,
As ragged as thy locks,
    In dark Cimmerian desert ever dwell.   10
But come thou goddess fair and free,
In Heav'n yclept Euphrosyne,
And by men, heart-easing Mirth,
Whom lovely Venus at a birth
With two sister Graces more
To ivy-crownèd Bacchus bore;
Or whether (as some sager sing)
The frolic wind that breathes the spring,
Zephyr with Aurora playing,
As he met her once a-Maying,   20
There on beds of violets blue,
And fresh-blown roses washed in dew,
Filled her with thee a daughter fair,
So buxom, blithe, and debonair.

Haste thee nymph, and bring with thee
Jest and youthful Jollity,
Quips and Cranks, and wanton Wiles,
Nods, and Becks, and wreathèd Smiles,
Such as hang on Hebe's cheek,
30 And love to live in dimple sleek;
Sport that wrinkled Care derides,
And Laughter holding both his sides.
Come, and trip it as ye go
On the light fantastic toe,
And in thy right hand lead with thee,
The mountain nymph, sweet Liberty;
And if I give thee honour due,
Mirth, admit me of thy crew
To live with her, and live with thee,
40 In unreprovèd pleasures free;
To hear the lark begin his flight,
And singing startle the dull night,
From his watch-tower in the skies,
Till the dappled dawn doth rise;
Then to come in spite of sorrow,
And at my window bid good morrow,
Through the sweet-briar, or the vine,
Or the twisted eglantine.
While the cock with lively din,
50 Scatters the rear of darkness thin,
And to the stack, or the barn door,
Stoutly struts his dames before,
Oft list'ning how the hounds and horn,
Cheerly rouse the slumb'ring morn,
From the side of some hoar hill,
Through the high wood echoing shrill.
Sometime walking not unseen
By hedgerow elms, on hillocks green,
Right against the eastern gate,
60 Where the great sun begins his state,
Robed in flames and amber light,
The clouds in thousand liveries dight.

While the ploughman near at hand,
Whistles o'er the furrowed land,
And the milkmaid singeth blithe,
And the mower whets his scythe,
And every shepherd tells his tale
Under the hawthorn in the dale.
Straight mine eye hath caught new pleasures
Whilst the landscape round it measures,   70
Russet lawns, and fallows grey,
Where the nibbling flocks do stray,
Mountains on whose barren breast
The labouring clouds do often rest:
Meadows trim with daisies pied,
Shallow brooks, and rivers wide.
Towers and battlements it sees
Bosomed high in tufted trees,
Where perhaps some beauty lies,
The Cynosure of neighbouring eyes.   80
Hard by, a cottage chimney smokes,
From betwixt two agèd oaks,
Where Corydon and Thyrsis met,
Are at their savoury dinner set
Of herbs, and other country messes,
Which the neat-handed Phyllis dresses;
And then in haste her bower she leaves,
With Thestylis to bind the sheaves;
Or if the earlier season lead
To the tanned haycock in the mead,   90
Sometimes with secure delight
The upland hamlets will invite,
When the merry bells ring round,
And the jocund rebecks sound
To many a youth, and many a maid,
Dancing in the chequered shade;
And young and old come forth to play
On a sunshine holiday,
Till the livelong daylight fail,
Then to the spicy nut-brown ale,   100

With stories told of many a feat,
How faery Mab the junkets ate;
She was pinched, and pulled she said,
And he by friar's lantern led,
Tells how the drudging goblin sweat,
To earn his cream-bowl duly set,
When in one night, ere glimpse of morn,
His shadowy flail hath threshed the corn
That ten day-labourers could not end,
Then lies him down the lubber fiend,
And stretched out all the chimney's length,
Basks at the fire his hairy strength;
And crop-full out of doors he flings,
Ere the first cock his matin rings.
Thus done the tales, to bed they creep,
By whispering winds soon lulled asleep.
Towered cities please us then,
And the busy hum of men,
Where throngs of knights and barons bold,
In weeds of peace high triumphs hold,
With store of ladies, whose bright eyes
Rain influence, and judge the prize
Of wit, or arms, while both contend
To win her grace, whom all commend.
There let Hymen oft appear
In saffron robe, with taper clear,
And pomp, and feast, and revelry,
With masque and antique pageantry;
Such sights as youthful poets dream
On summer eves by haunted stream.
Then to the well-trod stage anon,
If Jonson's learned sock be on,
Or sweetest Shakespeare, Fancy's child,
Warble his native wood-notes wild.
And ever against eating cares,
Lap me in soft Lydian airs,
Married to immortal verse
Such as the meeting soul may pierce

In notes, with many a winding bout
Of linkèd sweetness long drawn out,   140
With wanton heed, and giddy cunning,
The melting voice through mazes running;
Untwisting all the chains that tie
The hidden soul of harmony.
That Orpheus' self may heave his head
From golden slumber on a bed
Of heaped Elysian flow'rs, and hear
Such strains as would have won the ear
Of Pluto, to have quite set free
His half-regained Eurydice.   150
These delights, if thou canst give,
Mirth with thee, I mean to live.

Il Penseroso

Hence vain deluding joys,
    The brood of Folly without father bred,
How little you bestead,
    Or fill the fixèd mind with all your toys;
Dwell in some idle brain,
    And fancies fond with gaudy shapes possess,
As thick and numberless
    As the gay motes that people the sunbeams,
Or likest hovering dreams,
    The fickle pensioners of Morpheus' train.   10
But hail thou goddess, sage and holy,
Hail divinest Melancholy,
Whose saintly visage is too bright
To hit the sense of human sight;
And therefore to our weaker view,
O'erlaid with black, staid Wisdom's hue.
Black, but such as in esteem,
Prince Memnon's sister might beseem,
Or that starred Ethiop queen that strove
To set her beauty's praise above   20

The sea-nymphs, and their powers offended;
Yet thou art higher far descended,
Thee bright-haired Vesta long of yore,
To solitary Saturn bore;
His daughter she (in Saturn's reign,
Such mixture was not held a stain).
Oft in glimmering bow'rs and glades
He met her, and in secret shades
Of woody Ida's inmost grove,
While yet there was no fear of Jove.
Come pensive nun, devout and pure,
Sober, steadfast, and demure,
All in a robe of darkest grain,
Flowing with majestic train,
And sable stole of cypress lawn,
Over thy decent shoulders drawn.
Come, but keep thy wonted state,
With even step, and musing gait,
And looks commercing with the skies,
Thy rapt soul sitting in thine eyes:
There held in holy passion still,
Forget thyself to marble, till
With a sad leaden downward cast,
Thou fix them on the earth as fast.
And join with thee calm Peace, and Quiet,
Spare Fast, that oft with gods doth diet,
And hears the Muses in a ring,
Ay round about Jove's altar sing.
And add to these retired Leisure,
That in trim gardens takes his pleasure;
But first, and chiefest, with three bring
Him that yon soars on golden wing,
Guiding the fiery-wheelèd throne,
The Cherub Contemplatïon,
And the mute Silence hist along,
'Less Philomel will deign a song,
In her sweetest, saddest plight,
Smoothing the rugged brow of Night,

30

40

50

While Cynthia checks her dragon yoke,
Gently o'er th' accustomed oak;   60
Sweet bird that shunn'st the noise of folly,
Most musical, most melancholy!
Thee chantress oft the woods among,
I woo to hear thy even-song;
And missing thee, I walk unseen
On the dry smooth-shaven green,
To behold the wand'ring moon,
Riding near her highest noon,
Like one that had been led astray
Through the heav'n's wide pathless way;   70
And oft, as if her head she bowed,
Stooping through a fleecy cloud.
Oft on a plat of rising ground,
I hear the far-off curfew sound,
Over some wide-watered shore,
Swinging slow with sullen roar;
Or if the air will not permit,
Some still removèd place will fit,
Where glowing embers through the room
Teach light to counterfeit a gloom,   80
Far from all resort of mirth,
Save the cricket on the hearth,
Or the bellman's drowsy charm,
To bless the doors from nightly harm:
Or let my lamp at midnight hour,
Be seen in some high lonely tow'r,
Where I may oft outwatch the Bear,
With thrice-great Hermes, or unsphere
The spirit of Plato to unfold
What worlds, or what vast regions hold   90
The immortal mind that hath forsook
Her mansion in this fleshly nook:
And of those daemons that are found
In fire, air, flood, or under ground,
Whose power hath a true consent
With planet, or with element.

Sometime let gorgeous Tragedy
In sceptred pall come sweeping by,
Presenting Thebes, or Pelops' line,
Or the tale of Troy divine.
Or what (though rare) of later age,
Ennobled hath the buskined stage.
But, O sad virgin, that thy power
Might raise Musaeus from his bower,
Or bid the soul of Orpheus sing
Such notes as warbled to the string,
Drew iron tears down Pluto's cheek,
And made Hell grant what love did seek.
Or call up him that left half-told
The story of Cambuscan bold,
Of Camball, and of Algarsife,
And who had Canace to wife,
That owned the virtuous ring and glass,
And of the wondrous horse of brass,
On which the Tartar king did ride;
And if aught else great bards beside,
In sage and solemn tunes have sung,
Of tourneys and of trophies hung;
Of forests, and enchantments drear,
Where more is meant than meets the ear.
Thus Night oft see me in thy pale career,
Till civil-suited Morn appear,
Not tricked and frounced as she was wont,
With the Attic boy to hunt,
But kerchiefed in a comely cloud,
While rocking winds are piping loud,
Or ushered with a shower still,
When the gust hath blown his fill,
Ending on the rustling leaves,
With minute drops from off the eaves.
And when the sun begins to fling
His flaring beams, me goddess bring
To archèd walks of twilight groves,
And shadows brown that Sylvan loves

Of pine, or monumental oak,
Where the rude axe with heavèd stroke,
Was never heard the nymphs to daunt,
Or fright them from their hallowed haunt.
There in close covert by some brook,
Where no profaner eye may look,   140
Hide me from Day's garish eye,
While the bee with honeyed thigh,
That at her flow'ry work doth sing,
And the waters murmuring
With such consort as they keep,
Entice the dewy-feathered Sleep;
And let some strange mysterious dream,
Wave at his wings in airy stream,
Of lively portraiture displayed,
Softly on my eyelids laid.   150
And as I wake, sweet music breathe
Above, about, or underneath,
Sent by some spirit to mortals good,
Or th' unseen Genius of the wood.
But let my due feet never fail,
To walk the studious cloister's pale,
And love the high embowèd roof,
With antique pillars' massy proof,
And storied windows richly dight,
Casting a dim religious light.   160
There let the pealing organ blow,
To the full-voiced choir below,
In service high and anthems clear,
As may with sweetness, through mine ear,
Dissolve me into ecstasies,
And bring all Heav'n before mine eyes.
And may at last my weary age
Find out the peaceful hermitage,
The hairy gown and mossy cell,
Where I may sit and rightly spell,   170
Of every star that heav'n doth show,
And every herb that sips the dew;

Till old experience do attain
To something like prophetic strain.
These pleasures Melancholy give,
And I with thee will choose to live.

Sonnet I

O nightingale, that on yon bloomy spray
    Warblest at eve, when all the woods are still,
    Thou with fresh hope the lover's heart dost fill,
    While the jolly Hours lead on propitious May;
Thy liquid notes that close the eye of day,
    First heard before the shallow cuckoo's bill
    Portend success in love; O if Jove's will
    Have linked that amorous power to thy soft lay,
Now timely sing, ere the rude bird of hate
    Foretell my hopeless doom in some grove nigh:
    As thou from year to year hast sung too late
For my relief, yet hadst no reason why:
    Whether the Muse, or Love call thee his mate,
    Both them I serve, and of their train am I.

Sonnet VII

How soon hath Time, the subtle thief of youth,
    Stol'n on his wing my three-and-twentieth year!
    My hasting days fly on with full career,
    But my late spring no bud or blossom shew'th.
Perhaps my semblance might deceive the truth,
    That I to manhood am arrived so near,
    And inward ripeness doth much less appear,
    That some more timely-happy spirits endu'th.
Yet be it less or more, or soon or slow,
    It shall be still in strictest measure even

To that same lot, however mean, or high,
Toward which Time leads me, and the will of Heaven;
All is, if I have grace to use it so,
As ever in my great task-master's eye.

Sonnet VIII
When the Assault was Intended to the City

Captain or colonel, or knight in arms,
    Whose chance on these defenceless doors may seize,
    If deed of honour did thee ever please,
    Guard them, and him within protect from harms;
He can requite thee, for he knows the charms
    That call fame on such gentle acts as these,
    And he can spread thy name o'er lands and seas,
    Whatever clime the sun's bright circle warms.
Lift not thy spear against the Muses' bower:
    The great Emathian conqueror bid spare   10
    The house of Pindarus, when temple and tower
Went to the ground; and the repeated air
    Of sad Electra's poet had the power
    To save th' Athenian walls from ruin bare.

Sonnet IX

Lady that in the prime of earliest youth,
    Wisely hast shunned the broad way and the green,
    And with those few art eminently seen,
    That labour up the hill of heav'nly Truth,
The better part with Mary, and with Ruth,
    Chosen thou hast; and they that overween,
    And at thy growing virtues fret their spleen,
    No anger find in thee, but pity and ruth.

Thy care is fixed, and zealously attends
10   To fill thy odorous lamp with deeds of light,
        And hope that reaps not shame. Therefore be sure
Thou, when the bridegroom with his feastful friends
        Passes to bliss at the mid-hour of night,
        Hast gained thy entrance, virgin wise and pure.

Sonnet X

Daughter to that good Earl, once President
    Of England's Council, and her Treasury,
    Who lived in both, unstained with gold or fee,
    And left them both, more in himself content,
Till the sad breaking of that Parliament
    Broke him, as that dishonest victory
    At Chaeronea, fatal to liberty
    Killed with report that old man eloquent,
Though later born than to have known the days
10   Wherein your father flourished, yet by you
        Madam, methinks I see him living yet;
So well your words his noble virtues praise,
        That all both judge you to relate them true,
        And to possess them, honoured Margaret.

Lycidas

*In this monody the author bewails a learned
friend, unfortunately drowned in his passage from
Chester on the Irish Seas, 1637. And by occasion
foretells the ruin of our corrupted clergy then in
their height.*

Yet once more, O ye laurels, and once more
Ye myrtles brown, with ivy never sere,
I come to pluck your berries harsh and crude,
And with forced fingers rude,

Shatter your leaves before the mellowing year.
Bitter constraint, and sad occasion dear,
Compels me to disturb your season due:
For Lycidas is dead, dead ere his prime,
Young Lycidas, and hath not left his peer.
Who would not sing for Lycidas? He knew   10
Himself to sing, and build the lofty rhyme.
He must not float upon his wat'ry bier
Unwept, and welter to the parching wind,
Without the meed of some melodious tear.
    Begin then, Sisters of the sacred well,
That from beneath the seat of Jove doth spring;
Begin, and somewhat loudly sweep the string.
Hence with denial vain, and coy excuse;
So may some gentle Muse
With lucky words favour my destined urn,   20
And as he passes, turn
And bid fair peace be to my sable shroud.
For we were nursed upon the self-same hill,
Fed the same flock, by fountain, shade, and rill.
    Together both, ere the high lawns appeared
Under the opening eyelids of the morn,
We drove afield, and both together heard
What time the grey-fly winds her sultry horn,
Batt'ning our flocks with the fresh dews of night,
Oft till the star that rose, at evening, bright   30
Toward heav'n's descent had sloped his westering
        wheel.
Meanwhile the rural ditties were not mute;
Tempered to th' oaten flute,
Rough satyrs danced, and fauns with cloven heel
From the glad sound would not be absent long,
And old Damoetas loved to hear our song.
    But O the heavy change, now thou art gone,
Now thou art gone, and never must return!
Thee shepherd, thee the woods, and desert caves,
With wild thyme and the gadding vine o'ergrown,   40
And all their echoes mourn.

The willows, and the hazel copses green,
Shall now no more be seen,
Fanning their joyous leaves to thy soft lays.
As killing as the canker to the rose,
Or taint-worm to the weanling herds that graze,
Or frost to flowers, that their gay wardrobe wear,
When first the whitethorn blows;
Such, Lycidas, thy loss to shepherd's ear.

50   Where were ye nymphs when the remorseless deep
Closed o'er the head of your loved Lycidas?
For neither were ye playing on the steep,
Where your old Bards, the famous Druids lie,
Nor on the shaggy top of Mona high,
Nor yet where Deva spreads her wizard stream:
Ay me, I fondly dream!
Had ye been there – for what could that have done?
What could the Muse herself that Orpheus bore,
The Muse herself, for her enchanting son
60   Whom universal nature did lament,
When by the rout that made the hideous roar,
His gory visage down the stream was sent,
Down the swift Hebrus to the Lesbian shore?
      Alas! What boots it with uncessant care
To tend the homely slighted shepherd's trade,
And strictly meditate the thankless Muse?
Were it not better done as others use,
To sport with Amaryllis in the shade,
Or with the tangles of Neaera's hair?
70   Fame is the spur that the clear spirit doth raise
(That last infirmity of noble mind)
To scorn delights, and live laborious days;
But the fair guerdon when we hope to find,
And think to burst out into sudden blaze,
Comes the blind Fury with th' abhorrèd shears,
And slits the thin-spun life. 'But not the praise,'
Phoebus replied, and touched my trembling ears;
'Fame is no plant that grows on mortal soil,
Nor in the glistering foil

Set off to th' world, nor in broad rumour lies,   80
But lives and spreads aloft by those pure eyes
And perfect witness of all-judging Jove;
As he pronounces lastly on each deed,
Of so much fame in Heav'n expect thy meed.'
  O fountain Arethuse, and thou honoured flood,
Smooth-sliding Mincius, crowned with vocal reeds,
That strain I heard was of a higher mood:
But now my oat proceeds,
And listens to the herald of the sea
That came in Neptune's plea.   90
He asked the waves, and asked the felon winds,
'What hard mishap hath doomed this gentle swain?'
And questioned every gust of rugged wings
That blows from off each beakèd promontory:
They knew not of his story,
And sage Hippotades their answer brings,
That not a blast was from his dungeon strayed;
The air was calm, and on the level brine
Sleek Panope with all her sisters played.
It was that fatal and perfidious bark,   100
Built in th' eclipse, and rigged with curses dark,
That sunk so low that sacred head of thine.
  Next Camus, reverend sire, went footing slow,
His mantle hairy, and his bonnet sedge,
Inwrought with figures dim, and on the edge
Like to that sanguine flower inscribed with woe.
'Ah! who hath reft,' quoth he, 'my dearest pledge?'
Last came, and last did go,
The pilot of the Galilean lake;
Two massy keys he bore of metals twain,   110
(The golden opes, the iron shuts amain).
He shook his mitred locks, and stern bespake,
'How well could I have spared for thee, young swain,
Enow of such as for their bellies' sake
Creep, and intrude, and climb into the fold!
Of other care they little reck'ning make,

Than how to scramble at the shearers' feast,
And shove away the worthy bidden guest.
Blind mouths! that scarce themselves know how to
            hold
120   A sheep-hook, or have learnt aught else the least
That to the faithful herdsman's art belongs!
What recks it them? What need they? They are sped;
And when they list, their lean and flashy songs
Grate on their scrannel pipes of wretched straw;
The hungry sheep look up, and are not fed,
But swoll'n with wind, and the rank mist they draw,
Rot inwardly, and foul contagion spread:
Besides what the grim Wolf with privy paw
Daily devours apace, and nothing said.
130   But that two-handed engine at the door,
Stands ready to smite once, and smite no more.'
        Return, Alpheus, the dread voice is past,
That shrunk thy streams; return, Sicilian Muse,
And call the vales, and bid them hither cast
Their bells, and flow'rets of a thousand hues.
Ye valleys low, where the mild whispers use
Of shades, and wanton winds, and gushing brooks,
On whose fresh lap the swart star sparely looks,
Throw hither all your quaint enamelled eyes,
140   That on the green turf suck the honeyed showers,
And purple all the ground with vernal flowers.
Bring the rathe primrose that forsaken dies,
The tufted crow-toe, and pale jessamine,
The white pink, and the pansy freaked with jet,
The growing violet,
The musk-rose, and the well-attired woodbine,
With cowslips wan that hang the pensive head,
And every flower that sad embroidery wears:
Bid amaranthus all his beauty shed,
150   And daffadillies fill their cups with tears,
To strew the laureate hearse where Lycid lies.
For so to interpose a little ease,

Let our frail thoughts dally with false surmise;
Ay me! Whilst thee the shores, and sounding seas
Wash far away, where'er thy bones are hurled,
Whether beyond the stormy Hebrides,
Where thou perhaps under the whelming tide
Visit'st the bottom of the monstrous world;
Or whether thou to our moist vows denied,
Sleep'st by the fable of Bellerus old,   160
Where the great vision of the guarded mount
Looks toward Namancos and Bayona's hold;
Look homeward angel now, and melt with ruth.
And, O ye dolphins, waft the hapless youth.
  Weep no more, woeful shepherds, weep no more,
For Lycidas your sorrow is not dead,
Sunk though he be beneath the wat'ry floor,
So sinks the day-star in the ocean bed,
And yet anon repairs his drooping head,
And tricks his beams, and with new-spangled ore,   170
Flames in the forehead of the morning sky:
So Lycidas sunk low, but mounted high,
Through the dear might of him that walked the waves,
Where other groves, and other streams along,
With nectar pure his oozy locks he laves,
And hears the unexpressive nuptial song,
In the blest kingdoms meek of joy and love.
There entertain him all the saints above,
In solemn troops, and sweet societies
That sing, and singing in their glory move,   180
And wipe the tears for ever from his eyes.
Now, Lycidas, the shepherds weep no more;
Henceforth thou art the Genius of the shore
In thy large recompense, and shalt be good
To all that wander in that perilous flood.
  Thus sang the uncouth swain to th' oaks and rills,
While the still Morn went out with sandals grey;
He touched the tender stops of various quills,

With eager thought warbling his Doric lay:
190   And now the sun had stretched out all the hills,
And now was dropped into the western bay;
At last he rose, and twitched his mantle blue:
Tomorrow to fresh woods and pastures new.

A Masque of the Same Author
Presented at Ludlow Castle, 1634
before the Earl of Bridgewater
then President of Wales
['Comus']

The Persons

The Attendant Spirit, afterwards in the habit of Thyrsis.
Comus, with his crew.
The Lady.
First Brother.
Second Brother.
Sabrina the Nymph.

The chief persons which presented, were
The Lord Brackley,
Mr. Thomas Egerton his brother,
The Lady Alice Egerton.

The first scene discovers a wild wood.
The Attendant Spirit descends or enters.

Before the starry threshold of Jove's court
My mansion is, where those immortal shapes
Of bright aërial Spirits live insphered
In regions mild of calm and sérene air,
Above the smoke and stir of this dim spot
Which men call earth, and with low-thoughted care
Confined, and pestered in this pinfold here,
Strive to keep up a frail and feverish being

Unmindful of the crown that Virtue gives
After this mortal change, to her true servants   10
Amongst the énthroned gods on sainted seats.
Yet some there be that by due steps aspire
To lay their just hands on that golden key
That opes the palace of eternity:
To such my errand is, and but for such
I would not soil these pure ambrosial weeds
With the rank vapours of this sin-worn mould.
　　But to my task. Neptune besides the sway
Of every salt flood, and each ebbing stream,
Took in by lot 'twixt high and nether Jove,   20
Imperial rule of all the sea-girt isles
That like to rich and various gems inlay
The unadornèd bosom of the deep,
Which he to grace his tributary gods
By course commits to several government,
And gives them leave to wear their sapphire crowns
And wield their little tridents; but this isle
The greatest and the best of all the main
He quarters to his blue-haired deities;
And all this tract that fronts the falling sun   30
A noble peer of mickle trust and power
Has in his charge, with tempered awe to guide
An old and haughty nation proud in arms:
Where his fair offspring nursed in princely lore
Are coming to attend their father's state,
And new-entrusted sceptre. But their way
Lies through the pérplexed paths of this drear wood,
The nodding horror of whose shady brows
Threats the forlorn and wand'ring passenger.
And here their tender age might suffer peril,   40
But that by quick command from sov'reign Jove
I was despatched for their defence, and guard;
And listen why, for I will tell ye now
What never yet was heard in tale or song
From old or modern bard in hall, or bow'r.
　　Bacchus, that first from out the purple grape

Crushed the sweet poison of misusèd wine,
After the Tuscan mariners transformed,
Coasting the Tyrrhene shore, as the winds listed,
50   On Circe's island fell (who knows not Circe
The daughter of the Sun? Whose charmèd cup
Whoever tasted, lost his upright shape,
And downward fell into a grovelling swine).
This nymph that gazed upon his clust'ring locks
With ivy berries wreathed, and his blithe youth,
Had by him, ere he parted thence, a son
Much like his father, but his mother more,
Whom therefore she brought up and Comus named,
Who ripe, and frolic of his full-grown age,
60   Roving the Celtic and Iberian fields,
At last betakes him to this ominous wood,
And in thick shelter of black shades embowered,
Excels his mother at her mighty art,
Off'ring to every weary traveller,
His orient liquor in a crystal glass,
To quench the drouth of Phoebus, which as they taste
(For most do taste through fond intemperate thirst)
Soon as the potion works, their human count'nance,
Th' express resemblance of the gods, is changed
70   Into some brutish form of wolf, or bear,
Or ounce, or tiger, hog, or bearded goat,
All other parts remaining as they were;
And they, so perfect is their misery,
Not once perceive their foul disfigurement,
But boast themselves more comely than before,
And all their friends and native home forget,
To roll with pleasure in a sensual sty.
Therefore when any favoured of high Jove
Chances to pass through this advent'rous glade,
80   Swift as the sparkle of a glancing star
I shoot from Heav'n to give him safe convóy,
As now I do: but first I must put off
These my sky robes spun out of Iris' woof,
And take the weeds and likeness of a swain,

That to the service of this house belongs,
Who with his soft pipe, and smooth-dittied song,
Well knows to still the wild winds when they roar,
And hush the waving woods; nor of less faith,
And in this office of his mountain watch,
Likeliest, and nearest to the present aid   90
Of this occasion. But I hear the tread
Of hateful steps; I must be viewless now.

*Comus enters with a charming-rod in one hand, his glass in
the other, with him a rout of monsters headed like sundry
sorts of wild beasts, but otherwise like men and women, their
apparel glistering; they come in making a riotous and unruly
noise, with torches in their hands.*

  Comus. The star that bids the shepherd fold,
Now the top of heav'n doth hold,
And the gilded car of day,
His glowing axle doth allay
In the steep Atlantic stream,
And the slope sun his upward beam
Shoots against the dusky pole,
Pacing toward the other goal   100
Of his chamber in the east.
Meanwhile, welcome joy and feast,
Midnight shout, and revelry,
Tipsy dance and jollity.
Braid your locks with rosy twine,
Dropping odours, dropping wine.
Rigour now is gone to bed,
And Advice with scrupulous head,
Strict Age, and sour Severity
With their grave saws in slumber lie.   110
We that are of purer fire,
Imitate the starry choir,
Who in their nightly watchful spheres,
Lead in swift round the months and years.
The sounds and seas with all their finny drove,

Now to the moon in wavering morris move,
And on the tawny sands and shelves,
Trip the pert fairies and the dapper elves;
By dimpled brook, and fountain brim,
120 The wood-nymphs decked with daisies trim,
Their merry wakes and pastimes keep:
What hath night to do with sleep?
Night hath better sweets to prove,
Venus now wakes, and wakens Love.
Come let us our rites begin
'Tis only daylight that makes sin,
Which these dun shades will ne'er report.
Hail goddess of nocturnal sport
Dark-veiled Cotytto, t' whom the secret flame
130 Of midnight torches burns; mysterious dame
That ne'er art called, but when the dragon womb
Of Stygian darkness spits her thickest gloom,
And makes one blot of all the air,
Stay thy cloudy ebon chair,
Wherein thou rid'st with Hecat', and befriend
Us thy vowed priests, till utmost end
Of all thy dues be done, and none left out,
Ere the blabbing eastern scout,
The nice Morn on the Indian steep
140 From her cabined loophole peep,
And to the tell-tale sun descry
Our concealed solemnity.
Come, knit hands, and beat the ground,
In a light fantastic round.

The Measure in a wild, rude and wanton antic

Break off, break off, I feel the different pace
Of some chaste footing near about this ground.
Run to your shrouds, within these brakes, and trees;
Our number may affright: some virgin sure
(For so I can distinguish by mine art)
150 Benighted in these woods. Now to my charms

And to my wily trains; I shall ere long
Be well stocked with as fair a herd as grazed
About my mother Circe. Thus I hurl
My dazzling spells into the spongy air,
Of power to cheat the eye with blear illusion,
And give it false presentments, lest the place
And my quaint habits breed astonishment,
And put the damsel to suspicious flight,
Which must not be, for that's against my course;
I under fair pretence of friendly ends,   160
And well-placed words of glozing courtesy
Baited with reasons not unplausible
Wind me into the easy-hearted man,
And hug him into snares. When once her eye
Hath met the virtue of this magic dust,
I shall appear some harmless villager
Whom thrift keeps up about his country gear;
But here she comes, I fairly step aside
And hearken, if I may, her business here.

The Lady enters.

    Lady. This way the noise was, if mine ear be true,   170
My best guide now; methought it was the sound
Of riot and ill-managed merriment,
Such as the jocund flute or gamesome pipe
Stirs up among the loose unlettered hinds,
When for their teeming flocks, and granges full
In wanton dance they praise the bounteous Pan,
And thank the gods amiss. I should be loath
To meet the rudeness and swilled insolence
Of such late wassailers; yet O where else
Shall I inform my unacquainted feet   180
In the blind mazes of this tangled wood?
My brothers when they saw me wearied out
With this long way, resolving here to lodge
Under the spreading favour of these pines,

Stepped as they said to the next thicket side
To bring me berries, or such cooling fruit
As the kind hospitable woods provide.
They left me then, when the grey-hooded Ev'n
Like a sad votarist in palmer's weed
190 Rose from the hindmost wheels of Phoebus' wain.
But where they are, and why they came not back,
Is now the labour of my thoughts; 'tis likeliest
They had engaged their wand'ring steps too far,
And envious darkness, ere they could return,
Had stole them from me; else O thievish Night
Why shouldst thou, but for some felonious end,
In thy dark lantern thus close up the stars
That Nature hung in heav'n, and filled their lamps
With everlasting oil, to give due light
200 To the misled and lonely traveller?
This is the place, as well as I may guess,
Whence even now the tumult of loud mirth
Was rife, and perfect in my listening ear,
Yet nought but single darkness do I find.
What might this be? A thousand fantasies
Begin to throng into my memory
Of calling shapes, and beck'ning shadows dire,
And airy tongues that syllable men's names
On sands, and shores, and desert wildernesses.
210 These thoughts may startle well, but not astound
The virtuous mind, that ever walks attended
By a strong siding champion Conscïence. –
O welcome pure-eyed Faith, white-handed Hope,
Thou hovering angel girt with golden wings,
And thou unblemished form of Chastity,
I see ye visibly, and now believe
That he, the Súpreme Good, t' whom all things ill
Are but as slavish officers of vengeance,
Would send a glist'ring guardian if need were
220 To keep my life and honour unassailed.
Was I deceived, or did a sable cloud
Turn forth her silver lining on the night?

I did not err, there does a sable cloud
Turn forth her silver lining on the night,
And casts a gleam over this tufted grove.
I cannot hallo to my brothers, but
Such noise as I can make to be heard farthest
I'll venture, for my new enlivened spirits
Prompt me; and they perhaps are not far off.

Song

Sweet Echo, sweetest nymph that liv'st unseen   230
    Within thy airy shell
  By slow Meander's margent green,
And in the violet-embroidered vale
  Where the love-lorn nightingale
Nightly to thee her sad song mourneth well.
Canst thou not tell me of a gentle pair
  That likest thy Narcissus are?
    O if thou have
Hid them in some flow'ry cave,
  Tell me but where,   240
  Sweet queen of parley, daughter of the sphere.
So may'st thou be translated to the skies,
And give resounding grace to all heav'n's harmonies.

Comus. Can any mortal mixture of earth's mould
Breathe such divine enchanting ravishment?
Sure something holy lodges in that breast,
And with these raptures moves the vocal air
To testify his hidden residence;
How sweetly did they float upon the wings
Of silence, through the empty-vaulted night,   250
At every fall smoothing the raven down
Of darkness till it smiled: I have oft heard
My mother Circe with the Sirens three,
Amidst the flow'ry-kirtled Naiades
Culling their potent herbs, and baleful drugs,
Who as they sung, would take the prisoned soul,
And lap it in Elysium; Scylla wept,

And chid her barking waves into attention,
And fell Charybdis murmured soft applause:
260 Yet they in pleasing slumber lulled the sense,
And in sweet madness robbed it of itself,
But such a sacred, and home-felt delight,
Such sober certainty of waking bliss
I never heard till now. I'll speak to her
And she shall be my queen. Hail foreign wonder
Whom certain these rough shades did never breed –
Unless the goddess that in rural shrine
Dwell'st here with Pan, or Sylvan, by blest song
Forbidding every bleak unkindly fog
270 To touch the prosperous growth of this tall wood.
Lady. Nay gentle shepherd, ill is lost that praise
That is addressed to unattending ears;
Not any boast of skill, but extreme shift
How to regain my severed company
Compelled me to awake the courteous Echo
To give me answer from her mossy couch.
Comus. What chance good Lady hath bereft you thus?
Lady. Dim darkness, and this leavy labyrinth.
Comus. Could that divide you from near-ushering
     guides?
280 *Lady.* They left me weary on a grassy turf.
Comus. By falsehood, or discourtesy, or why?
Lady. To seek i' the valley some cool friendly spring.
Comus. And left your fair side all unguarded Lady?
Lady. They were but twain, and purposed quick return.
Comus. Perhaps forestalling night prevented them.
Lady. How easy my misfortune is to hit!
Comus. Imports their loss, beside the present need?
Lady. No less than if I should my brothers lose.
Comus. Were they of manly prime, or youthful bloom?
290 *Lady.* As smooth as Hebe's their unrazored lips.
Comus. Two such I saw, what time the laboured ox
In his loose traces from the furrow came,
And the swinked hedger at his supper sat;
I saw them under a green mantling vine

That crawls along the side of yon small hill,
Plucking ripe clusters from the tender shoots;
Their port was more than human, as they stood;
I took it for a faery visïon
Of some gay creatures of the element
That in the colours of the rainbow live   300
And play i' th' plighted clouds. I was awe-strook,
And as I passed, I worshipped; if those you seek,
It were a journey like the path to heav'n
To help you find them.
Lady.   Gentle villager
What readiest way would bring me to that place?
Comus. Due west it rises from this shrubby point.
Lady. To find out that, good shepherd, I suppose,
In such a scant allowance of star-light,
Would overtask the best land-pilot's art,
Without the sure guess of well-practised feet.   310
Comus. I know each lane, and every alley green,
Dingle, or bushy dell of this wild wood,
And every bosky bourn from side to side
My daily walks and ancient neighbourhood,
And if your stray attendance be yet lodged,
Or shroud within these limits, I shall know
Ere morrow wake, or the low-roosted lark
From her thatched pallet rouse; if otherwise,
I can conduct you Lady to a low
But loyal cottage, where you may be safe   320
Till further quest.
Lady.   Shepherd I take thy word,
And trust thy honest-offered courtesy,
Which oft is sooner found in lowly sheds
With smoky rafters, than in tap'stry halls
And courts of princes, where it first was named,
And yet is most pretended: in a place
Less warranted than this, or less secure
I cannot be, that I should fear to change it.
Eye me blest Providence, and square my trial
To my proportioned strength. Shepherd lead on. –   330

The Two Brothers

Elder Brother. Unmuffle ye faint stars, and thou fair moon
That wont'st to love the traveller's benison,
Stoop thy pale visage through an amber cloud,
And disinherit Chaos, that reigns here
In double night of darkness, and of shades;
Or if your influence be quite dammed up
With black usurping mists, some gentle taper
Though a rush-candle from the wicker hole
Of some clay habitation, visit us

340   With thy long levelled rule of streaming light,
And thou shalt be our star of Arcady,
Or Tyrian Cynosure.
Second Brother.   Or if our eyes
Be barred that happiness, might we but hear
The folded flocks penned in their wattled cotes,
Or sound of pastoral reed with oaten stops,
Or whistle from the lodge, or village cock
Count the night watches to his feathery dames,
'Twould be some solace yet, some little cheering
In this close dungeon of innumerous boughs.

350   But O that hapless virgin our lost sister,
Where may she wander now, whither betake her
From the chill dew, amongst rude burs and thistles?
Perhaps some cold bank is her bolster now
Or 'gainst the rugged bark of some broad elm
Leans her unpillowed head fraught with sad fears.
What if in wild amazement, and affright,
Or while we speak within the direful grasp
Of savage hunger, or of savage heat?
Elder Brother. Peace brother, be not over-exquisite

360   To cast the fashion of uncertain evils;
For grant they be so, while they rest unknown,
What need a man forestall his date of grief,
And run to meet what he would most avoid?
Or if they be but false alarms of fear,

How bitter is such self-delusïon!
I do not think my sister so to seek,
Or so unprincipled in virtue's book,
And the sweet peace that goodness bosoms ever,
As that the single want of light and noise
(Not being in danger, as I trust she is not)   370
Could stir the constant mood of her calm thoughts,
And put them into misbecoming plight.
Virtue could see to do what virtue would
By her own radiant light, though sun and moon
Were in the flat sea sunk. And Wisdom's self
Oft seeks to sweet retired solitude,
Where with her best nurse Contemplatïon
She plumes her feathers, and lets grow her wings
That in the various bustle of resort
Were all to-ruffled, and sometimes impaired.   380
He that has light within his own clear breast
May sit i' th' centre, and enjoy bright day,
But he that hides a dark soul and foul thoughts
Benighted walks under the midday sun;
Himself is his own dungeon.
Second Brother.   'Tis most true
That musing meditation most affects
The pensive secrecy of desert cell,
Far from the cheerful haunt of men and herds,
And sits as safe as in a senate-house;
For who would rob a hermit of his weeds,   390
His few books, or his beads, or maple dish,
Or do his grey hairs any violence?
But beauty like the fair Hesperian tree
Laden with blooming gold, had need the guard
Of dragon watch with unenchanted eye,
To save her blossoms, and defend her fruit
From the rash hand of bold Incontinence.
You may as well spread out the unsunned heaps
Of miser's treasure by an outlaw's den,
And tell me it is safe, as bid me hope   400
Danger will wink on opportunity,

And let a single helpless maiden pass
Uninjured in this wild surrounding waste.
Of night, or loneliness it recks me not;
I fear the dread events that dog them both,
Lest some ill-greeting touch attempt the person
Of our unownèd sister.
Elder Brother.   I do not, brother,
Infer, as if I thought my sister's state
Secure without all doubt, or controversy:
410   Yet where an equal poise of hope and fear
Does arbitrate th' event, my nature is
That I incline to hope, rather than fear,
And gladly banish squint suspicïon.
My sister is not so defenceless left
As you imagine; she has a hidden strength
Which you remember not.
Second Brother.   What hidden strength,
Unless the strength of Heav'n, if you mean that?
Elder Brother. I mean that too, but yet a hidden strength
Which if Heav'n gave it, may be termed her own:
420   'Tis chastity, my brother, chastity:
She that has that, is clad in cómplete steel,
And like a quivered nymph with arrows keen
May trace huge forests, and unharboured heaths,
Infamous hills, and sandy perilous wilds,
Where through the sacred rays of chastity,
No savage fierce, bandit, or mountaineer
Will dare to soil her virgin purity:
Yea there, where very desolation dwells,
By grots, and caverns shagged with horrid shades,
430   She may pass on with unblenched majesty,
Be it not done in pride, or in presumption.
Some say no evil thing that walks by night
In fog, or fire, by lake, or moorish fen,
Blue meagre hag, or stubborn unlaid ghost,
That breaks his magic chains at curfew time,
No goblin, or swart faery of the mine,
Hath hurtful power o'er true virginity.

Do ye believe me yet, or shall I call
Antiquity from the old schools of Greece
To testify the arms of chastity?   440
Hence had the huntress Dian her dread bow,
Fair silver-shafted queen for ever chaste,
Wherewith she tamed the brinded lioness
And spotted mountain pard, but set at nought
The frivolous bolt of Cupid; gods and men
Feared her stern frown, and she was queen o' th'
     woods.
What was that snaky-headed Gorgon shield
That wise Minerva wore, unconquered virgin,
Wherewith she freezed her foes to congealed stone,
But rigid looks of chaste austerity,   450
And noble grace that dashed brute violence
With sudden adoration, and blank awe?
So dear to Heav'n is saintly chastity,
That when a soul is found sincerely so,
A thousand liveried angels lackey her,
Driving far off each thing of sin and guilt,
And in clear dream and solemn visïon
Tell her of things that no gross ear can hear,
Till oft converse with Heav'nly habitants
Begin to cast a beam on th' outward shape,   460
The unpolluted temple of the mind,
And turns it by degrees to the soul's essence,
Till all be made immortal: but when lust
By unchaste looks, loose gestures, and foul talk,
But most by lewd and lavish act of sin,
Lets in defilement to the inward parts,
The soul grows clotted by contagïon,
Embodies, and imbrutes, till she quite lose
The divine property of her first being.
Such are those thick and gloomy shadows damp   470
Oft seen in charnel vaults, and sepulchres
Lingering and sitting by a new-made grave,
As loath to leave the body that it loved,
And linked itself by carnal sensualty

To a degenerate and degraded state.
Second Brother. How charming is divine philosophy!
Not harsh and crabbed, as dull fools suppose,
But musical as is Apollo's lute,
And a perpetual feast of nectared sweets,
Where no crude surfeit reigns.
480 *Elder Brother.*   List, list, I hear
Some far-off hallo break the silent air.
Second Brother. Methought so too; what should
     it be?
Elder Brother.   For certain
Either some one like us night-foundered here,
Or else some neighbour woodman, or at worst,
Some roving robber calling to his fellows.
Second Brother. Heav'n keep my sister. Again, again,
     and near.
Best draw, and stand upon our guard.
Elder Brother.   I'll hallo;
If he be friendly he comes well; if not,
Defence is a good cause, and Heav'n be for us.

The Attendant Spirit habited like a shepherd

490 That hallo I should know. What are you? Speak;
     Come not too near, you fall on iron stakes else.
Spirit. What voice is that, my young lord? Speak again.
Second Brother. O brother, 'tis my father's shepherd
     sure.
Elder Brother. Thyrsis? Whose artful strains have oft
     delayed
The huddling brook to hear his madrigal,
And sweetened every musk-rose of the dale,
How cam'st thou here good swain? Hath any ram
Slipped from the fold, or young kid lost his dam,
Or straggling wether the pent flock forsook?
500 How couldst thou find this dark sequestered nook?
Spirit. O my loved master's heir, and his next joy,
I came not here on such a trivial toy

As a strayed ewe, or to pursue the stealth
Of pilfering wolf; not all the fleecy wealth
That doth enrich these downs, is worth a thought
To this my errand, and the care it brought.
But O my virgin Lady, where is she?
How chance she is not in your company?
Elder Brother. To tell thee sadly shepherd, without
      blame,
Or our neglect, we lost her as we came.   510
Spirit. Ay me unhappy, then my fears are true.
Elder Brother. What fears good Thyrsis? Prithee
      briefly show.
Spirit. I'll tell ye. 'Tis not vain or fabulous
(Though so esteemed by shallow ignorance)
What the sage poets, taught by th' Heavenly Muse,
Storied of old in high immortal verse
Of dire Chimeras and enchanted isles,
And rifted rocks whose entrance leads to Hell,
For such there be, but unbelief is blind.
      Within the navel of this hideous wood,   520
Immured in cypress shades a sorcerer dwells
Of Bacchus and of Circe born, great Comus,
Deep skilled in all his mother's witcheries,
And here to every thirsty wanderer,
By sly enticement gives his baneful cup,
With many murmurs mixed, whose pleasing poison
The visage quite transforms of him that drinks,
And the inglorious likeness of a beast
Fixes instead, unmoulding reason's mintage
Charáctered in the face; this have I learnt   530
Tending my flocks hard by i' th' hilly crofts
That brow this bottom glade, whence night by night
He and his monstrous rout are heard to howl
Like stabled wolves, or tigers at their prey,
Doing abhorrèd rites to Hecate
In their obscurèd haunts of inmost bow'rs.
Yet have they many baits, and guileful spells
T' inveigle and invite th' unwary sense

Of them that pass unweeting by the way.
540   This evening late, by then the chewing flocks
Had ta'en their supper on the savoury herb
Of knot-grass dew-besprent, and were in fold,
I sat me down to watch upon a bank
With ivy canopied, and interwove
With flaunting honeysuckle, and began
Wrapped in a pleasing fit of melancholy
To meditate my rural minstrelsy
Till fancy had her fill; but ere a close
The wonted roar was up amidst the woods,
550   And filled the air with barbarous dissonance,
At which I ceased, and listened them a while,
Till an unusual stop of sudden silence
Gave respite to the drowsy-frighted steeds
That draw the litter of close-curtained sleep.
At last a soft and solemn-breathing sound
Rose like a steam of rich distilled perfumes,
And stole upon the air, that even Silence
Was took ere she was ware, and wished she might
Deny her nature, and be never more
560   Still to be so displaced. I was all ear,
And took in strains that might create a soul
Under the ribs of Death. But O ere long
Too well I did perceive it was the voice
Of my most honoured Lady, your dear sister.
Amazed I stood, harrowed with grief and fear,
And 'O poor hapless nightingale' thought I,
'How sweet thou sing'st, how near the deadly snare!'
Then down the lawns I ran with headlong haste
Through paths and turnings often trod by day,
570   Till guided by mine ear I found the place
Where that damned wizard, hid in sly disguise
(For so by certain signs I knew) had met
Already, ere my best speed could prevent,
The aidless innocent Lady his wished prey,
Who gently asked if he had seen such two,
Supposing him some neighbour villager;

Longer I durst not stay, but soon I guessed
Ye were the two she meant; with that I sprung
Into swift flight, till I had found you here,
But further know I not.   580
Second Brother.   O night and shades,
How are ye joined with Hell in triple knot
Against th' unarmèd weakness of one virgin
Alone, and helpless! Is this the confidence
You gave me brother?
Elder Brother.   Yes, and keep it still,
Lean on it safely; not a period
Shall be unsaid for me: against the threats
Of malice or of sorcery, or that power
Which erring men call Chance, this I hold firm,
Virtue may be assailed, but never hurt,
Surprised by unjust force, but not enthralled,   590
Yea even that which mischief meant most harm,
Shall in the happy trial prove most glory.
But evil on itself shall back recoil,
And mix no more with goodness, when at last
Gathered like scum, and settled to itself
It shall be in eternal restless change
Self-fed, and self-consumed. If this fail,
The pillared firmament is rottenness,
And earth's base built on stubble. But come, let's on.
Against th' opposing will and arm of Heav'n   600
May never this just sword be lifted up.
But for that damned magician, let him be girt
With all the grisly legïons that troop
Under the sooty flag of Acheron,
Harpies and Hydras, or all the monstrous forms
'Twixt Africa and Ind, I'll find him out,
And force him to restore his purchase back,
Or drag him by the curls to a foul death,
Cursed as his life.
Spirit.   Alas good vent'rous youth,
I love thy courage yet, and bold emprise,   610
But here thy sword can do thee little stead;

Far other arms, and other weapons must
Be those that quell the might of Hellish charms;
He with his bare wand can unthread thy joints,
And crumble all thy sinews.
Elder Brother.   Why prithee shepherd
How durst thou then thyself approach so near
As to make this relation?
Spirit.   Care and utmost shifts
How to secure the Lady from surprisal
Brought to my mind a certain shepherd lad
620 Of small regard to see to, yet well skilled
In every virtuous plant and healing herb
That spreads her verdant leaf to the morning ray;
He loved me well, and oft would beg me sing,
Which when I did, he on the tender grass
Would sit, and hearken even to ecstasy,
And in requital ope his leathern scrip,
And show me simples of a thousand names
Telling their strange and vigorous faculties;
Amongst the rest a small unsightly root,
630 But of divine effect, he culled me out;
The leaf was darkish, and had prickles on it,
But in another country, as he said,
Bore a bright golden flower, but not in this soil:
Unknown, and like esteemed, and the dull swain
Treads on it daily with his clouted shoon,
And yet more med'cinal is it than that Moly
That Hermes once to wise Ulysses gave;
He called it haemony, and gave it me,
And bade me keep it as of sov'reign use
640 'Gainst all enchantments, mildew blast, or damp
Or ghastly Furies' apparition;
I pursed it up, but little reck'ning made
Till now that this extremity compelled,
But now I find it true; for by this means
I knew the foul enchanter though disguised,
Entered the very lime-twigs of his spells,
And yet came off: if you have this about you

(As I will give you when we go) you may
Boldly assault the necromancer's hall;
Where if he be, with dauntless hardihood,   650
And brandished blade rush on him, break his glass,
And shed the luscious liquor on the ground,
But seize his wand. Though he and his cursed crew
Fierce sign of battle make, and menace high,
Or like the sons of Vulcan vomit smoke,
Yet will they soon retire, if he but shrink.
Elder Brother. Thyrsis lead on apace, I'll follow thee,
And some good angel bear a shield before us.

*The scene changes to a stately palace, set out with all manner
of deliciousness: soft music, tables spread with all dainties.
Comus appears with his rabble, and the Lady set in an
enchanted chair, to whom he offers his glass, which she puts
by, and goes about to rise.*

  Comus. Nay Lady sit; if I but wave this wand,
Your nerves are all chained up in alabaster,   660
And you a statue; or as Daphne was,
Root-bound, that fled Apollo.
  Lady.   Fool, do not boast;
Thou canst not touch the freedom of my mind
With all thy charms, although this corporal rind
Thou hast immanacled, while Heav'n sees good.
  Comus. Why are you vexed Lady? Why do you frown?
Here dwell no frowns, nor anger; from these gates
Sorrow flies far: see here be all the pleasures
That fancy can beget on youthful thoughts
When the fresh blood grows lively, and returns   670
Brisk as the April buds in primrose season.
And first behold this cordial julep here
That flames and dances in his crystal bounds
With spirits of balm and fragrant syrups mixed.
Not that Nepenthes which the wife of Thone
In Egypt gave to Jove-born Helena
Is of such power to stir up joy as this,

To life so friendly, or so cool to thirst.
Why should you be so cruel to yourself,
And to those dainty limbs which Nature lent
For gentle usage, and soft delicacy?
But you invert the cov'nants of her trust,
And harshly deal like an ill borrower
With that which you received on other terms,
Scorning the unexempt conditïon
By which all mortal frailty must subsist,
Refreshment after toil, ease after pain,
That have been tired all day without repast,
And timely rest have wanted; but fair virgin
This will restore all soon.
    Lady.   'Twill not false traitor,
'Twill not restore the truth and honesty
That thou hast banished from thy tongue with lies;
Was this the cottage and the safe abode
Thou told'st me of? What grim aspécts are these,
These ugly-headed monsters? Mercy guard me!
Hence with thy brewed enchantments, foul deceiver;
Hast thou betrayed my credulous innocence
With vizored falsehood, and base forgery,
And wouldst thou seek again to trap me here
With lickerish baits fit to ensnare a brute?
Were it a draught for Juno when she banquets,
I would not taste thy treasonous offer; none
But such as are good men can give good things,
And that which is not good, is not delicious
To a well-governed and wise appetite.
    Comus. O foolishness of men! that lend their ears
To those budge doctors of the Stoic fur,
And fetch their precepts from the Cynic tub,
Praising the lean and sallow Abstinence.
Wherefore did Nature pour her bounties forth
With such a full and unwithdrawing hand,
Covering the earth with odours, fruits, and flocks,
Thronging the seas with spawn innumerable,
But all to please, and sate the curious taste?

And set to work millions of spinning worms,
That in their green shops weave the smooth-haired silk
To deck her sons; and that no corner might
Be vacant of her plenty, in her own loins
She hutched th' all-worshipped ore and precious gems
To store her children with; if all the world   720
Should in a pet of temperance feed on pulse,
Drink the clear stream, and nothing wear but frieze,
Th' all-giver would be unthanked, would be unpraised,
Not half his riches known, and yet despised,
And we should serve him as a grudging master,
As a penurious niggard of his wealth,
And live like Nature's bastards, not her sons,
Who would be quite surcharged with her own weight,
And strangled with her waste fertility;
Th' earth cumbered, and the winged air darked
      with plumes,   730
The herds would over-multitude their lords,
The sea o'erfraught would swell, and th' unsought
      diamonds
Would so emblaze the forehead of the deep,
And so bestud with stars, that they below
Would grow inured to light, and come at last
To gaze upon the sun with shameless brows.
List Lady be not coy, and be not cozened
With that same vaunted name Virginity;
Beauty is Nature's coin, must not be hoarded,
But must be current, and the good thereof   740
Consists in mutual and partaken bliss,
Unsavoury in th' enjoyment of itself.
If you let slip time, like a neglected rose
It withers on the stalk with languished head.
Beauty is Nature's brag, and must be shown
In courts, at feasts, and high solemnities
Where most may wonder at the workmanship;
It is for homely features to keep home,
They had their name thence; coarse complexïons
And cheeks of sorry grain will serve to ply   750

The sampler, and to tease the housewife's wool.
What need a vermeil-tinctured lip for that,
Love-darting eyes, or tresses like the morn?
There was another meaning in these gifts,
Think what, and be advised; you are but young yet.
Lady. I had not thought to have unlocked my lips
In this unhallowed air, but that this juggler
Would think to charm my judgement, as mine eyes,
Obtruding false rules pranked in reason's garb.
760 I hate when vice can bolt her arguments,
And virtue has no tongue to check her pride:
Impostor, do not charge most innocent Nature,
As if she would her children should be riotous
With her abundance; she good cateress
Means her provision only to the good
That live according to her sober laws,
And holy dictate of spare Temperance:
If every just man that now pines with want
Had but a moderate and beseeming share
770 Of that which lewdly-pampered Luxury
Now heaps upon some few with vast excess,
Nature's full blessings would be well-dispensed
In unsuperfluous even proportion,
And she no whit encumbered with her store;
And then the Giver would be better thanked,
His praise due paid, for swinish gluttony
Ne'er looks to Heav'n amidst his gorgeous feast,
But with besotted base ingratitude
Crams, and blasphemes his feeder. Shall I go on?
780 Or have I said enough? To him that dares
Arm his profane tongue with contemptuous words
Against the sun-clad power of Chastity,
Fain would I something say, yet to what end?
Thou hast nor ear, nor soul to apprehend
The sublime notion, and high mystery
That must be uttered to unfold the sage
And serious doctrine of Virginity,
And thou art worthy that thou shouldst not know

More happiness than this thy present lot.
Enjoy your dear wit, and gay rhetoric   790
That hath so well been taught her dazzling fence;
Thou art not fit to hear thyself convinced;
Yet should I try, the uncontrollèd worth
Of this pure cause would kindle my rapt spirits
To such a flame of sacred vehemence,
That dumb things would be moved to sympathize,
And the brute Earth would lend her nerves, and shake,
Till all thy magic structures reared so high,
Were shattered into heaps o'er thy false head.
Comus. She fables not, I feel that I do fear   800
Her words set off by some superior power;
And though not mortal, yet a cold shudd'ring dew
Dips me all o'er, as when the wrath of Jove
Speaks thunder, and the chains of Erebus
To some of Saturn's crew. I must dissemble,
And try her yet more strongly. Come, no more,
This is mere moral babble, and direct
Against the canon laws of our foundation;
I must not suffer this; yet 'tis but the lees
And settlings of a melancholy blood;   810
But this will cure all straight; one sip of this
Will bathe the drooping spirits in delight
Beyond the bliss of dreams. Be wise, and taste.

*The Brothers rush in with swords drawn, wrest his glass out
of his hand, and break it against the ground; his rout make
sign of resistance, but are all driven in; the Attendant Spirit
comes in.*

Spirit. What, have you let the false enchanter 'scape?
O ye mistook, ye should have snatched his wand
And bound him fast; without his rod reversed,
And backward mutters of dissevering power,
We cannot free the Lady that sits here
In stony fetters fixed, and motionless;
Yet stay, be not disturbed, now I bethink me,   820

Some other means I have which may be used,
Which once of Meliboeus old I learnt,
The soothest shepherd that e'er piped on plains.
    There is a gentle nymph not far from hence,
That with moist curb sways the smooth Severn stream,
Sabrina is her name, a virgin pure;
Whilom she was the daughter of Locrine,
That had the sceptre from his father Brute.
She, guiltless damsel, flying the mad pursuit
830   Of her enragèd stepdame Guendolen,
Commended her fair innocence to the flood
That stayed her flight with his cross-flowing course;
The water nymphs that in the bottom played,
Held up their pearlèd wrists and took her in,
Bearing her straight to agèd Nereus' hall,
Who piteous of her woes, reared her lank head,
And gave her to his daughters to imbathe
In nectared lavers strewed with asphodel,
And through the porch and inlet of each sense
840   Dropped in ambrosial oils till she revived,
And underwent a quick immortal change,
Made goddess of the river; still she retains
Her maiden gentleness, and oft at eve
Visits the herds along the twilight meadows,
Helping all urchin blasts, and ill-luck signs
That the shrewd meddling elf delights to make,
Which she with precious vialed liquors heals.
For which the shepherds at their festivals
Carol her goodness loud in rustic lays,
850   And throw sweet garland wreaths into her stream
Of pansies, pinks, and gaudy daffodils.
And, as the old swain said, she can unlock
The clasping charm, and thaw the numbing spell,
If she be right invoked in warbled song,
For maidenhood she loves, and will be swift
To aid a virgin, such as was herself
In hard-besetting need; this will I try,
And add the power of some adjuring verse.

Song

Sabrina fair,
   Listen where thou art sitting   860
Under the glassy, cool, translucent wave,
   In twisted braids of lilies knitting
The loose train of thy amber-dropping hair;
   Listen for dear honour's sake,
   Goddess of the silver lake,
     Listen and save.

Listen and appear to us
In name of great Oceanus,
By th' earth-shaking Neptune's mace,
And Tethys' grave majestic pace,   870
By hoary Nereus' wrinkled look,
And the Carpathian wizard's hook,
By scaly Triton's winding shell,
And old soothsaying Glaucus' spell,
By Leucothea's lovely hands,
And her son that rules the strands,
By Thetis' tinsel-slippered feet,
And the songs of Sirens sweet,
By dead Parthenope's dear tomb,
And fair Ligea's golden comb,   880
Wherewith she sits on diamond rocks
Sleeking her soft alluring locks,
By all the nymphs that nightly dance
Upon thy streams with wily glance,
Rise, rise, and heave thy rosy head
From thy coral-paven bed,
And bridle in thy headlong wave,
Till thou our summons answered have.
                 Listen and save.

Sabrina rises, attended by water-nymphs, and sings.

890   *By the rushy-fringèd bank,*
         Where grows the willow and the osier dank,
            My sliding chariot stays,
         Thick set with agate, and the azurn sheen
         Of turquoise blue, and emerald green
            That in the channel strays,
         Whilst from off the waters fleet
         Thus I set my printless feet
         O'er the cowslip's velvet head,
            That bends not as I tread;
900   *Gentle swain at thy request*
            I am here.
         Spirit. Goddess dear,
         We implore thy powerful hand
         To undo the charmèd band
         Of true virgin here distressed,
         Through the force and through the wile
         Of unblest enchanter vile.
         Sabrina. Shepherd 'tis my office best
         To help ensnarèd chastity;
910   Brightest Lady look on me;
         Thus I sprinkle on thy breast
         Drops that from my fountain pure,
         I have kept of precious cure;
         Thrice upon thy finger's tip,
         Thrice upon thy rubied lip;
         Next this marble venomed seat
         Smeared with gums of glutinous heat
         I touch with chaste palms moist and cold.
         Now the spell hath lost his hold;
920   And I must haste ere morning hour
         To wait in Amphitrite's bower.

Sabrina descends, and the Lady rises out of her seat.

         Spirit. Virgin, daughter of Locrine,
         Sprung of old Anchises' line,
         May thy brimmèd waves for this

Their full tribute never miss
From a thousand petty rills,
That tumble down the snowy hills:
Summer drought, or singèd air
Never scorch thy tresses fair,
Nor wet October's torrent flood   930
Thy molten crystal fill with mud;
May thy billows roll ashore
The beryl, and the golden ore;
May thy lofty head be crowned
With many a tower and terrace round,
And here and there thy banks upon
With groves of myrrh, and cinnamon.

   Come Lady while Heaven lends us grace,
Let us fly this cursèd place,
Lest the sorcerer us entice   940
With some other new device.
Not a waste or needless sound
Till we come to holier ground;
I shall be your faithful guide
Through this gloomy covert wide,
And not many furlongs thence
Is your father's residence,
Where this night are met in state
Many a friend to gratulate
His wished presence, and beside   950
All the swains that there abide,
With jigs, and rural dance resort;
We shall catch them at their sport,
And our sudden coming there
Will double all their mirth and cheer;
Come let us haste, the stars grow high,
But Night sits monarch yet in the mid sky.

*The scene changes, presenting Ludlow Town and the
President's Castle, then come in country dancers, after them
the Attendant Spirit, with the two Brothers and the Lady.*

Song
Spirit. *Back shepherds, back, enough your play,*
Till next sunshine holiday,
960 *Here be without duck or nod*
Other trippings to be trod
Of lighter toes, and such court guise
As Mercury did first devise
With the mincing Dryades
On the lawns and on the leas.

This second song presents them to their father and mother.

Noble Lord, and Lady bright,
I have brought ye new delight.
Here behold so goodly grown
Three fair branches of your own;
970 *Heav'n hath timely tried their youth,*
Their faith, their patience, and their truth.
And sent them here through hard assays
With a crown of deathless praise,
    To triumph in victorious dance
O'er sensual folly and intemperance.

The dances ended, the Spirit epiloguizes.

Spirit. To the Ocean now I fly,
And those happy climes that lie
Where day never shuts his eye,
Up in the broad fields of the sky:
980 There I suck the liquid air
All amidst the gardens fair
Of Hesperus, and his daughters three
That sing about the golden tree:
Along the crispèd shades and bow'rs
Revels the spruce and jocund Spring;
The Graces, and the rosy-bosomed Hours,
Thither all their bounties bring,
That there eternal Summer dwells,

And west winds with musky wing
About the cedarn alleys fling   990
Nard and cassia's balmy smells.
Iris there with humid bow,
Waters the odorous banks that blow
Flowers of more mingled hue
Than her purfled scarf can show,
And drenches with Elysian dew
(List mortals, if your ears be true)
Beds of hyacinth, and roses,
Where young Adonis oft reposes,
Waxing well of his deep wound   1000
In slumber soft, and on the ground
Sadly sits th' Assyrian queen;
But far above in spangled sheen
Celestial Cupid, her famed son advanced,
Holds his dear Psyche sweet entranced
After her wand'ring labours long,
Till free consent the gods among
Make her his eternal bride,
And from her fair unspotted side
Two blissful twins are to be born,   1010
Youth and Joy; so Jove hath sworn.
    But now my task is smoothly done,
I can fly, or I can run
Quickly to the green earth's end,
Where the bowed welkin slow doth bend,
And from thence can soar as soon
To the corners of the moon.
    Mortals that would follow me,
Love Virtue, she alone is free,
She can teach ye how to climb   1020
Higher than the sphery chime;
Or if Virtue feeble were,
Heav'n itself would stoop to her.

from ENGLISH POEMS
ADDED IN 1673

Sonnet XI
On the Detraction Which Followed Upon My Writing Certain Treatises

A book was writ of late called *Tetrachordon*;
   And woven close, both matter, form and style;
   The subject new: it walked the town a while,
   Numb'ring good intellects; now seldom pored on.
Cries the stall-reader, 'Bless us! What a word on
   A title-page is this!' And some in file
   Stand spelling false, while one might walk to Mile-
End Green. Why is it harder sirs than Gordon,
Colkitto, or Macdonnel, or Galasp?
   Those rugged names to our like mouths grow sleek
   That would have made Quintilian stare and gasp.
Thy age, like ours, O soul of Sir John Cheke,
   Hated not learning worse than toad or asp,
   When thou taught'st Cambridge and King Edward
      Greek.

Sonnet XII
On the Same

I did but prompt the age to quit their clogs
  By the known rules of ancient liberty,
  When straight a barbarous noise environs me
  Of owls and cuckoos, asses, apes and dogs.
As when those hinds that were transformed to frogs
  Railed at Latona's twin-born progeny
  Which after held the sun and moon in fee.
  But this is got by casting pearl to hogs;
That bawl for freedom in their senseless mood,
  And still revolt when truth would set them free.   10
  Licence they mean when they cry liberty;
For who loves that, must first be wise and good;
  But from that mark how far they rove we see
  For all this waste of wealth, and loss of blood.

Sonnet XIII
To Mr. H. Lawes, on his Airs

Harry, whose tuneful and well-measured song
  First taught our English music how to span
  Words with just note and accent, not to scan
  With Midas' ears, committing short and long,
Thy worth and skill exempts thee from the throng,
  With praise enough for envy to look wan;
  To after age thou shalt be writ the man
  That with smooth air couldst humour best our tongue.
Thou honour'st verse, and verse must lend her wing
  To honour thee, the priest of Phoebus' choir   10
  That tun'st their happiest lines in hymn, or story.
Dante shall give Fame leave to set thee higher
  Than his Casella, whom he wooed to sing
  Met in the milder shades of Purgatory.

Sonnet XIV
On the religious memory of Mrs. Catharine
Thomason, my Christian friend,
deceased December 1646

When Faith and Love which parted from thee never,
    Had ripened thy just soul to dwell with God,
    Meekly thou didst resign this earthy load
Of death, called life; which us from life doth sever.
Thy works and alms and all thy good endeavour
    Stayed not behind, nor in the grave were trod;
    But as Faith pointed with her golden rod,
Followed thee up to joy and bliss for ever.
Love led them on, and Faith who knew them best
10   Thy handmaids, clad them o'er with purple beams
    And azure wings, that up they flew so dressed,
And spake the truth of thee on glorious themes
    Before the Judge, who thenceforth bid thee rest
    And drink thy fill of pure immortal streams.

Sonnet XV
On the Late Massacre in Piedmont

Avenge O Lord thy slaughtered saints, whose bones
    Lie scattered on the Alpine mountains cold,
    Ev'n them who kept thy truth so pure of old
When all our fathers worshipped stocks and stones,
Forget not: in thy book record their groans
    Who were thy sheep and in their ancient fold
    Slain by the bloody Piedmontese that rolled
Mother with infant down the rocks. Their moans
The vales redoubled to the hills, and they
10   To Heav'n. Their martyred blood and ashes sow

O'er all th' Italian fields where still doth sway
The triple Tyrant: that from these may grow
  A hundredfold, who having learnt thy way
  Early may fly the Babylonian woe.

Sonnet XVI

When I consider how my light is spent,
  Ere half my days, in this dark world and wide,
  And that one talent which is death to hide,
  Lodged with me useless, though my soul more bent
To serve therewith my Maker, and present
  My true account, lest he returning chide,
  'Doth God exact day-labour, light denied?'
  I fondly ask; but Patience to prevent
That murmur, soon replies, 'God doth not need
  Either man's work or his own gifts; who best   10
  Bear his mild yoke, they serve him best; his state
Is kingly. Thousands at his bidding speed
  And post o'er land and ocean without rest:
  They also serve who only stand and wait.'

Sonnet XVII

Lawrence of virtuous father virtuous son,
  Now that the fields are dank, and ways are mire,
  Where shall we sometimes meet, and by the fire
  Help waste a sullen day, what may be won
From the hard season gaining? Time will run
  On smoother, till Favonius reinspire
  The frozen earth, and clothe in fresh attire
  The lily and rose, that neither sowed nor spun.

What neat repast shall feast us, light and choice,
10   Of Attic taste, with wine, whence we may rise
To hear the lute well touched, or artful voice
Warble immortal notes and Tuscan air?
He who of those delights can judge, and spare
To interpose them oft, is not unwise.

Sonnet XVIII

Cyriack, whose grandsire on the Royal Bench
Of British Themis, with no mean applause
Pronounced and in his volumes taught our laws,
Which others at their bar so often wrench;
Today deep thoughts resolve with me to drench
In mirth, that after no repenting draws;
Let Euclid rest and Archimedes pause,
And what the Swede intend, and what the French.
To measure life learn thou betimes, and know
10   Toward solid good what leads the nearest way;
For other things mild Heav'n a time ordains,
And disapproves that care, though wise in show,
That with superfluous burden loads the day,
And when God sends a cheerful hour, refrains.

Sonnet XIX

Methought I saw my late espousèd saint
Brought to me like Alcestis from the grave,
Whom Jove's great son to her glad husband gave,
Rescued from death by force though pale and faint.
Mine as whom washed from spot of childbed taint
Purification in the old Law did save,
And such, as yet once more I trust to have
Full sight of her in heaven without restraint,

Came vested all in white, pure as her mind:
Her face was veiled, yet to my fancied sight, 10
Love, sweetness, goodness, in her person shined
So clear, as in no face with more delight.
But O as to embrace me she inclined,
I waked, she fled, and day brought back my night.

On the New Forcers of Conscience under the Long Parliament

Because you have thrown off your prelate lord,
And with stiff vows renounced his liturgy
To seize the widowed whore Plurality
From them whose sin ye envied, not abhorred,
Dare ye for this adjure the civil sword
To force our consciences that Christ set free,
And ride us with a classic hierarchy
Taught ye by mere A. S. and Rutherford?
Men whose life, learning, faith and pure intent
Would have been held in high esteem with Paul 10
Must now be named and printed heretics
By shallow Edwards and Scotch What-d'ye-call:
But we do hope to find out all your tricks,
Your plots and packing worse than those of Trent,
                 That so the Parliament
May with their wholesome and preventive shears
Clip your phylacteries, though balk your ears,
                        And succour our just fears
When they shall read this clearly in your charge:
New *Presbyter* is but old *Priest* writ large. 20

UNCOLLECTED ENGLISH SONNETS

On the Lord General Fairfax at the
Siege of Colchester

Fairfax, whose name in arms through Europe rings
    Filling each mouth with envy or with praise,
    And all her jealous monarchs with amaze,
    And rumours loud, that daunt remotest kings,
Thy firm unshaken virtue ever brings
    Victory home, though new rebellions raise
    Their Hydra heads, and the false North displays
    Her broken league to imp their serpent wings,
O yet a nobler task awaits thy hand;
10   For what can war but endless war still breed,
    Till truth, and right from violence be freed,
And public faith cleared from the shameful brand
    Of public fraud? In vain doth valour bleed
    While avarice and rapine share the land.

To the Lord General Cromwell, May 1652, on the Proposals of Certain Ministers at the Committee for Propagation of the Gospel

Cromwell, our chief of men, who through a cloud
    Not of war only, but detractions rude,
    Guided by faith and matchless fortitude
    To peace and truth thy glorious way hast ploughed,
And on the neck of crownèd Fortune proud
    Hast reared God's trophies and his work pursued,
    While Darwen stream with blood of Scots imbrued,
    And Dunbar field resounds thy praises loud,
And Worcester's laureate wreath; yet much remains
    To conquer still; peace hath her victories   10
    No less renowned than war, new foes arise
Threat'ning to bind our souls with secular chains:
    Help us to save free conscience from the paw
    Of hireling wolves whose Gospel is their maw.

To Sir Henry Vane the Younger

Vane, young in years, but in sage counsel old,
    Than whom a better senator ne'er held
    The helm of Rome, when gowns not arms repelled
    The fierce Epirot and the African bold:
Whether to settle peace or to unfold
    The drift of hollow states, hard to be spelled,
    Then to advise how war may best, upheld,
    Move by her two main nerves, iron and gold,

In all her equipage; besides to know
10   Both spiritual power and civil, what each means,
        What severs each, thou hast learnt, which few have
                done.
The bounds of either sword to thee we owe;
        Therefore on thy firm hand religion leans
        In peace, and reckons thee her eldest son.

To Mr. Cyriack Skinner upon his Blindness

Cyriack, this three years' day these eyes, though clear
        To outward view, of blemish or of spot;
        Bereft of light their seeing have forgot,
        Nor to their idle orbs doth sight appear
Of sun or moon or star throughout the year,
        Or man or woman. Yet I argue not
        Against Heaven's hand or will, nor bate a jot
        Of heart or hope; but still bear up and steer
Right onward. What supports me dost thou ask?
10   The conscience, friend, to have lost them overplied
        In liberty's defence, my noble task,
Of which all Europe talks from side to side.
        This thought might lead me through the world's vain
                masque
        Content though blind, had I no better guide.

from PARADISE LOST

The Verse

The measure is English heroic verse without rhyme, as that of Homer in Greek, and of Virgil in Latin; rhyme being no necessary adjunct or true ornament of poem or good verse, in longer works especially, but the invention of a barbarous age, to set off wretched matter and lame metre; graced indeed since by the use of some famous modern poets, carried away by custom, but much to their own vexation, hindrance, and constraint to express many things otherwise, and for the most part worse than else they would have expressed them. Not without cause therefore some both Italian and Spanish poets of prime note have rejected rhyme both in longer and shorter works, as have also long since our best English tragedies, as a thing of itself, to all judicious ears, trivial and of no true musical delight; which consists only in apt numbers, fit quantity of syllables, and the sense variously drawn out from one verse into another, not in the jingling sound of like endings, a fault avoided by the learned ancients both in poetry and all good oratory. This neglect then of rhyme so little is to be taken for a defect, though it may seem so perhaps to vulgar readers, that it rather is to be esteemed an example set, the first in English, of ancient liberty recovered to heroic poem from the troublesome and modern bondage of rhyming.

BOOK I

Of man's first disobedience, and the fruit
Of that forbidden tree, whose mortal taste
Brought death into the world, and all our woe,
With loss of Eden, till one greater man
Restore us, and regain the blissful seat,
Sing Heav'nly Muse, that on the secret top
Of Oreb, or of Sinai, didst inspire
That shepherd, who first taught the chosen seed,
In the beginning how the heav'ns and earth
Rose out of Chaos: or if Sion hill
Delight thee more, and Siloa's brook that flowed
Fast by the oracle of God; I thence
Invoke thy aid to my advent'rous song,
That with no middle flight intends to soar
Above th' Aonian mount, while it pursues
Things unattempted yet in prose or rhyme.
And chiefly thou O Spirit, that dost prefer
Before all temples th' upright heart and pure,
Instruct me, for thou know'st; thou from the first
Wast present, and with mighty wings outspread
Dove-like sat'st brooding on the vast abyss
And mad'st it pregnant: what in me is dark
Illumine, what is low raise and support;
That to the heighth of this great argument
I may assert Eternal Providence,
And justify the ways of God to men.
    Say first, for Heav'n hides nothing from thy
      view
Nor the deep tract of Hell, say first what cause
Moved our grand parents in that happy state,
Favoured of Heav'n so highly, to fall off
From their Creator, and transgress his will
For one restraint, lords of the world besides?
Who first seduced them to that foul revolt?

Th' infernal Serpent; he it was, whose guile
Stirred up with envy and revenge, deceived
The mother of mankind, what time his pride
Had cast him out from Heav'n, with all his host
Of rebel angels, by whose aid aspiring
To set himself in glory above his peers,
He trusted to have equalled the Most High,   40
If he opposed; and with ambitious aim
Against the throne and monarchy of God
Raised impious war in Heav'n and battle proud
With vain attempt. Him the Almighty Power
Hurled headlong flaming from th' ethereal sky
With hideous ruin and combustion down
To bottomless perdition, there to dwell
In adamantine chains and penal fire,
Who durst defy th' Omnipotent to arms.
Nine times the space that measures day and night   50
To mortal men, he with his horrid crew
Lay vanquished, rolling in the fiery gulf
Confounded though immortal: but his doom
Reserved him to more wrath; for now the thought
Both of lost happiness and lasting pain
Torments him; round he throws his baleful eyes
That witnessed huge affliction and dismay
Mixed with obdúrate pride and steadfast hate:
At once as far as angels' ken he views
The dismal situation waste and wild,   60
A dungeon horrible, on all sides round
As one great furnace flamed, yet from those flames
No light, but rather darkness visible
Served only to discover sights of woe,
Regions of sorrow, doleful shades, where peace
And rest can never dwell, hope never comes
That comes to all; but torture without end
Still urges, and a fiery deluge, fed
With ever-burning sulphur unconsumed:
Such place Eternal Justice had prepared   70
For those rebellious, here their prison ordained

In utter darkness, and their portion set
As far removed from God and light of Heav'n
As from the centre thrice to th' utmost pole.
O how unlike the place from whence they fell!
There the companions of his fall, o'erwhelmed
With floods and whirlwinds of tempestuous fire,
He soon discerns, and welt'ring by his side
One next himself in power, and next in crime,
80 Long after known in Palestine, and named
Beëlzebub. To whom th' Arch-Enemy,
And thence in Heav'n called Satan, with bold words
Breaking the horrid silence thus began.

    'If thou beest he; but O how fall'n! how changed
From him, who in the happy realms of light
Clothed with transcendent brightness didst outshine
Myriads though bright: if he whom mutual league,
United thoughts and counsels, equal hope
And hazard in the glorious enterprise,
90 Joined with me once, now misery hath joined
In equal ruin: into what pit thou seest
From what heighth fall'n, so much the stronger proved
He with his thunder: and till then who knew
The force of those dire arms? Yet not for those,
Nor what the potent Victor in his rage
Can else inflict, do I repent or change,
Though changed in outward lustre, that fixed mind
And high disdain, from sense of injured merit,
That with the mightiest raised me to contend,
100 And to the fierce contention brought along
Innumerable force of Spirits armed
That durst dislike his reign, and me preferring,
His utmost power with adverse power opposed
In dubious battle on the plains of Heav'n,
And shook his throne. What though the field be lost?
All is not lost; the unconquerable will,
And study of revenge, immortal hate,
And courage never to submit or yield:
And what is else not to be overcome?

That glory never shall his wrath or might   110
Extort from me. To bow and sue for grace
With suppliant knee, and deify his power
Who from the terror of this arm so late
Doubted his empire, that were low indeed,
That were an ignominy and shame beneath
This downfall; since by Fate the strength of gods
And this empyreal substance cannot fail,
Since through experience of this great event
In arms not worse, in foresight much advanced,
We may with more successful hope resolve   120
To wage by force or guile eternal war
Irreconcilable, to our grand Foe,
Who now triúmphs, and in th' excess of joy
Sole reigning holds the tyranny of Heav'n.'
    So spake th' apostate angel, though in pain,
Vaunting aloud, but racked with deep despair:
And him thus answered soon his bold compeer.
    'O Prince, O chief of many thronèd Powers
That led th' embattled Seraphim to war
Under thy conduct, and in dreadful deeds   130
Fearless, endangered Heav'n's perpetual King;
And put to proof his high supremacy,
Whether upheld by strength, or Chance, or Fate;
Too well I see and rue the dire event,
That with sad overthrow and foul defeat
Hath lost us Heav'n, and all this mighty host
In horrible destruction laid thus low,
As far as gods and Heav'nly essences
Can perish: for the mind and spirit remains
Invincible, and vigour soon returns,   140
Though all our glory extinct, and happy state
Here swallowed up in endless misery.
But what if he our Conqueror (whom I now
Of force believe Almighty, since no less
Than such could have o'erpow'red such force as ours)
Have left us this our spirit and strength entire
Strongly to suffer and support our pains,

That we may so suffice his vengeful ire,
Or do him mightier service as his thralls
150   By right of war, whate'er his business be,
Here in the heart of Hell to work in fire,
Or do his errands in the gloomy deep;
What can it then avail though yet we feel
Strength undiminished, or eternal being
To undergo eternal punishment?'
Whereto with speedy words th'Arch-Fiend replied.

     'Fall'n Cherub, to be weak is miserable
Doing or suffering: but of this be sure,
To do aught good never will be our task,
160   But ever to do ill our sole delight,
As being the contrary to his high will
Whom we resist. If then his Providence
Out of our evil seek to bring forth good,
Our labour must be to pervert that end,
And out of good still to find means of evil;
Which oft-times may succeed, so as perhaps
Shall grieve him, if I fail not, and disturb
His inmost counsels from their destined aim.
But see the angry Victor hath recalled
170   His ministers of vengeance and pursuit
Back to the gates of Heav'n: the sulphurous hail
Shot after us in storm, o'erblown hath laid
The fiery surge, that from the precipice
Of Heav'n received us falling, and the thunder,
Winged with red lightning and impetuous rage,
Perhaps hath spent his shafts, and ceases now
To bellow through the vast and boundless deep.
Let us not slip th' occasion, whether scorn,
Or satiate fury yield it from our Foe.
180   Seest thou yon dreary plain, forlorn and wild,
The seat of desolation, void of light,
Save what the glimmering of these livid flames
Casts pale and dreadful? Thither let us tend
From off the tossing of these fiery waves,
There rest, if any rest can harbour there,

And reassembling our afflicted powers,
Consult how we may henceforth most offend
Our Enemy, our own loss how repair,
How overcome this dire calamity,
What reinforcement we may gain from hope,   190
If not what resolution from despair.'
   Thus Satan talking to his nearest mate
With head uplift above the wave, and eyes
That sparkling blazed; his other parts besides
Prone on the flood, extended long and large
Lay floating many a rood, in bulk as huge
As whom the fables name of monstrous size,
Titanian, or Earth-born, that warred on Jove,
Briareos or Typhon, whom the den
By ancient Tarsus held, or that sea-beast   200
Leviathan, which God of all his works
Created hugest that swim th' Océan stream:
Him haply slumb'ring on the Norway foam
The pilot of some small night-foundered skiff,
Deeming some island, oft, as seamen tell,
With fixèd anchor in his scaly rind
Moors by his side under the lee, while night
Invests the sea, and wishèd morn delays:
So stretched out huge in length the Arch-Fiend lay
Chained on the burning lake, nor ever thence   210
Had ris'n or heaved his head, but that the will
And high permission of all-ruling Heaven
Left him at large to his own dark designs,
That with reiterated crimes he might
Heap on himself damnation, while he sought
Evil to others, and enraged might see
How all his malice served but to bring forth
Infinite goodness, grace and mercy shown
On man by him seduced, but on himself
Treble confusion, wrath and vengeance poured.   220
Forthwith upright he rears from off the pool
His mighty stature; on each hand the flames
Driv'n backward slope their pointing spires, and rolled

In billows, leave i' th' midst a horrid vale.
Then with expanded wings he steers his flight
Aloft, incumbent on the dusky air
That felt unusual weight, till on dry land
He lights, if it were land that ever burned
With solid, as the lake with liquid fire,
230   And such appeared in hue; as when the force
Of subterranean wind transports a hill
Torn from Pelorus, or the shattered side
Of thund'ring Etna, whose combustible
And fuelled entrails thence conceiving fire,
Sublimed with mineral fury, aid the winds,
And leave a singèd bottom all involved
With stench and smoke: such resting found the sole
Of unblest feet. Him followed his next mate,
Both glorying to have 'scaped the Stygian flood
240   As gods, and by their own recovered strength,
Not by the sufferance of supernal power.
    'Is this the region, this the soil, the clime,'
Said then the lost Archangel, 'this the seat
That we must change for Heav'n, this mournful gloom
For that celestial light? Be it so, since he
Who now is sov'reign can dispose and bid
What shall be right: farthest from him is best
Whom reason hath equalled, force hath made supreme
Above his equals. Farewell happy fields
250   Where joy for ever dwells: hail horrors, hail
Infernal world, and thou profoundest Hell
Receive thy new possessor: one who brings
A mind not to be changed by place or time.
The mind is its own place, and in itself
Can make a Heav'n of Hell, a Hell of Heav'n.
What matter where, if I be still the same,
And what I should be, all but less than he
Whom thunder hath made greater? Here at least
We shall be free; th' Almighty hath not built
260   Here for his envy, will not drive us hence:
Here we may reign secure, and in my choice

To reign is worth ambition, though in Hell:
Better to reign in Hell than serve in Heav'n.
But wherefore let we then our faithful friends,
Th' associates and copartners of our loss
Lie thus astonished on th' oblivious pool,
And call them not to share with us their part
In this unhappy mansion; or once more
With rallied arms to try what may be yet
Regained in Heav'n, or what more lost in Hell?'   270
    So Satan spake, and him Beëlzebub
Thus answered. 'Leader of those armies bright,
Which but th' Omnipotent none could have foiled,
If once they hear that voice, their liveliest pledge
Of hope in fears and dangers, heard so oft
In worst extremes, and on the perilous edge
Of battle when it raged, in all assaults
Their surest signal, they will soon resume
New courage and revive, though now they lie
Grovelling and prostrate on yon lake of fire,   280
As we erewhile, astounded and amazed,
No wonder, fall'n such a pernicious heighth.'
    He scarce had ceased when the superior Fiend
Was moving toward the shore; his ponderous shield
Ethereal temper, massy, large, and round,
Behind him cast; the broad circumference
Hung on his shoulders like the moon, whose orb
Through optic glass the Tuscan artist views
At evening from the top of Fesole,
Or in Valdarno, to descry new lands,   290
Rivers or mountains in her spotty globe.
His spear, to equal which the tallest pine
Hewn on Norwegian hills, to be the mast
Of some great ammiral, were but a wand,
He walked with to support uneasy steps
Over the burning marl, not like those steps
On Heaven's azure; and the torrid clime
Smote on him sore besides, vaulted with fire;
Nathless he so endured, till on the beach

300   Of that inflamèd sea, he stood and called
        His legions, angel forms, who lay entranced
        Thick as autumnal leaves that strow the brooks
        In Vallombrosa, where th' Etrurian shades
        High overarched embow'r; or scattered sedge
        Afloat, when with fierce winds Orion armed
        Hath vexed the Red Sea coast, whose waves o'erthrew
        Busiris and his Memphian chivalry,
        While with perfidious hatred they pursued
        The sojourners of Goshen, who beheld
310   From the safe shore their floating carcasses
        And broken chariot wheels. So thick bestrown
        Abject and lost lay these, covering the flood,
        Under amazement of their hideous change.
        He called so loud, that all the hollow deep
        Of Hell resounded. 'Princes, Potentates,
        Warriors, the flow'r of Heav'n, once yours, now lost,
        If such astonishment as this can seize
        Eternal Spirits: or have ye chos'n this place
        After the toil of battle to repose
320   Your wearied virtue, for the ease you find
        To slumber here, as in the vales of Heav'n?
        Or in this abject posture have ye sworn
        To adore the Conqueror? who now beholds
        Cherub and Seraph rolling in the flood
        With scattered arms and ensigns, till anon
        His swift pursuers from Heav'n gates discern
        Th' advantage, and descending tread us down
        Thus drooping, or with linkèd thunderbolts
        Transfix us to the bottom of this gulf.
330   Awake, arise, or be for ever fall'n.'
                They heard, and were abashed, and up they sprung
        Upon the wing, as when men wont to watch
        On duty, sleeping found by whom they dread,
        Rouse and bestir themselves ere well awake.
        Nor did they not perceive the evil plight
        In which they were, or the fierce pains not feel;
        Yet to their General's voice they soon obeyed

Innumerable. As when the potent rod
Of Amram's son in Egypt's evil day
Waved round the coast, up called a pitchy cloud   340
Of locusts, warping on the eastern wind,
That o'er the realm of impious Pharaoh hung
Like night, and darkened all the land of Nile:
So numberless were those bad angels seen
Hovering on wing under the cope of Hell
'Twixt upper, nether, and surrounding fires;
Till, as a signal giv'n, th' uplifted spear
Of their great Sultan waving to direct
Their course, in even balance down they light
On the firm brimstone, and fill all the plain;   350
A multitude, like which the populous North
Poured never from her frozen loins, to pass
Rhene or the Danaw, when her barbarous sons
Came like a deluge on the South, and spread
Beneath Gibraltar to the Libyan sands.
Forthwith from every squadron and each band
The heads and leaders thither haste where stood
Their great Commander; godlike shapes and forms
Excelling human, Princely dignities,
And Powers that erst in Heaven sat on thrones;   360
Though of their names in Heav'nly records now
Be no memorial, blotted out and razed
By their rebellion, from the Books of Life.
Nor had they yet among the sons of Eve
Got them new names, till wand'ring o'er the earth,
Through God's high sufferance for the trial of man,
By falsities and lies the greatest part
Of mankind they corrupted to forsake
God their Creator, and th' invisible
Glory of him that made them, to transform   370
Oft to the image of a brute, adorned
With gay religions full of pomp and gold,
And devils to adore for deities:
Then were they known to men by various names,
And various idols through the heathen world.

Say, Muse, their names then known, who first, who
        last,
Roused from the slumber on that fiery couch,
At their great Emperor's call, as next in worth
Came singly where he stood on the bare strand,
380 While the promiscuous crowd stood yet aloof?
The chief were those who from the pit of Hell
Roaming to seek their prey on earth, durst fix
Their seats, long after, next the seat of God,
Their altars by his altar, gods adored
Among the nations round, and durst abide
Jehovah thund'ring out of Sion, throned
Between the Cherubim; yea, often placed
Within his sanctuary itself their shrines,
Abominations; and with cursèd things
390 His holy rites, and solemn feasts profaned,
And with their darkness durst affront his light.
First Moloch, horrid king besmeared with blood
Of human sacrifice, and parents' tears,
Though for the noise of drums and timbrels loud
Their children's cries unheard, that passed through fire
To his grim idol. Him the Ammonite
Worshipped in Rabba and her wat'ry plain,
In Argob and in Basan, to the stream
Of utmost Arnon. Nor content with such
400 Audacious neighbourhood, the wisest heart
Of Solomon he led by fraud to build
His temple right against the temple of God
On that opprobrious hill, and made his grove
The pleasant valley of Hinnom, Tophet thence
And black Gehenna called, the type of Hell.
Next Chemos, th' óbscene dread of Moab's sons,
From Aroer to Nebo, and the wild
Of southmost Abarim; in Hesebon
And Horonaim, Seon's realm, beyond
410 The flow'ry dale of Sibma clad with vines,
And Elealè to th' Asphaltic pool.
Peor his other name, when he enticed

Israel in Sittim on their march from Nile
To do him wanton rites, which cost them woe.
Yet thence his lustful orgies he enlarged
Even to that hill of scandal, by the grove
Of Moloch homicide, lust hard by hate;
Till good Josiah drove them thence to Hell.
With these came they, who from the bord'ring flood
Of old Euphrates to the brook that parts   420
Egypt from Syrian ground, had general names
Of Baälim and Ashtaroth, those male,
These feminine. For Spirits when they please
Can either sex assume, or both; so soft
And uncompounded is their essence pure;
Not tied or manacled with joint or limb,
Nor founded on the brittle strength of bones,
Like cumbrous flesh; but in what shape they choose
Dilated or condensed, bright or obscure,
Can execute their airy purposes,   430
And works of love or enmity fulfil.
For those the race of Israel oft forsook
Their Living Strength, and unfrequented left
His righteous altar, bowing lowly down
To bestial gods; for which their heads as low
Bowed down in battle, sunk before the spear
Of déspicable foes. With these in troop
Came Astoreth, whom the Phoenicians called
Astarte, queen of Heav'n, with crescent horns;
To whose bright image nightly by the moon   440
Sidonian virgins paid their vows and songs,
In Sion also not unsung, where stood
Her temple on th' offensive mountain, built
By that uxorious king, whose heart though large,
Beguiled by fair idolatresses, fell
To idols foul. Thammuz came next behind,
Whose annual wound in Lebanon allured
The Syrian damsels to lament his fate
In amorous ditties all a summer's day,
While smooth Adonis from his native rock   450

Ran purple to the sea, supposed with blood
Of Thammuz yearly wounded: the love-tale
Infected Sion's daughters with like heat,
Whose wanton passions in the sacred porch
Ezekiel saw, when by the vision led
His eye surveyed the dark idolatries
Of alienated Judah. Next came one
Who mourned in earnest, when the captive ark
Maimed his brute image, head and hands lopped off
460 In his own temple, on the grunsel edge,
Where he fell flat, and shamed his worshippers:
Dagon his name, sea monster, upward man
And downward fish: yet had his temple high
Reared in Azotus, dreaded through the coast
Of Palestine, in Gath and Ascalon,
And Accaron and Gaza's frontier bounds.
Him followed Rimmon, whose delightful seat
Was fair Damascus, on the fertile banks
Of Abbana and Pharphar, lucid streams.
470 He also against the house of God was bold:
A leper once he lost and gained a king,
Ahaz his sottish conqueror, whom he drew
God's altar to disparage and displace
For one of Syrian mode, whereon to burn
His odious off'rings, and adore the gods
Whom he had vanquished. After these appeared
A crew who under names of old renown,
Osiris, Isis, Orus and their train
With monstrous shapes and sorceries abused
480 Fanatic Egypt and her priests, to seek
Their wand'ring gods disguised in brutish forms
Rather than human. Nor did Israel 'scape
Th' infection when their borrowed gold composed
The calf in Oreb: and the rebel king
Doubled that sin in Bethel and in Dan,
Lik'ning his Maker to the grazèd ox,
Jehovah, who in one night when he passed
From Egypt marching, equalled with one stroke

Both her first born and all her bleating gods.
Belial came last, than whom a Spirit more lewd   490
Fell not from Heaven, or more gross to love
Vice for itself: to him no temple stood
Or altar smoked; yet who more oft than he
In temples and at altars, when the priest
Turns atheist, as did Eli's sons, who filled
With lust and violence the house of God.
In courts and palaces he also reigns
And in luxurious cities, where the noise
Of riot ascends above their loftiest tow'rs,
And injury and outrage: and when night   500
Darkens the streets, then wander forth the sons
Of Belial, flown with insolence and wine.
Witness the streets of Sodom, and that night
In Gibeah, when the hospitable door
Exposed a matron to avoid worse rape.
These were the prime in order and in might;
The rest were long to tell, though far renowned,
Th' Ionian gods, of Javan's issue held
Gods, yet confessed later than Heav'n and Earth
Their boasted parents; Titan Heav'n's first-born   510
With his enormous brood, and birthright seized
By younger Saturn, he from mightier Jove
His own and Rhea's son like measure found;
So Jove usurping reigned: these first in Crete
And Ida known, thence on the snowy top
Of cold Olympus ruled the middle air
Their highest heav'n; or on the Delphian cliff,
Or in Dodona, and through all the bounds
Of Doric land; or who with Saturn old
Fled over Adria to th' Hesperian fields,   520
And o'er the Celtic roamed the utmost isles.
All these and more came flocking; but with looks
Downcast and damp, yet such wherein appeared
Obscure some glimpse of joy, to have found their chief
Not in despair, to have found themselves not lost
In loss itself; which on his count'nance cast

Like doubtful hue: but he his wonted pride
Soon recollecting, with high words, that bore
Semblance of worth, not substance, gently raised
530 Their fainting courage, and dispelled their fears.
Then straight commands that at the warlike sound
Of trumpets loud and clarions be upreared
His mighty standard; that proud honour claimed
Azazel as his right, a Cherub tall:
Who forthwith from the glittering staff unfurled
Th' imperial ensign, which full high advanced
Shone like a meteor streaming to the wind
With gems and golden lustre rich emblazed,
Seraphic arms and trophies: all the while
540 Sonórous metal blowing martial sounds:
At which the universal host upsent
A shout that tore Hell's concave, and beyond
Frighted the reign of Chaos and old Night.
All in a moment through the gloom were seen
Ten thousand banners rise into the air
With orient colours waving: with them rose
A forest huge of spears: and thronging helms
Appeared, and serried shields in thick array
Of depth immeasurable: anon they move
550 In perfect phalanx to the Dorian mood
Of flutes and soft recorders; such as raised
To heighth of noblest temper heroes old
Arming to battle, and instead of rage
Deliberate valour breathed, firm and unmoved
With dread of death to flight or foul retreat,
Nor wanting power to mitigate and swage
With solemn touches, troubled thoughts, and chase
Anguish and doubt and fear and sorrow and pain
From mortal or immortal minds. Thus they
560 Breathing united force with fixèd thought
Moved on in silence to soft pipes that charmed
Their painful steps o'er the burnt soil; and now
Advanced in view they stand, a horrid front
Of dreadful length and dazzling arms, in guise

Of warriors old with ordered spear and shield,
Awaiting what command their mighty chief
Had to impose: he through the armèd files
Darts his experienced eye, and soon traverse
The whole battalion views; their order due,
Their visages and stature as of gods,   570
Their number last he sums. And now his heart
Distends with pride, and hard'ning in his strength
Glories: for never since created man,
Met such embodied force, as named with these
Could merit more than that small infantry
Warred on by cranes: though all the Giant brood
Of Phlegra with th' heroic race were joined
That fought at Thebes and Ilium, on each side
Mixed with auxiliar gods; and what resounds
In fable or romance of Uther's son   580
Begirt with British and Armoric knights;
And all who since, baptized or infidel
Jousted in Aspramont or Montalban,
Damasco, or Morocco, or Trebizond,
Or whom Biserta sent from Afric shore
When Charlemagne with all his peerage fell
By Fontarabbia. Thus far these beyond
Compare of mortal prowess, yet observed
Their dread commander: he above the rest
In shape and gesture proudly eminent   590
Stood like a tow'r; his form had yet not lost
All her original brightness, nor appeared
Less than Archangel ruined, and th' excess
Of glory obscured: as when the sun new ris'n
Looks through the horizontal misty air
Shorn of his beams, or from behind the moon
In dim eclipse disastrous twilight sheds
On half the nations, and with fear of change
Perplexes monarchs. Darkened so, yet shone
Above them all th' Archangel: but his face   600
Deep scars of thunder had intrenched, and care
Sat on his faded cheek, but under brows

Of dauntless courage, and considerate pride
Waiting revenge: cruel his eye, but cast
Signs of remorse and passion to behold
The fellows of his crime, the followers rather
(Far other once beheld in bliss) condemned
For ever now to have their lot in pain,
Millions of Spirits for his fault amerced
610 Of Heav'n, and from eternal splendours flung
For his revolt, yet faithful how they stood,
Their glory withered. As when Heaven's fire
Hath scathed the forest oaks or mountain pines,
With singèd top their stately growth though bare
Stands on the blasted heath. He now prepared
To speak; whereat their doubled ranks they bend
From wing to wing, and half enclose him round
With all his peers: attention held them mute.
Thrice he assayed, and thrice in spite of scorn,
620 Tears such as angels weep, burst forth: at last
Words interwove with sighs found out their way.
    'O myriads of immortal Spirits, O Powers
Matchless, but with th' Almighty, and that strife
Was not inglorious, though th' event was dire,
As this place testifies, and this dire change
Hateful to utter: but what power of mind
Foreseeing or presaging, from the depth
Of knowledge past or present, could have feared
How such united force of gods, how such
630 As stood like these, could ever know repulse?
For who can yet believe, though after loss,
That all these puissant legions, whose exíle
Hath emptied Heav'n, shall fail to reascend
Self-raised, and repossess their native seat?
For me be witness all the host of Heav'n,
If counsels different, or danger shunned
By me, have lost our hopes. But he who reigns
Monarch in Heav'n, till then as one secure
Sat on his throne, upheld by old repute,
640 Consent or custom, and his regal state

Put forth at full, but still his strength concealed,
Which tempted our attempt, and wrought our fall.
Henceforth his might we know, and know our own
So as not either to provoke, or dread
New war, provoked; our better part remains
To work in close design, by fraud or guile
What force effected not: that he no less
At length from us may find, who overcomes
By force, hath overcome but half his foe.
Space may produce new worlds; whereof so rife   650
There went a fame in Heav'n that he ere long
Intended to create, and therein plant
A generation, whom his choice regard
Should favour equal to the sons of Heav'n:
Thither, if but to pry, shall be perhaps
Our first eruption; thither or elsewhere:
For this infernal pit shall never hold
Celestial Spirits in bondage, nor th' abyss
Long under darkness cover. But these thoughts
Full counsel must mature: peace is despaired,   660
For who can think submission? War then, war
Open or understood must be resolved.'
    He spake: and to confirm his words, out flew
Millions of flaming swords, drawn from the thighs
Of mighty Cherubim; the sudden blaze
Far round illumined Hell: highly they raged
Against the Highest, and fierce with graspèd arms
Clashed on their sounding shields the din of war,
Hurling defiance toward the vault of Heav'n.
    There stood a hill not far whose grisly top   670
Belched fire and rolling smoke; the rest entire
Shone with a glossy scurf, undoubted sign
That in his womb was hid metallic ore,
The work of sulphur. Thither winged with speed
A numerous brígade hastened. As when bands
Of pioneers with spade and pickaxe armed
Forerun the royal camp, to trench a field
Or cast a rampart. Mammon led them on,

Mammon, the least erected Spirit that fell
680 From Heav'n, for ev'n in Heav'n his looks and thoughts
Were always downward bent, admiring more
The riches of Heav'n's pavement, trodden gold,
Than aught divine or holy else enjoyed
In vision beatific: by him first
Men also, and by his suggestion taught,
Ransacked the centre, and with impious hands
Rifled the bowels of their mother Earth
For treasures better hid. Soon had his crew
Opened into the hill a spacious wound
690 And digged out ribs of gold. Let none admire
That riches grow in Hell; that soil may best
Deserve the precious bane. And here let those
Who boast in mortal things, and wond'ring tell
Of Babel, and the works of Memphian kings,
Learn how their greatest monuments of fame,
And strength and art are easily outdone
By Spirits reprobate, and in an hour
What in an age they with incessant toil
And hands innumerable scarce perform.
700 Nigh on the plain in many cells prepared,
That underneath had veins of liquid fire
Sluiced from the lake, a second multitude
With wondrous art founded the massy ore,
Severing each kind, and scummed the bullion dross:
A third as soon had formed within the ground
A various mould, and from the boiling cells
By strange conveyance filled each hollow nook,
As in an organ from one blast of wind
To many a row of pipes the sound-board breathes.
710 Anon out of the earth a fabric huge
Rose like an exhalation, with the sound
Of dulcet symphonies and voices sweet,
Built like a temple, where pilasters round
Were set, and Doric pillars overlaid
With golden architrave; nor did there want
Cornice or frieze with bossy sculptures grav'n;

The roof was fretted gold. Not Babylon,
Nor great Alcairo such magnificence
Equalled in all their glories, to enshrine
Belus or Serapis their gods, or seat   720
Their kings, when Egypt with Assyria strove
In wealth and luxury. Th' ascending pile
Stood fixed her stately heighth, and straight the doors
Op'ning their brazen folds discover wide
Within, her ample spaces, o'er the smooth
And level pavement: from the archèd roof
Pendent by subtle magic many a row
Of starry lamps and blazing cressets fed
With naphtha and asphaltus yielded light
As from a sky. The hasty multitude   730
Admiring entered, and the work some praise
And some the architect: his hand was known
In Heav'n by many a towered structure high,
Where sceptred angels held their residence,
And sat as princes, whom the súpreme King
Exalted to such power, and gave to rule,
Each in his hierarchy, the orders bright.
Nor was his name unheard or unadored
In ancient Greece; and in Ausonian land
Men called him Mulciber; and how he fell   740
From Heav'n, they fabled, thrown by angry Jove
Sheer o'er the crystal battlements: from morn
To noon he fell, from noon to dewy eve,
A summer's day: and with the setting sun
Dropped from the zenith like a falling star,
On Lemnos th' Aégean isle: thus they relate,
Erring; for he with this rebellious rout
Fell long before; nor aught availed him now
To have built in Heav'n high tow'rs; nor did he 'scape
By all his engines, but was headlong sent   750
With his industrious crew to build in Hell.
Meanwhile the wingèd heralds by command
Of sov'reign power, with awful ceremony
And trumpets' sound throughout the host proclaim

A solemn council forthwith to be held
At Pandaemonium, the high capital
Of Satan and his peers: their summons called
From every band and squarèd regiment
By place or choice the worthiest; they anon
760 With hundreds and with thousands trooping came
Attended: all accéss was thronged, the gates
And porches wide, but chief the spacious hall
(Though like a covered field, where champions bold
Wont ride in armed, and at the Soldan's chair
Defied the best of paynim chivalry
To mortal combat or career with lance)
Thick swarmed, both on the ground and in the air,
Brushed with the hiss of rustling wings. As bees
In springtime, when the sun with Taurus rides,
770 Pour forth their populous youth about the hive
In clusters; they among fresh dews and flowers
Fly to and fro, or on the smoothèd plank,
The suburb of their straw-built citadel,
New rubbed with balm, expatiate and confer
Their state affairs. So thick the airy crowd
Swarmed and were straitened; till the signal giv'n,
Behold a wonder! They but now who seemed
In bigness to surpass Earth's Giant sons
Now less than smallest dwarfs, in narrow room
780 Throng numberless, like that Pygméan race
Beyond the Indian mount, or faery elves,
Whose midnight revels, by a forest side
Or fountain some belated peasant sees,
Or dreams he sees, while overhead the moon
Sits arbitress, and nearer to the earth
Wheels her pale course: they on their mirth and dance
Intent, with jocund music charm his ear;
At once with joy and fear his heart rebounds.
Thus incorporeal Spirits to smallest forms
790 Reduced their shapes immense, and were at large,
Though without number still amidst the hall
Of that infernal Court. But far within

And in their own dimensions like themselves
The great Seraphic Lords and Cherubim
In close recess and secret conclave sat
A thousand demi-gods on golden seats,
Frequent and full. After short silence then
And summons read, the great consult began.

BOOK II

High on a throne of royal state, which far
Outshone the wealth of Ormus and of Ind,
Or where the gorgeous East with richest hand
Show'rs on her kings barbaric pearl and gold,
Satan exalted sat, by merit raised
To that bad eminence; and from despair
Thus high uplifted beyond hope, aspires
Beyond thus high, insatiate to pursue
Vain war with Heav'n, and by success untaught
His proud imaginations thus displayed.   10
    'Powers and Dominions, deities of Heaven,
For since no deep within her gulf can hold
Immortal vigour, though oppressed and fall'n,
I give not Heav'n for lost. From this descent
Celestial Virtues rising, will appear
More glorious and more dread than from no fall,
And trust themselves to fear no second fate:
Me though just right, and the fixed laws of Heav'n
Did first create your leader, next, free choice,
With what besides, in counsel or in fight,   20
Hath been achieved of merit, yet this loss
Thus far at least recovered, hath much more
Established in a safe unenvied throne
Yielded with full consent. The happier state
In Heav'n, which follows dignity, might draw

Envy from each inferior; but who here
Will envy whom the highest place exposes
Foremost to stand against the Thunderer's aim
Your bulwark, and condemns to greatest share
30   Of endless pain? Where there is then no good
For which to strive, no strife can grow up there
From faction; for none sure will claim in Hell
Precédence, none, whose portion is so small
Of present pain, that with ambitious mind
Will covet more. With this advantage then
To union, and firm faith, and firm accord,
More than can be in Heav'n, we now return
To claim our just inheritance of old,
Surer to prosper than prosperity
40   Could have assured us; and by what best way,
Whether of open war or covert guile,
We now debate; who can advise, may speak.'
          He ceased, and next him Moloch, sceptred king
Stood up, the strongest and the fiercest Spirit
That fought in Heav'n; now fiercer by despair:
His trust was with th' Eternal to be deemed
Equal in strength, and rather than be less
Cared not to be at all; with that care lost
Went all his fear: of God, or Hell, or worse
50   He recked not, and these words thereafter spake.
          'My sentence is for open war: of wiles,
More unexpért, I boast not: them let those
Contrive who need, or when they need, not now.
For while they sit contriving, shall the rest,
Millions that stand in arms, and longing wait
The signal to ascend, sit ling'ring here
Heav'n's fugitives, and for their dwelling place
Accept this dark opprobrious den of shame,
The prison of his tyranny who reigns
60   By our delay? No, let us rather choose
Armed with Hell flames and fury all at once
O'er Heav'n's high tow'rs to force resistless way,
Turning our tortures into horrid arms

Against the Torturer; when to meet the noise
Of his almighty engine he shall hear
Infernal thunder, and for lightning see
Black fire and horror shot with equal rage
Among his angels; and his throne itself
Mixed with Tartarean sulphur, and strange fire,
His own invented torments. But perhaps   70
The way seems difficult and steep to scale
With upright wing against a higher foe.
Let such bethink them, if the sleepy drench
Of that forgetful lake benumb not still,
That in our proper motion we ascend
Up to our native seat: descent and fall
To us is adverse. Who but felt of late
When the fierce foe hung on our broken rear
Insulting, and pursued us through the deep,
With what compulsion and laborious flight   80
We sunk thus low? Th' ascent is easy then;
Th' event is feared; should we again provoke
Our stronger, some worse way his wrath may find
To our destruction: if there be in Hell
Fear to be worse destroyed: what can be worse
Than to dwell here, driv'n out from bliss, condemned
In this abhorrèd deep to utter woe;
Where pain of unextinguishable fire
Must exercise us without hope of end
The vassals of his anger, when the scourge   90
Inexorably, and the torturing hour
Calls us to penance? More destroyed than thus
We should be quite abolished and expire.
What fear we then? What doubt we to incense
His utmost ire? Which to the heighth enraged,
Will either quite consume us, and reduce
To nothing this essential, happier far
Than miserable to have eternal being:
Or if our substance be indeed divine,
And cannot cease to be, we are at worst   100
On this side nothing; and by proof we feel

Our power sufficient to disturb his Heav'n,
And with perpetual inroads to alarm,
Though inaccessible, his fatal throne:
Which if not victory is yet revenge.'
   He ended frowning, and his look denounced
Desperate revenge, and battle dangerous
To less than gods. On th' other side up rose
Belial, in act more graceful and humane:
A fairer person lost not Heav'n; he seemed
For dignity composed and high explóit:
But all was false and hollow; though his tongue
Dropped manna, and could make the worse appear
The better reason, to perplex and dash
Maturest counsels: for his thoughts were low;
To vice industrious, but to nobler deeds
Timorous and slothful: yet he pleased the ear,
And with persuasive accent thus began.
   'I should be much for open war, O Peers,
As not behind in hate; if what was urged
Main reason to persuade immediate war,
Did not dissuade me most, and seem to cast
Ominous conjecture on the whole success:
When he who most excels in fact of arms,
In what he counsels and in what excels
Mistrustful, grounds his courage on despair
And utter dissolution, as the scope
Of all his aim, after some dire revenge.
First, what revenge? The tow'rs of Heav'n are filled
With armèd watch, that render all accéss
Impregnable; oft on the bordering deep
Encamp their legions, or with óbscure wing
Scout far and wide into the realm of Night,
Scorning surprise. Or could we break our way
By force, and at our heels all Hell should rise
With blackest insurrection, to confound
Heav'n's purest light, yet our great Enemy
All incorruptible would on his throne
Sit unpolluted, and th' ethereal mould

110

120

130

Incapable of stain would soon expel   140
Her mischief, and purge off the baser fire
Victorious. Thus repulsed, our final hope
Is flat despair: we must exasperate
Th' Almighty Victor to spend all his rage,
And that must end us, that must be our cure,
To be no more; sad cure; for who would lose,
Though full of pain, this intellectual being,
Those thoughts that wander through eternity,
To perish rather, swallowed up and lost
In the wide womb of uncreated Night,   150
Devoid of sense and motion? And who knows,
Let this be good, whether our angry Foe
Can give it, or will ever? How he can
Is doubtful; that he never will is sure.
Will he, so wise, let loose at once his ire,
Belike through impotence, or unaware,
To give his enemies their wish, and end
Them in his anger, whom his anger saves
To punish endless? "Wherefore cease we then?"
Say they who counsel war, "We are decreed,   160
Reserved and destined to eternal woe;
Whatever doing, what can we suffer more,
What can we suffer worse?" Is this then worst,
Thus sitting, thus consulting, thus in arms?
What when we fled amain, pursued and strook
With Heav'n's afflicting thunder, and besought
The deep to shelter us? This Hell then seemed
A refuge from those wounds: or when we lay
Chained on the burning lake? That sure was worse.
What if the breath that kindled those grim fires   170
Awaked should blow them into sevenfold rage
And plunge us in the flames? Or from above
Should intermitted vengeance arm again
His red right hand to plague us? What if all
Her stores were opened, and this firmament
Of Hell should spout her cataracts of fire,
Impendent horrors, threat'ning hideous fall

One day upon our heads; while we perhaps
Designing or exhorting glorious war,
180   Caught in a fiery tempest shall be hurled
Each on his rock transfixed, the sport and prey
Of racking whirlwinds, or for ever sunk
Under yon boiling ocean, wrapped in chains;
There to converse with everlasting groans,
Unrespited, unpitied, unreprieved,
Ages of hopeless end; this would be worse.
War therefore, open or concealed, alike
My voice dissuades; for what can force or guile
With him, or who deceive his mind, whose eye
190   Views all things at one view? He from Heav'n's heighth
All these our motions vain, sees and derides;
Not more Almighty to resist our might
Than wise to frustrate all our plots and wiles.
Shall we then live thus vile, the race of Heav'n
Thus trampled, thus expelled to suffer here
Chains and these torments? Better these than worse
By my advice; since Fate inevitable
Subdues us, and omnipotent decree,
The Victor's will. To suffer, as to do,
200   Our strength is equal, nor the law unjust
That so ordains: this was at first resolved,
If we were wise, against so great a foe
Contending, and so doubtful what might fall.
I laugh, when those who at the spear are bold
And vent'rous, if that fail them, shrink and fear
What yet they know must follow, to endure
Exile, or ignominy, or bonds, or pain,
The sentence of their Conqueror: this is now
Our doom; which if we can sustain and bear,
210   Our súpreme Foe in time may much remit
His anger, and perhaps thus far removed
Not mind us not offending, satisfied
With what is punished; whence these raging fires
Will slacken, if his breath stir not their flames.
Our purer essence then will overcome

Their noxious vapour, or inured not feel,
Or changed at length, and to the place conformed
In temper and in nature, will receive
Familiar the fierce heat, and void of pain;
This horror will grow mild, this darkness light,   220
Besides what hope the never-ending flight
Of future days may bring, what chance, what change
Worth waiting, since our present lot appears
For happy though but ill, for ill not worst,
If we procure not to ourselves more woe.'
   Thus Belial with words clothed in reason's garb
Counselled ignoble ease, and peaceful sloth,
Not peace: and after him thus Mammon spake.
   'Either to disenthrone the King of Heav'n
We war, if war be best, or to regain   230
Our own right lost: him to unthrone we then
May hope when everlasting Fate shall yield
To fickle Chance, and Chaos judge the strife:
The former vain to hope argues as vain
The latter: for what place can be for us
Within Heav'n's bound, unless Heav'n's Lord supreme
We overpower? Suppose he should relent
And publish grace to all, on promise made
Of new subjection; with what eyes could we
Stand in his presence humble, and receive   240
Strict laws imposed, to celebrate his throne
With warbled hymns, and to his Godhead sing
Forced hallelujahs; while he lordly sits
Our envied sov'reign, and his altar breathes
Ambrosial odours and ambrosial flowers,
Our servile offerings? This must be our task
In Heav'n, this our delight: how wearisome
Eternity so spent in worship paid
To whom we hate. Let us not then pursue
By force impossible, by leave obtained   250
Unácceptáble, though in Heav'n, our state
Of splendid vassalage, but rather seek
Our own good from ourselves, and from our own

Live to ourselves, though in this vast recess,
Free, and to none accountable, preferring
Hard liberty before the easy yoke
Of servile pomp. Our greatness will appear
Then most conspicuous, when great things of small,
Useful of hurtful, prosperous of adverse
260 We can create, and in what place soe'er
Thrive under evil, and work ease out of pain
Through labour and endurance. This deep world
Of darkness do we dread? How oft amidst
Thick clouds and dark doth Heav'n's all-ruling Sire
Choose to reside, his glory unobscured,
And with the majesty of darkness round
Covers his throne; from whence deep thunders roar
Must'ring their rage, and Heav'n resembles Hell?
As he our darkness, cannot we his light
270 Imitate when we please? This desert soil
Wants not her hidden lustre, gems and gold;
Nor want we skill or art, from whence to raise
Magnificence; and what can Heav'n show more?
Our torments also may in length of time
Become our elements, these piercing fires
As soft as now severe, our temper changed
Into their temper; which must needs remove
The sensible of pain. All things invite
To peaceful counsels, and the settled state
280 Of order, how in safety best we may
Compose our present evils, with regard
Of what we are and where, dismissing quite
All thoughts of war: ye have what I advise.'
      He scarce had finished, when such murmur filled
Th' assembly, as when hollow rocks retain
The sound of blust'ring winds, which all night long
Had roused the sea, now with hoarse cadence lull
Seafaring men o'erwatched, whose bark by chance
Or pinnace anchors in a craggy bay
290 After the tempest: such applause was heard
As Mammon ended, and his sentence pleased,

Advising peace: for such another field
They dreaded worse than Hell: so much the fear
Of thunder and the sword of Michaël
Wrought still within them; and no less desire
To found this nether empire, which might rise
By policy, and long procéss of time,
In emulation opposite to Heav'n.
Which when Beëlzebub perceived, than whom,
Satan except, none higher sat, with grave   300
Aspéct he rose, and in his rising seemed
A pillar of state; deep on his front engraven
Deliberation sat and public care;
And princely counsel in his face yet shone,
Majestic though in ruin: sage he stood
With Atlantéan shoulders fit to bear
The weight of mightiest monarchies; his look
Drew audience and attention still as night
Or summer's noontide air, while thus he spake.
　'Thrones and imperial Powers, offspring of
　　　Heav'n   310
Ethereal Virtues; or these titles now
Must we renounce, and changing style be called
Princes of Hell? For so the popular vote
Inclines, here to continue, and build up here
A growing empire; doubtless; while we dream,
And know not that the King of Heav'n hath doomed
This place our dungeon, not our safe retreat
Beyond his potent arm, to live exempt
From Heav'n's high jurisdiction, in new league
Banded against his throne, but to remain   320
In strictest bondage, though thus far removed,
Under th' inevitable curb, reserved
His captive multitude: for he, be sure
In heighth or depth, still first and last will reign
Sole King, and of his kingdom lose no part
By our revolt, but over Hell extend
His empire, and with iron sceptre rule
Us here, as with his golden those in Heav'n.

What sit we then projecting peace and war?
330 War hath determined us, and foiled with loss
Irreparable; terms of peace yet none
Vouchsafed or sought; for what peace will be giv'n
To us enslaved, but custody severe,
And stripes, and arbitrary punishment
Inflicted? And what peace can we return,
But to our power hostility and hate,
Untamed reluctance, and revenge though slow,
Yet ever plotting how the Conqueror least
May reap his conquest, and may least rejoice
340 In doing what we most in suffering feel?
Nor will occasion want, nor shall we need
With dangerous expedition to invade
Heav'n, whose high walls fear no assault or siege,
Or ambush from the deep. What if we find
Some easier enterprise? There is a place
(If ancient and prophetic fame in Heav'n
Err not) another world, the happy seat
Of some new race called *Man*, about this time
To be created like to us, though less
350 In power and excellence, but favoured more
Of him who rules above; so was his will
Pronounced among the gods, and by an oath,
That shook Heav'n's whole circumference, confirmed.
Thither let us bend all our thoughts, to learn
What creatures there inhabit, of what mould,
Or substance, how endued, and what their power,
And where their weakness, how attempted best,
By force or subtlety: though Heav'n be shut,
And Heav'n's high Arbitrator sit secure
360 In his own strength, this place may lie exposed
The utmost border of his kingdom, left
To their defence who hold it: here perhaps
Some advantageous act may be achieved
By sudden onset, either with Hell fire
To waste his whole Creation, or possess
All as our own, and drive as we were driven,

The puny habitants, or if not drive,
Seduce them to our party, that their God
May prove their foe, and with repenting hand
Abolish his own works. This would surpass   370
Common revenge, and interrupt his joy
In our confusion, and our joy upraise
In his disturbance; when his darling sons
Hurled headlong to partake with us, shall curse
Their frail original, and faded bliss,
Faded so soon. Advise if this be worth
Attempting, or to sit in darkness here
Hatching vain empires.' Thus Beëlzebub
Pleaded his devilish counsel, first devised
By Satan, and in part proposed: for whence,   380
But from the author of all ill could spring
So deep a malice, to confound the race
Of mankind in one root, and earth with Hell
To mingle and involve, done all to spite
The great Creator? But their spite still serves
His glory to augment. The bold design
Pleased highly those infernal States, and joy
Sparkled in all their eyes; with full assent
They vote: whereat his speech he thus renews.
    'Well have ye judged, well ended long debate,   390
Synod of gods, and like to what ye are,
Great things resolved, which from the lowest deep
Will once more lift us up, in spite of Fate,
Nearer our ancient seat; perhaps in view
Of those bright confines, whence with neighbouring
        arms
And opportune excursion we may chance
Re-enter Heav'n; or else in some mild zone
Dwell not unvisited of Heav'n's fair light
Secure, and at the bright'ning orient beam
Purge off this gloom; the soft delicious air,   400
To heal the scar of these corrosive fires
Shall breathe her balm. But first whom shall we send
In search of this new world, whom shall we find

Sufficient? Who shall tempt with wand'ring feet
The dark unbottomed infinite abyss
And through the palpable obscure find out
His uncouth way, or spread his airy flight
Upborne with indefatigable wings
Over the vast abrupt, ere he arrive
410   The happy isle; what strength, what art can then
Suffice, or what evasion bear him safe
Through the strict senteries and stations thick
Of angels watching round? Here he had need
All circumspection, and we now no less
Choice in our suffrage; for on whom we send,
The weight of all and our last hope relies.'
　　This said, he sat; and expectation held
His look suspense, awaiting who appeared
To second, or oppose, or undertake
420   The perilous attempt: but all sat mute,
Pondering the danger with deep thoughts; and each
In other's count'nance read his own dismay
Astonished: none among the choice and prime
Of those Heav'n-warring champions could be found
So hardy as to proffer or accept
Alone the dreadful voyage; till at last
Satan, whom now transcendent glory raised
Above his fellows, with monarchal pride
Conscious of highest worth, unmoved thus spake.
430   'O progeny of Heav'n, empyreal Thrones,
With reason hath deep silence and demur
Seized us, though undismayed: long is the way
And hard, that out of Hell leads up to light;
Our prison strong, this huge convéx of fire,
Outrageous to devour, immures us round
Ninefold, and gates of burning adamant
Barred over us prohibit all egress.
These passed, if any pass, the void profound
Of unessential Night receives him next
440   Wide gaping, and with utter loss of being
Threatens him, plunged in that abortive gulf.

If thence he 'scape into whatever world,
Or unknown region, what remains him less
Than unknown dangers and as hard escape.
But I should ill become this throne, O Peers,
And this imperial sov'reignty, adorned
With splendour, armed with power, if aught
    proposed
And judged of public moment, in the shape
Of difficulty or danger could deter
Me from attempting. Wherefore do I assume   450
These royalties, and not refuse to reign,
Refusing to accept as great a share
Of hazard as of honour, due alike
To him who reigns, and so much to him due
Of hazard more, as he above the rest
High honoured sits? Go therefore mighty Powers,
Terror of Heav'n, though fall'n; intend at home,
While here shall be our home, what best may ease
The present misery, and render Hell
More tolerable; if there be cure or charm   460
To respite or deceive, or slack the pain
Of this ill mansion: intermit no watch
Against a wakeful Foe, while I abroad
Through all the coasts of dark destruction seek
Deliverance for us all: this enterprise
None shall partake with me.' Thus saying rose
The monarch, and prevented all reply,
Prudent, lest from his resolution raised
Others among the chief might offer now
(Certain to be refused) what erst they feared;   470
And so refused might in opinion stand
His rivals, winning cheap the high repute
Which he through hazard huge must earn. But they
Dreaded not more th' adventure than his voice
Forbidding; and at once with him they rose;
Their rising all at once was as the sound
Of thunder heard remote. Towards him they bend
With awful reverence prone; and as a god

Extol him equal to the highest in Heav'n.
480 Nor failed they to express how much they praised,
That for the general safety he despised
His own: for neither do the Spirits damned
Lose all their virtue; lest bad men should boast
Their specious deeds on earth, which glory excites,
Or close ambition varnished o'er with zeal.
Thus they their doubtful consultations dark
Ended rejoicing in their matchless chief:
As when from mountain tops the dusky clouds
Ascending, while the north wind sleeps, o'erspread
490 Heav'n's cheerful face, the louring element
Scowls o'er the darkened landscape snow, or show'r;
If chance the radiant sun with farewell sweet
Extend his ev'ning beam, the fields revive,
The birds their notes renew, and bleating herds
Attest their joy, that hill and valley rings.
O shame to men! Devil with devil damned
Firm concord holds, men only disagree
Of creatures rational, though under hope
Of Heav'nly grace: and God proclaiming peace,
500 Yet live in hatred, enmity, and strife
Among themselves, and levy cruel wars,
Wasting the earth, each other to destroy:
As if (which might induce us to accord)
Man had not Hellish foes enow besides,
That day and night for his destruction wait.
     The Stygian Council thus dissolved; and forth
In order came the grand infernal Peers:
Midst came their mighty Paramount, and seemed
Alone th' Antagonist of Heav'n, nor less
510 Than Hell's dread Emperor with pomp supreme,
And God-like imitated state; him round
A globe of fiery Seraphim enclosed
With bright emblazonry, and horrent arms.
Then of their session ended they bid cry
With trumpets' regal sound the great result:
Toward the four winds four speedy Cherubim

Put to their mouths the sounding alchemy
By herald's voice explained: the hollow abyss
Heard far and wide, and all the host of Hell
With deaf'ning shout returned them loud acclaim.   520
Thence more at ease their minds and somewhat raised
By false presumptuous hope, the rangèd powers
Disband, and wand'ring, each his several way
Pursues, as inclination or sad choice
Leads him perplexed, where he may likeliest find
Truce to his restless thoughts, and entertain
The irksome hours, till his great chief return.
Part on the plain, or in the air sublime
Upon the wing, or in swift race contend,
As at th' Olympian games or Pythian fields;   530
Part curb their fiery steeds, or shun the goal
With rapid wheels, or fronted brígades form.
As when to warn proud cities war appears
Waged in the troubled sky, and armies rush
To battle in the clouds, before each van
Prick forth the airy knights, and couch their spears
Till thickest legions close; with feats of arms
From either end of heav'n the welkin burns.
Others with vast Typhoean rage more fell
Rend up both rocks and hills, and ride the air   540
In whirlwind; Hell scarce holds the wild uproar.
As when Alcides from Oechalia crowned
With conquest, felt th' envenomed robe, and tore
Through pain up by the roots Thessalian pines,
And Lichas from the top of Oeta threw
Into th' Euboic Sea. Others more mild,
Retreated in a silent valley, sing
With notes angelical to many a harp
Their own heroic deeds and hapless fall
By doom of battle; and complain that Fate   550
Free virtue should enthrall to Force or Chance.
Their song was partial, but the harmony
(What could it less when Spirits immortal sing?)
Suspended Hell, and took with ravishment

The thronging audience. In discourse more sweet
(For eloquence the soul, song charms the sense)
Others apart sat on a hill retired,
In thoughts more elevate, and reasoned high
Of Providence, Foreknowledge, Will, and Fate,
560 Fixed Fate, Free Will, Foreknowledge absolute,
And found no end, in wand'ring mazes lost.
Of good and evil much they argued then,
Of happiness and final misery,
Passion and apathy, and glory and shame,
Vain wisdom all, and false philosophy:
Yet with a pleasing sorcery could charm
Pain for a while or anguish, and excite
Fallacious hope, or arm th' obdurèd breast
With stubborn patience as with triple steel.
570 Another part in squadrons and gross bands,
On bold adventure to discover wide
That dismal world, if any clime perhaps
Might yield them easier habitation, bend
Four ways their flying march, along the banks
Of four infernal rivers that disgorge
Into the burning lake their baleful streams;
Abhorrèd Styx the flood of deadly hate,
Sad Acheron of sorrow, black and deep;
Cocytus, named of lamentation loud
580 Heard on the rueful stream; fierce Phlegethon
Whose waves of torrent fire inflame with rage.
Far off from these a slow and silent stream,
Lethe the river of oblivion rolls
Her wat'ry labyrinth, whereof who drinks,
Forthwith his former state and being forgets,
Forgets both joy and grief, pleasure and pain.
Beyond this flood a frozen continent
Lies dark and wild, beat with perpetual storms
Of whirlwind and dire hail, which on firm land
590 Thaws not, but gathers heap, and ruin seems
Of ancient pile; all else deep snow and ice,
A gulf profound as that Serbonian bog

Betwixt Damiata and Mount Casius old,
Where armies whole have sunk: the parching air
Burns frore, and cold performs th' effect of fire.
Thither by Harpy-footed Furies haled,
At certain revolutions all the damned
Are brought: and feel by turns the bitter change
Of fierce extremes, extremes by change more fierce,
From beds of raging fire to starve in ice   600
Their soft ethereal warmth, and there to pine
Immovable, infixed, and frozen round,
Periods of time, thence hurried back to fire.
They ferry over this Lethean sound
Both to and fro, their sorrow to augment,
And wish and struggle, as they pass, to reach
The tempting stream, with one small drop to lose
In sweet forgetfulness all pain and woe,
All in one moment, and so near the brink;
But Fate withstands, and to oppose th' attempt   610
Medusa with Gorgonian terror guards
The ford, and of itself the water flies
All taste of living wight, as once it fled
The lip of Tantalus. Thus roving on
In cónfused march forlorn, th' adventurous bands
With shudd'ring horror pale, and eyes aghast
Viewed first their lamentable lot, and found
No rest: through many a dark and dreary vale
They passed, and many a region dolorous,
O'er many a frozen, many a fiery alp,   620
Rocks, caves, lakes, fens, bogs, dens, and shades of
        death,
A universe of death, which God by curse
Created evil, for evil only good,
Where all life dies, death lives, and nature breeds,
Perverse, all monstrous, all prodigious things,
Abominable, inutterable, and worse
Than fables yet have feigned, or fear conceived,
Gorgons and Hydras, and Chimeras dire.
   Meanwhile the Adversary of God and man,

630   Satan with thoughts inflamed of highest design,
      Puts on swift wings, and toward the gates of Hell
      Explores his solitary flight; sometimes
      He scours the right-hand coast, sometimes the left,
      Now shaves with level wing the deep, then soars
      Up to the fiery concave tow'ring high.
      As when far off at sea a fleet descried
      Hangs in the clouds, by equinoctial winds
      Close sailing from Bengala, or the isles
      Of Ternate and Tidore, whence merchants bring
640   Their spicy drugs: they on the trading flood
      Through the wide Ethiopian to the Cape
      Ply stemming nightly toward the pole. So seemed
      Far off the flying Fiend: at last appear
      Hell bounds high reaching to the horrid roof,
      And thrice threefold the gates; three folds were brass,
      Three iron, three of adamantine rock,
      Impenetrable, impaled with circling fire,
      Yet unconsumed. Before the gates there sat
      On either side a formidable shape;
650   The one seemed woman to the waist, and fair,
      But ended foul in many a scaly fold
      Voluminous and vast, a serpent armed
      With mortal sting: about her middle round
      A cry of Hell hounds never ceasing barked
      With wide Cerberean mouths full loud, and rung
      A hideous peal: yet, when they list, would creep,
      If aught disturbed their noise, into her womb,
      And kennel there, yet there still barked and howled
      Within unseen. Far less abhorred than these
660   Vexed Scylla bathing in the sea that parts
      Calabria from the hoarse Trinacrian shore:
      Nor uglier follow the night-hag, when called
      In secret, riding through the air she comes
      Lured with the smell of infant blood, to dance
      With Lapland witches, while the labouring moon
      Eclipses at their charms. The other shape,
      If shape it might be called that shape had none

Distinguishable in member, joint, or limb,
Or substance might be called that shadow seemed,
For each seemed either; black it stood as Night,   670
Fierce as ten Furies, terrible as Hell,
And shook a dreadful dart; what seemed his head
The likeness of a kingly crown had on.
Satan was now at hand, and from his seat
The monster moving onward came as fast
With horrid strides, Hell trembled as he strode.
Th' undaunted Fiend what this might be admired,
Admired, not feared; God and his Son except,
Created thing naught valued he nor shunned;
And with disdainful look thus first began.   680
    'Whence and what art thou, execrable shape,
That dar'st, though grim and terrible, advance
Thy miscreated front athwart my way
To yonder gates? Through them I mean to pass,
That be assured, without leave asked of thee:
Retire, or taste thy folly, and learn by proof,
Hell-born, not to contend with Spirits of Heav'n.'
    To whom the goblin full of wrath replied,
'Art thou that traitor angel, art thou he,
Who first broke peace in Heav'n and faith, till then   690
Unbroken, and in proud rebellious arms
Drew after him the third part of Heav'n's sons
Conjúred against the Highest, for which both thou
And they outcást from God, are here condemned
To waste eternal days in woe and pain?
And reckon'st thou thyself with Spirits of Heav'n,
Hell-doomed, and breath'st defiance here and scorn,
Where I reign king, and to enrage thee more,
Thy king and lord? Back to thy punishment,
False fugitive, and to thy speed add wings,   700
Lest with a whip of scorpions I pursue
Thy ling'ring, or with one stroke of this dart
Strange horror seize thee, and pangs unfelt before.'
    So spake the grisly terror, and in shape,
So speaking and so threat'ning, grew tenfold

More dreadful and deform: on th' other side
Incensed with indignation Satan stood
Unterrified, and like a comet burned,
That fires the length of Ophiucus huge
710   In th' Arctic sky, and from his horrid hair
Shakes pestilence and war. Each at the head
Levelled his deadly aim; their fatal hands
No second stroke intend, and such a frown
Each cast at th' other, as when two black clouds
With heav'n's artillery fraught, come rattling on
Over the Caspian, then stand front to front
Hov'ring a space, till winds the signal blow
To join their dark encounter in mid air:
So frowned the mighty combatants, that Hell
720   Grew darker at their frown, so matched they stood;
For never but once more was either like
To meet so great a foe: and now great deeds
Had been achieved, whereof all Hell had rung,
Had not the snaky sorceress that sat
Fast by Hell gate, and kept the fatal key,
Ris'n, and with hideous outcry rushed between.
   'O father, what intends thy hand,' she cried,
'Against thy only son? What fury O son,
Possesses thee to bend that mortal dart
730   Against thy father's head? And know'st for whom?
For him who sits above and laughs the while
At thee ordained his drudge, to execute
Whate'er his wrath, which he calls justice, bids,
His wrath which one day will destroy ye both.'
   She spake, and at her words the Hellish pest
Forbore, then these to her Satan returned:
   'So strange thy outcry, and thy words so strange
Thou interposest, that my sudden hand
Prevented spares to tell thee yet by deeds
740   What it intends; till first I know of thee,
What thing thou art, thus double-formed, and why
In this infernal vale first met thou call'st
Me father, and that phantasm call'st my son?

I know thee not, nor ever saw till now
Sight more detestable than him and thee.'
   T' whom thus the portress of Hell gate replied;
'Hast thou forgot me then, and do I seem
Now in thine eye so foul, once deemed so fair
In Heav'n, when at th' assembly, and in sight
Of all the Seraphim with thee combined   750
In bold conspiracy against Heav'n's King,
All on a sudden miserable pain
Surprised thee, dim thine eyes, and dizzy swum
In darkness, while thy head flames thick and fast
Threw forth, till on the left side op'ning wide,
Likest to thee in shape and count'nance bright,
Then shining Heav'nly fair, a goddess armed
Out of thy head I sprung: amazement seized
All th' host of Heav'n; back they recoiled afraid
At first, and called me *Sin*, and for a Sign   760
Portentous held me; but familiar grown,
I pleased, and with attractive graces won
The most averse, thee chiefly, who full oft
Thyself in me thy perfect image viewing
Becam'st enamoured, and such joy thou took'st
With me in secret, that my womb conceived
A growing burden. Meanwhile war arose,
And fields were fought in Heav'n; wherein remained
(For what could else) to our Almighty Foe
Clear victory, to our part loss and rout   770
Through all the Empyrean: down they fell
Driv'n headlong from the pitch of Heaven, down
Into this deep, and in the general fall
I also; at which time this powerful key
Into my hand was giv'n, with charge to keep
These gates for ever shut, which none can pass
Without my op'ning. Pensive here I sat
Alone, but long I sat not, till my womb
Pregnant by thee, and now excessive grown
Prodigious motion felt and rueful throes.   780
At last this odious offspring whom thou seest

Thine own begotten, breaking violent way
Tore through my entrails, that with fear and pain
Distorted, all my nether shape thus grew
Transformed: but he my inbred enemy
Forth issued, brandishing his fatal dart
Made to destroy: I fled, and cried out *Death*;
Hell trembled at the hideous name, and sighed
From all her caves, and back resounded *Death*.

790   I fled, but he pursued (though more, it seems,
Inflamed with lust than rage) and swifter far,
Me overtook his mother all dismayed,
And in embraces forcible and foul
Engend'ring with me, of that rape begot
These yelling monsters that with ceaseless cry
Surround me, as thou saw'st, hourly conceived
And hourly born, with sorrow infinite
To me, for when they list, into the womb
That bred them they return, and howl and gnaw

800 My bowels, their repast; then bursting forth
Afresh with conscious terrors vex me round,
That rest or intermission none I find.
Before mine eyes in opposition sits
Grim Death my son and foe, who sets them on,
And me his parent would full soon devour
For want of other prey, but that he knows
His end with mine involved; and knows that I
Should prove a bitter morsel, and his bane,
Whenever that shall be; so Fate pronounced.

810 But thou O father, I forewarn thee, shun
His deadly arrow; neither vainly hope
To be invulnerable in those bright arms,
Though tempered Heav'nly, for that mortal dint,
Save he who reigns above, none can resist.'
    She finished, and the subtle Fiend his lore
Soon learned, now milder, and thus answered smooth:
'Dear daughter, since thou claim'st me for thy sire,
And my fair son here show'st me, the dear pledge
Of dalliance had with thee in Heav'n, and joys

Then sweet, now sad to mention, through dire
   change   820
Befall'n us unforeseen, unthought of, know
I come no enemy, but to set free
From out this dark and dismal house of pain,
Both him and thee, and all the Heav'nly host
Of Spirits that in our just pretences armed
Fell with us from on high: from them I go
This uncouth errand sole, and one for all
Myself expose, with lonely steps to tread
Th' unfounded deep, and through the void immense
To search with wand'ring quest a place foretold 830
Should be, and, by concurring signs, ere now
Created vast and round, a place of bliss
In the purlieus of Heav'n, and therein placed
A race of upstart creatures, to supply
Perhaps our vacant room, though more removed,
Lest Heav'n surcharged with potent multitude
Might hap to move new broils: be this or aught
Than this more secret now designed, I haste
To know, and this once known, shall soon return,
And bring ye to the place where thou and Death 840
Shall dwell at ease, and up and down unseen
Wing silently the buxom air, embalmed
With odours; there ye shall be fed and filled
Immeasurably, all things shall be your prey.'
He ceased, for both seemed highly pleased, and Death
Grinned horrible a ghastly smile, to hear
His famine should be filled, and blessed his maw
Destined to that good hour: no less rejoiced
His mother bad, and thus bespake her sire.
 'The key of this infernal pit by due,   850
And by command of Heav'n's all-powerful King
I keep, by him forbidden to unlock
These adamantine gates; against all force
Death ready stands to interpose his dart,
Fearless to be o'ermatched by living might.
But what owe I to his commands above

Who hates me, and hath hither thrust me down
Into this gloom of Tartarus profound,
To sit in hateful office here confined,
860 Inhabitant of Heav'n, and Heav'nly-born,
Here in perpetual agony and pain,
With terrors and with clamours compassed round
Of mine own brood, that on my bowels feed?
Thou art my father, thou my author, thou
My being gav'st me; whom should I obey
But thee, whom follow? Thou wilt bring me soon
To that new world of light and bliss, among
The gods who live at ease, where I shall reign
At thy right hand voluptuous, as beseems
870 Thy daughter and thy darling, without end.'
        Thus saying, from her side the fatal key,
Sad instrument of all our woe, she took;
And towards the gate rolling her bestial train,
Forthwith the huge portcullis high up drew,
Which but herself not all the Stygian powers
Could once have moved; then in the key-hole turns
Th' intricate wards, and every bolt and bar
Of massy iron or solid rock with ease
Unfastens: on a sudden open fly
880 With impetuous recoil and jarring sound
Th' infernal doors, and on their hinges grate
Harsh thunder, that the lowest bottom shook
Of Erebus. She opened, but to shut
Excelled her power; the gates wide open stood,
That with extended wings a bannered host
Under spread ensigns marching might pass through
With horse and chariots ranked in loose array;
So wide they stood, and like a furnace mouth
Cast forth redounding smoke and ruddy flame.
890 Before their eyes in sudden view appear
The secrets of the hoary deep, a dark
Illimitable Ocean without bound,
Without dimension, where length, breadth, and
            heighth,

And time and place are lost; where eldest Night
And Chaos, ancestors of Nature, hold
Eternal anarchy, amidst the noise
Of endless wars, and by confusion stand.
For Hot, Cold, Moist, and Dry, four champions
        fierce
Strive here for mast'ry, and to battle bring
Their embryon atoms; they around the flag   900
Of each his faction, in their several clans,
Light-armed or heavy, sharp, smooth, swift or slow,
Swarm populous, unnumbered as the sands
Of Barca or Cyrene's torrid soil,
Levied to side with warring winds, and poise
Their lighter wings. To whom these most adhere,
He rules a moment; Chaos umpire sits,
And by decision more embroils the fray
By which he reigns: next him high arbiter
Chance governs all. Into this wild abyss,   910
The womb of Nature and perhaps her grave,
Of neither sea, nor shore, nor air, nor fire,
But all these in their pregnant causes mixed
Confus'dly, and which thus must ever fight,
Unless th' Almighty Maker them ordain
His dark materials to create more worlds,
Into this wild abyss the wary Fiend
Stood on the brink of Hell and looked a while,
Pondering his voyage; for no narrow frith
He had to cross. Nor was his ear less pealed   920
With noises loud and ruinous (to compare
Great things with small) than when Bellona storms,
With all her battering engines bent to raze
Some capital city; or less than if this frame
Of heav'n were falling, and these elements
In mutiny had from her axle torn
The steadfast earth. At last his sail-broad vans
He spreads for flight, and in the surging smoke
Uplifted spurns the ground, thence many a league
As in a cloudy chair ascending rides   930

Audacious, but that seat soon failing, meets
A vast vacuity: all unawares
Flutt'ring his pennons vain plumb down he drops
Ten thousand fathom deep, and to this hour
Down had been falling, had not by ill chance
The strong rebuff of some tumultuous cloud
Instínct with fire and nitre hurried him
As many miles aloft: that fury stayed,
Quenched in a boggy Syrtis, neither sea,
940   Nor good dry land: nigh foundered on he fares,
Treading the crude consistence, half on foot,
Half flying; behoves him now both oar and sail.
As when a gryphon through the wilderness
With wingèd course o'er hill or moory dale,
Pursues the Arimaspian, who by stealth
Had from his wakeful custody purloined
The guarded gold: so eagerly the Fiend
O'er bog or steep, through strait, rough, dense,
          or rare,
With head, hands, wings, or feet pursues his way,
950   And swims or sinks, or wades, or creeps, or flies:
At length a universal hubbub wild
Of stunning sounds and voices all confused
Borne through the hollow dark assaults his ear
With loudest vehemence: thither he plies,
Undaunted to meet there whatever Power
Or Spirit of the nethermost abyss
Might in that noise reside, of whom to ask
Which way the nearest coast of darkness lies
Bordering on light; when straight behold the throne
960   Of Chaos, and his dark pavilion spread
Wide on the wasteful deep; with him enthroned
Sat sable-vested Night, eldest of things,
The consort of his reign; and by them stood
Orcus and Ades, and the dreaded name
Of Demogorgon; Rumour next and Chance,
And Tumult and Confusion all embroiled,
And Discord with a thousand various mouths.

T' whom Satan turning boldly, thus. 'Ye Powers
And Spirits of this nethermost abyss,
Chaos and ancient Night, I come no spy,   970
With purpose to explore or to disturb
The secrets of your realm, but by constraint
Wand'ring this darksome desert, as my way
Lies through your spacious empire up to light,
Alone, and without guide, half lost, I seek
What readiest path leads where your gloomy bounds
Confine with Heav'n; or if some other place
From your dominion won, th' Ethereal King
Possesses lately, thither to arrive
I travel this profound, direct my course;   980
Directed, no mean recompense it brings
To your behoof, if I that region lost,
All usurpation thence expelled, reduce
To her original darkness and your sway
(Which is my present journey) and once more
Erect the standard there of ancient Night;
Yours be th' advantage all, mine the revenge.'
    Thus Satan; and him thus the Anarch old
With falt'ring speech and visage incomposed
Answered. 'I know thee, stranger, who thou art,   990
That mighty leading angel, who of late
Made head against Heav'n's King, though overthrown.
I saw and heard, for such a numerous host
Fled not in silence through the frighted deep
With ruin upon ruin, rout on rout,
Confusion worse confounded; and Heav'n gates
Poured out by millions her victorious bands
Pursuing. I upon my frontiers here
Keep residence; if all I can will serve,
That little which is left so to defend,   1000
Encroached on still through our intestine broils
Weak'ning the sceptre of old Night: first Hell
Your dungeon stretching far and wide beneath;
Now lately heav'n and earth, another world

Hung o'er my realm, linked in a golden chain
To that side Heav'n from whence your legions fell:
If that way be your walk, you have not far;
So much the nearer danger; go and speed;
Havoc and spoil and ruin are my gain.'

1010   He ceased; and Satan stayed not to reply,
But glad that now his sea should find a shore,
With fresh alacrity and force renewed
Springs upward like a pyramid of fire
Into the wide expanse, and through the shock
Of fighting elements, on all sides round
Environed wins his way; harder beset
And more endangered, than when Argo passed
Through Bosporus betwixt the justling rocks:
Or when Ulysses on the larboard shunned
1020   Charybdis, and by th' other whirlpool steered.
So he with difficulty and labour hard
Moved on, with difficulty and labour he;
But he once passed, soon after when man fell,
Strange alteration! Sin and Death amain
Following his track, such was the will of Heav'n,
Paved after him a broad and beaten way
Over the dark abyss, whose boiling gulf
Tamely endured a bridge of wondrous length
From Hell continued reaching th' utmost orb
1030   Of this frail world; by which the Spirits perverse
With easy intercourse pass to and fro
To tempt or punish mortals, except whom
God and good angels guard by special grace.
But now at last the sacred influence
Of light appears, and from the walls of Heav'n
Shoots far into the bosom of dim Night
A glimmering dawn; here Nature first begins
Her farthest verge, and Chaos to retire
As from her outmost works a broken foe
1040   With tumult less and with less hostile din,
That Satan with less toil, and now with ease
Wafts on the calmer wave by dubious light

And like a weather-beaten vessel holds
Gladly the port, though shrouds and tackle torn;
Or in the emptier waste, resembling air,
Weighs his spread wings, at leisure to behold
Far off th' empyreal Heav'n, extended wide
In circuit, undetermined square or round,
With opal tow'rs and battlements adorned
Of living sapphire, once his native seat;   1050
And fast by hanging in a golden chain
This pendent world, in bigness as a star
Of smallest magnitude close by the moon.
Thither full fraught with mischievous revenge,
Accursed, and in a cursèd hour he hies.

BOOK IV

O for that warning voice, which he who saw
Th' Apocalypse, heard cry in Heav'n aloud,
Then when the Dragon, put to second rout,
Came furious down to be revenged on men,
'Woe to the inhabitants on earth!' that now,
While time was, our first parents had been warned
The coming of their secret foe, and 'scaped
Haply so 'scaped his mortal snare; for now,
Satan, now first inflamed with rage, came down,
The Tempter ere th' Accuser of mankind,   10
To wreck on innocent frail man his loss
Of that first battle, and his flight to Hell:
Yet not rejoicing in his speed, though bold,
Far off and fearless, nor with cause to boast,
Begins his dire attempt, which nigh the birth
Now rolling, boils in his tumultuous breast,
And like a devilish engine back recoils
Upon himself; horror and doubt distract

His troubled thoughts, and from the bottom stir
20   The Hell within him, for within him Hell
He brings, and round about him, nor from Hell
One step no more than from himself can fly
By change of place: now conscience wakes despair
That slumbered, wakes the bitter memory
Of what he was, what is, and what must be
Worse; of worse deeds worse sufferings must ensue.
Sometimes towards Eden which now in his view
Lay pleasant, his grieved look he fixes sad,
Sometimes towards heav'n and the full-blazing sun,
30   Which now sat high in his meridian tower:
Then much revolving, thus in sighs began.
     'O thou that with surpassing glory crowned,
Look'st from thy sole dominion like the god
Of this new world; at whose sight all the stars
Hide their diminished heads; to thee I call,
But with no friendly voice, and add thy name
O sun, to tell thee how I hate thy beams
That bring to my remembrance from what state
I fell, how glorious once above thy sphere;
40   Till pride and worse ambition threw me down
Warring in Heav'n against Heav'n's matchless King:
Ah wherefore! He deserved no such return
From me, whom he created what I was
In that bright eminence, and with his good
Upbraided none; nor was his service hard.
What could be less than to afford him praise,
The easiest recompense, and pay him thanks,
How due! Yet all his good proved ill in me,
And wrought but malice; lifted up so high
50   I 'sdained subjection, and thought one step higher
Would set me highest, and in a moment quit
The debt immense of endless gratitude,
So burdensome, still paying, still to owe;
Forgetful what from him I still received,
And understood not that a grateful mind
By owing owes not, but still pays, at once

Indebted and discharged; what burden then?
O had his powerful destiny ordained
Me some inferior angel, I had stood
Then happy; no unbounded hope had raised   60
Ambition. Yet why not? Some other Power
As great might have aspired, and me though mean
Drawn to his part; but other Powers as great
Fell not, but stand unshaken, from within
Or from without, to all temptations armed.
Hadst thou the same free will and power to stand?
Thou hadst: whom hast thou then or what to accuse,
But Heav'n's free love dealt equally to all?
Be then his love accursed, since love or hate,
To me alike, it deals eternal woe.   70
Nay cursed be thou; since against his thy will
Chose freely what it now so justly rues.
Me miserable! Which way shall I fly
Infinite wrath, and infinite despair?
Which way I fly is Hell; myself am Hell;
And in the lowest deep a lower deep
Still threat'ning to devour me opens wide,
To which the Hell I suffer seems a Heav'n.
O then at last relent: is there no place
Left for repentance, none for pardon left?   80
None left but by submission; and that word
Disdain forbids me, and my dread of shame
Among the Spirits beneath, whom I seduced
With other promises and other vaunts
Than to submit, boasting I could subdue
Th' Omnipotent. Ay me, they little know
How dearly I abide that boast so vain,
Under what torments inwardly I groan;
While they adore me on the throne of Hell,
With diadem and sceptre high advanced   90
The lower still I fall, only supreme
In misery; such joy ambition finds.
But say I could repent and could obtain
By act of grace my former state; how soon

Would heighth recall high thoughts, how soon unsay
What feigned submission swore: ease would recant
Vows made in pain, as violent and void.
For never can true reconcilement grow
Where wounds of deadly hate have pierced so deep:
100   Which would but lead me to a worse relapse
And heavier fall: so should I purchase dear
Short intermission bought with double smart.
This knows my punisher; therefore as far
From granting he, as I from begging peace:
All hope excluded thus, behold instead
Of us outcást, exíled, his new delight,
Mankind created, and for him this world.
So farewell hope, and with hope farewell fear,
Farewell remorse: all good to me is lost;
110   Evil be thou my good; by thee at least
Divided empire with Heav'n's King I hold
By thee, and more than half perhaps will reign;
As man ere long, and this new world shall know.'
      Thus while he spake, each passion dimmed his face
Thrice changed with pale, ire, envy and despair,
Which marred his borrowed visage, and betrayed
Him counterfeit, if any eye beheld.
For Heav'nly minds from such distempers foul
Are ever clear. Whereof he soon aware,
120   Each perturbation smoothed with outward calm,
Artificer of fraud; and was the first
That practised falsehood under saintly show,
Deep malice to conceal, couched with revenge:
Yet not enough had practised to deceive
Uriel once warned; whose eye pursued him down
The way he went, and on th' Assyrian mount
Saw him disfigured, more than could befall
Spirit of happy sort: his gestures fierce
He marked and mad demeanour, then alone,
130   As he supposed, all unobserved, unseen.
So on he fares, and to the border comes

Of Eden, where delicious Paradise,
Now nearer, crowns with her enclosure green,
As with a rural mound the champaign head
Of a steep wilderness, whose hairy sides
With thicket overgrown, grotesque and wild,
Access denied; and overhead up grew
Insuperable heighth of loftiest shade,
Cedar, and pine, and fir, and branching palm,
A sylvan scene, and as the ranks ascend   140
Shade above shade, a woody theatre
Of stateliest view. Yet higher than their tops
The verdurous wall of Paradise up sprung:
Which to our general sire gave prospect large
Into his nether empire neighbouring round.
And higher than that wall a circling row
Of goodliest trees loaden with fairest fruit,
Blossoms and fruits at once of golden hue
Appeared, with gay enamelled colours mixed:
On which the sun more glad impressed his beams   150
Than in fair evening cloud, or humid bow,
When God hath show'red the earth; so lovely seemed
That landscape: and of pure now purer air
Meets his approach, and to the heart inspires
Vernal delight and joy, able to drive
All sadness but despair: now gentle gales
Fanning their odoriferous wings dispense
Native perfumes, and whisper whence they stole
Those balmy spoils. As when to them who sail
Beyond the Cape of Hope, and now are past   160
Mozámbique, off at sea north-east winds blow
Sabéan odours from the spicy shore
Of Araby the Blest, with such delay
Well pleased they slack their course, and many a league
Cheered with the grateful smell old Ocean smiles.
So entertained those odorous sweets the Fiend
Who came their bane, though with them better pleased
Than Asmodéus with the fishy fume,

That drove him, though enamoured, from the spouse
170   Of Tobit's son, and with a vengeance sent
From Media post to Egypt, there fast bound.
    Now to th' ascent of that steep savage hill
Satan had journeyed on, pensive and slow;
But further way found none, so thick entwined,
As one continued brake, the undergrowth
Of shrubs and tangling bushes had perplexed
All path of man or beast that passed that way:
One gate there only was, and that looked east
On th' other side: which when th' Arch-felon saw
180   Due entrance he disdained, and in contempt,
At one slight bound high overleaped all bound
Of hill or highest wall, and sheer within
Lights on his feet. As when a prowling wolf,
Whom hunger drives to seek new haunt for prey,
Watching where shepherds pen their flocks at eve
In hurdled cotes amid the field secure,
Leaps o'er the fence with ease into the fold:
Or as a thief bent to unhoard the cash
Of some rich burgher, whose substantial doors,
190   Cross-barred and bolted fast, fear no assault,
In at the window climbs, or o'er the tiles;
So clomb this first grand thief into God's fold:
So since into his Church lewd hirelings climb.
Thence up he flew, and on the Tree of Life,
The middle tree and highest there that grew,
Sat like a cormorant; yet not true life
Thereby regained, but sat devising death
To them who lived; nor on the virtue thought
Of that life-giving plant, but only used
200   For prospect, what well used had been the pledge
Of immortality. So little knows
Any, but God alone, to value right
The good before him, but perverts best things
To worst abuse, or to their meanest use.
Beneath him with new wonder now he views
To all delight of human sense exposed

In narrow room Nature's whole wealth, yea more,
A Heav'n on earth: for blissful Paradise
Of God the garden was, by him in the east
Of Eden planted; Eden stretched her line   210
From Auran eastward to the royal towers
Of great Seleucia, built by Grecian kings,
Or where the sons of Eden long before
Dwelt in Telassar: in this pleasant soil
His far more pleasant garden God ordained;
Out of this fertile ground he caused to grow
All trees of noblest kind for sight, smell, taste;
And all amid them stood the Tree of Life,
High eminent, blooming ambrosial fruit
Of vegetable gold; and next to life   220
Our death the Tree of Knowledge grew fast by,
Knowledge of Good bought dear by knowing ill.
Southward through Eden went a river large,
Nor changed his course, but through the shaggy hill
Passed underneath ingulfed, for God had thrown
That mountain as his garden mould high raised
Upon the rapid current, which through veins
Of porous earth with kindly thirst up drawn,
Rose a fresh fountain, and with many a rill
Watered the garden; thence united fell   230
Down the steep glade, and met the nether flood,
Which from his darksome passage now appears,
And now divided into four main streams,
Runs diverse, wand'ring many a famous realm
And country whereof here needs no account,
But rather to tell how, if art could tell,
How from that sapphire fount the crispèd brooks,
Rolling on orient pearl and sands of gold,
With mazy error under pendent shades
Ran nectar, visiting each plant, and fed   240
Flow'rs worthy of Paradise which not nice art
In beds and curious knots, but Nature boon
Poured forth profuse on hill and dale and plain,
Both where the morning sun first warmly smote

The open field, and where the unpierced shade
Embrowned the noontide bow'rs: thus was this place,
A happy rural seat of various view;
Groves whose rich trees wept odorous gums and balm,
Others whose fruit burnished with golden rind
250 Hung amiable, Hesperian fables true,
If true, here only, and of delicious taste:
Betwixt them lawns, or level downs, and flocks
Grazing the tender herb, were interposed,
Or palmy hillock, or the flow'ry lap
Of some irriguous valley spread her store,
Flow'rs of all hue, and without thorn the rose:
Another side, umbrageous grots and caves
Of cool recess, o'er which the mantling vine
Lays forth her purple grape, and gently creeps
260 Luxuriant; meanwhile murmuring waters fall
Down the slope hills, dispersed, or in a lake,
That to the fringèd bank with myrtle crowned,
Her crystal mirror holds, unite their streams.
The birds their choir apply; airs, vernal airs,
Breathing the smell of field and grove, attune
The trembling leaves, while universal Pan
Knit with the Graces and the Hours in dance
Led on th' eternal spring. Not that fair field
Of Enna, where Prosérpine gath'ring flow'rs
270 Herself a fairer flow'r by gloomy Dis
Was gathered, which cost Ceres all that pain
To seek her through the world; nor that sweet grove
Of Daphne by Orontes, and th' inspired
Castalian spring, might with this Paradise
Of Eden strive; nor that Nyseian isle
Girt with the river Triton, where old Cham,
Whom Gentiles Ammon call and Libyan Jove,
Hid Amalthea and her florid son
Young Bacchus from his stepdame Rhea's eye;
280 Nor where Abássin kings their issue guard,
Mount Amara, though this by some supposed
True Paradise under the Ethiop line

By Nilus' head, enclosed with shining rock,
A whole day's journey high, but wide remote
From this Assyrian garden, where the Fiend
Saw undelighted all delight, all kind
Of living creatures new to sight and strange:
Two of far nobler shape erect and tall,
Godlike erect, with native honour clad
In naked majesty seemed lords of all,   290
And worthy seemed, for in their looks divine
The image of their glorious Maker shone,
Truth, wisdom, sanctitude severe and pure,
Severe, but in true filial freedom placed;
Whence true authority in men; though both
Not equal, as their sex not equal seemed;
For contemplation he and valour formed,
For softness she and sweet attractive grace,
He for God only, she for God in him:
His fair large front and eye sublime declared   300
Absolute rule; and hyacinthine locks
Round from his parted forelock manly hung
Clust'ring, but not beneath his shoulders broad:
She as a veil down to the slender waist
Her unadornèd golden tresses wore
Dishevelled, but in wanton ringlets waved
As the vine curls her tendrils, which implied
Subjection, but required with gentle sway,
And by her yielded, by him best received,
Yielded with coy submission, modest pride,   310
And sweet reluctant amorous delay.
Nor those mysterious parts were then concealed;
Then was not guilty shame, dishonest shame
Of nature's works, honour dishonourable,
Sin-bred, how have ye troubled all mankind
With shows instead, mere shows of seeming pure,
And banished from man's life his happiest life,
Simplicity and spotless innocence.
So passed they naked on, nor shunned the sight
Of God or angel, for they thought no ill: 320

So hand in hand they passed, the loveliest pair
That ever since in love's embraces met,
Adam the goodliest man of men since born
His sons, the fairest of her daughters Eve.
Under a tuft of shade that on a green
Stood whispering soft, by a fresh fountain side
They sat them down, and after no more toil
Of their sweet gard'ning labour than sufficed
To recommend cool Zephyr, and made ease
More easy, wholesome thirst and appetite
More grateful, to their supper fruits they fell,
Nectarine fruits which the compliant boughs
Yielded them, sidelong as they sat recline
On the soft downy bank damasked with flow'rs:
The savoury pulp they chew, and in the rind
Still as they thirsted scoop the brimming stream;
Nor gentle purpose, nor endearing smiles
Wanted, nor youthful dalliance as beseems
Fair couple, linked in happy nuptial league,
Alone as they. About them frisking played
All beasts of th' earth, since wild, and of all chase
In wood or wilderness, forest or den;
Sporting the lion ramped, and in his paw
Dandled the kid; bears, tigers, ounces, pards
Gambolled before them, th' unwieldy elephant
To make them mirth used all his might, and wreathed
His lithe proboscis; close the serpent sly
Insinuating, wove with Gordian twine
His braided train, and of his fatal guile
Gave proof unheeded; others on the grass
Couched, and now filled with pasture gazing sat,
Or bedward ruminating: for the sun
Declined was hasting now with prone career
To th' Ocean Isles, and in th' ascending Scale
Of heav'n the stars that usher evening rose:
When Satan still in gaze, as first he stood,
Scarce thus at length failed speech recovered sad.
        'O Hell! What do mine eyes with grief behold,

330

340

350

Into our room of bliss thus high advanced
Creatures of other mould, earth-born perhaps,   360
Not Spirits, yet to Heav'nly Spirits bright
Little inferior; whom my thoughts pursue
With wonder, and could love, so lively shines
In them divine resemblance, and such grace
The hand that formed them on their shape hath poured.
Ah gentle pair, ye little think how nigh
Your change approaches, when all these delights
Will vanish and deliver ye to woe,
More woe, the more your taste is now of joy;
Happy, but for so happy ill secured   370
Long to continue, and this high seat your Heav'n
Ill fenced for Heav'n to keep out such a foe
As now is entered; yet no purposed foe
To you whom I could pity thus forlorn
Though I unpitied: league with you I seek,
And mutual amity so strait, so close,
That I with you must dwell, or you with me
Henceforth; my dwelling haply may not please
Like this fair Paradise, your sense, yet such
Accept your Maker's work; he gave it me,   380
Which I as freely give; Hell shall unfold,
To entertain you two, her widest gates,
And send forth all her kings; there will be room,
Not like these narrow limits, to receive
Your numerous offspring; if no better place,
Thank him who puts me loath to this revenge
On you who wrong me not for him who wronged.
And should I at your harmless innocence
Melt, as I do, yet public reason just,
Honour and empire with revenge enlarged,   390
By conquering this new world, compels me now
To do what else though damned I should abhor.'
  So spake the Fiend, and with necessity,
The tyrant's plea, excused his devilish deeds.
Then from his lofty stand on that high tree
Down he alights among the sportful herd

Of those four-footed kinds, himself now one,
Now other, as their shape served best his end
Nearer to view his prey, and unespied
400   To mark what of their state he more might learn
By word or action marked: about them round
A lion now he stalks with fiery glare,
Then as a tiger, who by chance hath spied
In some purlieu two gentle fawns at play,
Straight couches close, then rising changes oft
His couchant watch, as one who chose his ground
Whence rushing he might surest seize them both
Gripped in each paw: when Adam first of men
To first of women Eve thus moving speech,
410   Turned him all ear to hear new utterance flow.
      'Sole partner and sole part of all these joys,
Dearer thyself than all; needs must the power
That made us, and for us this ample world
Be infinitely good, and of his good
As liberal and free as infinite,
That raised us from the dust and placed us here
In all this happiness, who at his hand
Have nothing merited, nor can perform
Aught whereof he hath need, he who requires
420   From us no other service than to keep
This one, this easy charge, of all the trees
In Paradise that bear delicious fruit
So various, not to taste that only Tree
Of Knowledge, planted by the Tree of Life,
So near grows death to life, whate'er death is,
Some dreadful thing no doubt; for well thou know'st
God hath pronounced it death to taste that Tree,
The only sign of our obedience left
Among so many signs of power and rule
430   Conferred upon us, and dominion giv'n
Over all other creatures that possess
Earth, air, and sea. Then let us not think hard
One easy prohibition, who enjoy
Free leave so large to all things else, and choice

Unlimited of manifold delights:
But let us ever praise him, and extol
His bounty, following our delightful task
To prune these growing plants, and tend these
    flow'rs,
Which were it toilsome, yet with thee were sweet.'
    To whom thus Eve replied. 'O thou for whom   440
And from whom I was formed flesh of thy flesh,
And without whom am to no end, my guide
And head, what thou hast said is just and right.
For we to him indeed all praises owe,
And daily thanks, I chiefly who enjoy
So far the happier lot, enjoying thee
Pre-eminent by so much odds, while thou
Like consort to thyself canst nowhere find.
That day I oft remember, when from sleep
I first awaked, and found myself reposed   450
Under a shade of flow'rs, much wond'ring where
And what I was, whence thither brought, and how.
Not distant far from thence a murmuring sound
Of waters issued from a cave and spread
Into a liquid plain, then stood unmoved
Pure as th' expanse of heav'n; I thither went
With unexperienced thought, and laid me down
On the green bank, to look into the clear
Smooth lake, that to me seemed another sky.
As I bent down to look, just opposite,   460
A shape within the wat'ry gleam appeared
Bending to look on me: I started back,
It started back, but pleased I soon returned,
Pleased it returned as soon with answering looks
Of sympathy and love; there I had fixed
Mine eyes till now, and pined with vain desire,
Had not a voice thus warned me, "What thou seest,
What there thou seest fair creature is thyself,
With thee it came and goes; but follow me,
And I will bring thee where no shadow stays   470
Thy coming, and thy soft embraces, he

Whose image thou art, him thou shall enjoy
Inseparably thine, to him shalt bear
Multitudes like thyself, and thence be called
Mother of human race": what could I do,
But follow straight, invisibly thus led?
Till I espied thee, fair indeed and tall,
Under a platan, yet methought less fair,
Less winning soft, less amiably mild,
480   Than that smooth wat'ry image; back I turned,
Thou following cried'st aloud, "Return, fair Eve;
Whom fli'st thou? Whom thou fli'st, of him thou art,
His flesh, his bone; to give thee being I lent
Out of my side to thee, nearest my heart
Substantial life, to have thee by my side
Henceforth an individual solace dear;
Part of my soul I seek thee, and thee claim
My other half": with that thy gentle hand
Seized mine, I yielded, and from that time see
490   How beauty is excelled by manly grace
And wisdom, which alone is truly fair.'
    So spake our general mother, and with eyes
Of conjugal attraction unreproved,
And meek surrender, half embracing leaned
On our first father; half her swelling breast
Naked met his under the flowing gold
Of her loose tresses hid: he in delight
Both of her beauty and submissive charms
Smiled with superior love, as Jupiter
500   On Juno smiles, when he impregns the clouds
That shed May flowers; and pressed her matron lip
With kisses pure: aside the Devil turned
For envy, yet with jealous leer malign
Eyed them askance, and to himself thus plained.
    'Sight hateful, sight tormenting! Thus these two
Imparadised in one another's arms
The happier Eden, shall enjoy their fill
Of bliss on bliss, while I to Hell am thrust,
Where neither joy nor love, but fierce desire,

Among our other torments not the least,   510
Still unfulfilled with pain of longing pines;
Yet let me not forget what I have gained
From their own mouths; all is not theirs it seems:
One fatal Tree there stands of Knowledge called,
Forbidden them to taste: knowledge forbidd'n?
Suspicious, reasonless. Why should their Lord
Envy them that? Can it be sin to know,
Can it be death? And do they only stand
By ignorance, is that their happy state,
The proof of their obedience and their faith?   520
O fair foundation laid whereon to build
Their ruin! Hence I will excite their minds
With more desire to know, and to reject
Envious commands, invented with design
To keep them low whom knowledge might exalt
Equal with gods; aspiring to be such,
They taste and die: what likelier can ensue?
But first with narrow search I must walk round
This garden, and no corner leave unspied;
A chance but chance may lead where I may meet   530
Some wand'ring Spirit of Heav'n, by fountain side,
Or in thick shade retired, from him to draw
What further would be learnt. Live while ye may,
Yet happy pair; enjoy, till I return,
Short pleasures, for long woes are to succeed.'
    So saying, his proud step he scornful turned,
But with sly circumspection, and began
Through wood, through waste, o'er hill, o'er dale his
        roam.
Meanwhile in utmost longitude, where heav'n
With earth and ocean meets, the setting sun   540
Slowly descended, and with right aspéct
Against the eastern gate of Paradise
Levelled his evening rays: it was a rock
Of alabaster, piled up to the clouds,
Conspicuous far, winding with one ascent
Accessible from earth, one entrance high;

The rest was craggy cliff, that overhung
Still as it rose, impossible to climb.
Betwixt these rocky pillars Gabriel sat
550   Chief of th' angelic guards, awaiting night;
About him exercised heroic games
Th' unarmèd youth of Heav'n, but nigh at hand
Celestial armoury, shields, helms, and spears,
Hung high with diamond flaming, and with gold.
Thither came Uriel, gliding through the even
On a sunbeam, swift as a shooting star
In autumn thwarts the night, when vapours fired
Impress the air, and shows the mariner
From what point of his compass to beware
560   Impetuous winds: he thus began in haste.
       'Gabriel, to thee thy course by lot hath giv'n
Charge and strict watch that to this happy place
No evil thing approach or enter in;
This day at heighth of noon came to my sphere
A Spirit, zealous, as he seemed, to know
More of th' Almighty's works, and chiefly man
God's latest image: I described his way
Bent all on speed, and marked his airy gait;
But in the mount that lies from Eden north,
570   Where he first lighted, soon discerned his looks
Alien from Heav'n, with passions foul obscured:
Mine eye pursued him still, but under shade
Lost sight of him; one of the banished crew
I fear, hath ventured from the deep, to raise
New troubles; him thy care must be to find.'
       To whom the wingèd warrior thus returned:
'Uriel, no wonder if thy perfect sight,
Amid the sun's bright circle where thou sitt'st,
See far and wide: in at this gate none pass
580   The vigilance here placed, but such as come
Well known from Heav'n; and since meridian hour
No creature thence: if Spirit of other sort,
So minded, have o'erleaped these earthy bounds
On purpose, hard thou know'st it to exclude

Spiritual substance with corporeal bar.
But if within the circuit of these walks,
In whatsoever shape he lurk, of whom
Thou tell'st, by morrow dawning I shall know.'
    So promised he, and Uriel to his charge
Returned on that bright beam, whose point now
        raised   590
Bore him slope downward to the sun now fall'n
Beneath the Azores; whether the prime orb,
Incredible how swift, had thither rolled
Diurnal, or this less volúble earth
By shorter flight to th' east, had left him there
Arraying with reflected purple and gold
The clouds that on his western throne attend:
Now came still ev'ning on, and twilight grey
Had in her sober livery all things clad;
Silence accompanied, for beast and bird,   600
They to their grassy couch, these to their nests
Were slunk, all but the wakeful nightingale;
She all night long her amorous descant sung;
Silence was pleased: now glowed the firmament
With living sapphires: Hesperus that led
The starry host, rode brightest, till the moon
Rising in clouded majesty, at length
Apparent queen unveiled her peerless light,
And o'er the dark her silver mantle threw.
    When Adam thus to Eve: 'Fair consort, th' hour   610
Of night, and all things now retired to rest
Mind us of like repose, since God hath set
Labour and rest, as day and night to men
Successive, and the timely dew of sleep
Now falling with soft slumb'rous weight inclines
Our eyelids; other creatures all day long
Rove idle unemployed, and less need rest;
Man hath his daily work of body or mind
Appointed, which declares his dignity,
And the regard of Heav'n on all his ways;   620
While other animals unactive range,

And of their doings God takes no account.
Tomorrow ere fresh morning streak the east
With first approach of light, we must be ris'n,
And at our pleasant labour, to reform
Yon flow'ry arbours, yonder alleys green,
Our walk at noon, with branches overgrown,
That mock our scant manuring, and require
More hands than ours to lop their wanton growth:
630   Those blossoms also, and those dropping gums,
That lie bestrewn unsightly and unsmooth,
Ask riddance, if we mean to tread with ease;
Meanwhile, as nature wills, night bids us rest.'
      To whom thus Eve with perfect beauty adorned.
'My author and disposer, what thou bidd'st
Unargued I obey; so God ordains,
God is thy law, thou mine: to know no more
Is woman's happiest knowledge and her praise.
With thee conversing I forget all time,
640   All seasons and their change, all please alike.
Sweet is the breath of morn, her rising sweet,
With charm of earliest birds; pleasant the sun
When first on this delightful land he spreads
His orient beams, on herb, tree, fruit, and flow'r,
Glist'ring with dew; fragrant the fertile earth
After soft showers; and sweet the coming on
Of grateful ev'ning mild, then silent night
With this her solemn bird and this fair moon,
And these the gems of heav'n, her starry train:
650   But neither breath of morn when she ascends
With charm of earliest birds, nor rising sun
On this delightful land, nor herb, fruit, flow'r,
Glist'ring with dew, nor fragrance after showers,
Nor grateful ev'ning mild, nor silent night
With this her solemn bird, nor walk by moon,
Or glittering starlight without thee is sweet.
But wherefore all night long shine these, for whom
This glorious sight, when sleep hath shut all eyes?'
      To whom our general ancestor replied.

'Daughter of God and man, accomplished Eve,   660
Those have their course to finish, round the earth,
By morrow ev'ning, and from land to land
In order, though to nations yet unborn,
Minist'ring light prepared, they set and rise;
Lest total darkness should by night regain
Her old possession, and extinguish life
In nature and all things, which these soft fires
Not only enlighten, but with kindly heat
Of various influence foment and warm,
Temper or nourish, or in part shed down   670
Their stellar virtue on all kinds that grow
On earth, made hereby apter to receive
Perfection from the sun's more potent ray.
These then, though unbeheld in deep of night,
Shine not in vain, nor think, though men were none,
That heav'n would want spectators, God want
          praise;
Millions of spiritual creatures walk the earth
Unseen, both when we wake, and when we sleep:
All these with ceaseless praise his works behold
Both day and night: how often from the steep   680
Of echoing hill or thicket have we heard
Celestial voices to the midnight air,
Sole, or responsive each to other's note
Singing their great Creator: oft in bands
While they keep watch, or nightly rounding walk
With Heav'nly touch of instrumental sounds
In full harmonic number joined, their songs
Divide the night, and lift our thoughts to Heaven.'
     Thus talking hand in hand alone they passed
On to their blissful bower; it was a place   690
Chos'n by the sov'reign Planter, when he framed
All things to man's delightful use; the roof
Of thickest covert was inwoven shade
Laurel and myrtle, and what higher grew
Of firm and fragrant leaf; on either side
Acanthus, and each odorous bushy shrub

Fenced up the verdant wall; each beauteous flow'r,
Iris all hues, roses, and jessamine
Reared high their flourished heads between, and
    wrought
700   Mosaic; underfoot the violet,
Crocus, and hyacinth with rich inlay
Broidered the ground, more coloured than with stone
Of costliest emblem: other creature here
Beast, bird, insect, or worm durst enter none;
Such was their awe of man. In shadier bower
More sacred and sequestered, though but feigned,
Pan or Silvanus never slept, nor nymph,
Nor Faunus haunted. Here in close recess
With flowers, garlands, and sweet-smelling herbs
710   Espousèd Eve decked first her nuptial bed,
And Heav'nly choirs the hymenean sung,
What day the genial angel to our sire
Brought her in naked beauty more adorned,
More lovely than Pandora, whom the gods
Endowed with all their gifts, and O too like
In sad event, when to th' unwiser son
Of Japhet brought by Hermes, she ensnared
Mankind with her fair looks, to be avenged
On him who had stole Jove's authentic fire.

720   Thus at their shady lodge arrived, both stood,
Both turned, and under open sky adored
The God that made both sky, air, earth and heav'n
Which they beheld, the moon's resplendent globe
And starry pole: 'Thou also mad'st the night,
Maker omnipotent, and thou the day,
Which we in our appointed work employed
Have finished happy in our mutual help
And mutual love, the crown of all our bliss
Ordained by thee, and this delicious place
730   For us too large, where thy abundance wants
Partakers, and uncropped falls to the ground.
But thou hast promised from us two a race
To fill the earth, who shall with us extol

Thy goodness infinite, both when we wake,
And when we seek, as now, thy gift of sleep.'
  This said unanimous, and other rites
Observing none, but adoration pure
Which God likes best, into their inmost bower
Handed they went; and eased the putting off
These troublesome disguises which we wear,   740
Straight side by side were laid, nor turned I ween
Adam from his fair spouse, nor Eve the rites
Mysterious of connubial love refused:
Whatever hypocrites austerely talk
Of purity and place and innocence,
Defaming as impure what God declares
Pure, and commands to some, leaves free to all.
Our Maker bids increase, who bids abstain
But our destroyer, foe to God and man?
Hail wedded love, mysterious law, true source   750
Of human offspring, sole propriety,
In Paradise of all things common else.
By thee adulterous lust was driv'n from men
Among the bestial herds to range, by thee
Founded in reason, loyal, just, and pure,
Relations dear, and all the charities
Of father, son, and brother first were known.
Far be it, that I should write thee sin or blame,
Or think thee unbefitting holiest place,
Perpetual fountain of domestic sweets,   760
Whose bed is undefiled and chaste pronounced,
Present, or past, as saints and patriarchs used.
Here Love his golden shafts employs, here lights
His constant lamp, and waves his purple wings,
Reigns here and revels; not in the bought smile
Of harlots, loveless, joyless, unendeared,
Casual fruition, nor in court amours
Mixed dance, or wanton masque, or midnight ball,
Or serenade, which the starved lover sings
To his proud fair, best quitted with disdain.   770
These lulled by nightingales embracing slept,

And on their naked limbs the flow'ry roof
Show'red roses, which the morn repaired. Sleep on,
Blest pair; and O yet happiest if ye seek
No happier state, and know to know no more.
    Now had night measured with her shadowy cone
Half way up hill this vast sublunar vault,
And from their ivory port the Cherubim
Forth issuing at th' accustomed hour stood armed
780   To their night watches in warlike parade,
When Gabriel to his next in power thus spake.
    'Uzziel, half these draw off, and coast the south
With strictest watch; these other wheel the north,
Our circuit meets full west.' As flame they part
Half wheeling to the shield, half to the spear.
From these, two strong and subtle Spirits he called
That near him stood, and gave them thus in charge.
    'Ithuriel and Zephon, with winged speed
Search through this garden, leave unsearched no nook,
790   But chiefly where those two fair creatures lodge,
Now laid perhaps asleep secure of harm.
This ev'ning from the sun's decline arrived
Who tells of some infernal Spirit seen
Hitherward bent (who could have thought?) escaped
The bars of Hell, on errand bad no doubt:
Such where ye find, seize fast, and hither bring.'
    So saying, on he led his radiant files,
Dazzling the moon; these to the bower direct
In search of whom they sought: him there they found
800   Squat like a toad, close at the ear of Eve;
Assaying by his devilish art to reach
The organs of her Fancy, and with them forge
Illusions as he list, phantasms and dreams,
Or if, inspiring venom, he might taint
Th' animal spirits that from pure blood arise
Like gentle breaths from rivers pure, thence raise
At least distempered, discontented thoughts,
Vain hopes, vain aims, inordinate desires
Blown up with high conceits engend'ring pride.

Him thus intent Ithuriel with his spear   810
Touched lightly; for no falsehood can endure
Touch of celestial temper, but returns
Of force to its own likeness: up he starts
Discovered and surprised. As when a spark
Lights on a heap of nitrous powder, laid
Fit for the tun some magazine to store
Against a rumoured war, the smutty grain
With sudden blaze diffused, inflames the air:
So started up in his own shape the Fiend.
Back stepped those two fair angels half amazed   820
So sudden to behold the grisly King;
Yet thus, unmoved with fear, accost him soon.

   'Which of those rebel Spirits adjudged to Hell
Com'st thou, escaped thy prison, and transformed,
Why sat'st thou like an enemy in wait
Here watching at the head of these that sleep?'

   'Know ye not then,' said Satan, filled with scorn,
'Know ye not me? Ye knew me once no mate
For you, there sitting where ye durst not soar;
Not to know me argues yourselves unknown,   830
The lowest of your throng; or if ye know,
Why ask ye, and superfluous begin
Your message, like to end as much in vain?'
To whom thus Zephon, answering scorn with scorn.
'Think not, revolted Spirit, thy shape the same,
Or undiminished brightness, to be known
As when thou stood'st in Heav'n upright and pure;
That glory then, when thou no more wast good,
Departed from thee, and thou resemblest now
Thy sin and place of doom obscure and foul.   840
But come, for thou, be sure, shalt give account
To him who sent us, whose charge is to keep
This place inviolable, and these from harm.'

   So spake the Cherub, and his grave rebuke
Severe in youthful beauty, added grace
Invincible: abashed the Devil stood,
And felt how awful goodness is, and saw

Virtue in her shape how lovely, saw, and pined
His loss; but chiefly to find here observed
His lustre visibly impaired; yet seemed
Undaunted. 'If I must contend,' said he,
'Best with the best, the sender not the sent,
Or all at once; more glory will be won,
Or less be lost.' 'Thy fear,' said Zephon bold,
'Will save us trial what the least can do
Single against thee wicked, and thence weak.'
      The Fiend replied not, overcome with rage;
But like a proud steed reined, went haughty on,
Champing his iron curb: to strive or fly
He held it vain; awe from above had quelled
His heart, not else dismayed. Now drew they nigh
The western point, where those half-rounding guards
Just met, and closing stood in squadron joined
Awaiting next command. To whom their chief
Gabriel from the front thus called aloud.
      'O friends, I hear the tread of nimble feet
Hasting this way, and now by glimpse discern
Ithuriel and Zephon through the shade,
And with them comes a third of regal port,
But faded splendour wan; who by his gait
And fierce demeanour seems the Prince of Hell,
Not likely to part hence without contést;
Stand firm, for in his look defiance lours.'
      He scarce had ended, when those two approached
And brief related whom they brought, where found,
How busied, in what form and posture couched.
      To whom with stern regard thus Gabriel spake.
'Why hast thou, Satan, broke the bounds prescribed
To thy transgressions, and disturbed the charge
Of others, who approve not to transgress
By thy example, but have power and right
To question thy bold entrance on this place;
Employed it seems to violate sleep, and those
Whose dwelling God hath planted here in bliss?'
      To whom thus Satan, with contemptuous brow.

850

860

870

880

'Gabriel, thou hadst in Heav'n th' esteem of wise,
And such I held thee; but this question asked
Puts me in doubt. Lives there who loves his pain?
Who would not, finding way, break loose from Hell,
Though thither doomed? Thou wouldst thyself, no
              doubt,   890
And boldly venture to whatever place
Farthest from pain, where thou might'st hope to change
Torment with ease, and soonest recompense
Dole with delight, which in this place I sought;
To thee no reason; who know'st only good,
But evil hast not tried: and wilt object
His will who bound us? Let him surer bar
His iron gates, if he intends our stay
In that dark durance: thus much what was asked.
The rest is true, they found me where they say;   900
But that implies not violence or harm.'
    Thus he in scorn. The warlike angel moved,
Disdainfully half smiling thus replied.
'O loss of one in Heav'n to judge of wise,
Since Satan fell, whom folly overthrew,
And now returns him from his prison 'scaped,
Gravely in doubt whether to hold them wise
Or not, who ask what boldness brought him hither
Unlicensed from his bounds in Hell prescribed;
So wise he judges it to fly from pain   910
However, and to 'scape his punishment.
So judge thou still, presumptuous, till the wrath,
Which thou incurr'st by flying, meet thy flight
Sevenfold, and scourge that wisdom back to Hell,
Which taught thee yet no better, that no pain
Can equal anger infinite provoked.
But wherefore thou alone? Wherefore with thee
Came not all Hell broke loose? Is pain to them
Less pain, less to be fled, or thou than they
Less hardy to endure? Courageous chief,   920
The first in flight from pain, hadst thou alleged
To thy deserted host this cause of flight,

Thou surely hadst not come sole fugitive.'
　　To which the Fiend thus answered frowning stern.
'Not that I less endure, or shrink from pain,
Insulting angel, well thou know'st I stood
Thy fiercest, when in battle to thy aid
The blasting volleyed thunder made all speed
And seconded thy else not dreaded spear.

930　But still thy words at random, as before,
Argue thy inexperience what behoves
From hard assays and ill successes past
A faithful leader, not to hazard all
Through ways of danger by himself untried.
I therefore, I alone first undertook
To wing the desolate abyss, and spy
This new-created world, whereof in Hell
Fame is not silent, here in hope to find
Better abode, and my afflicted powers

940　To settle here on earth, or in mid air;
Though for possession put to try once more
What thou and thy gay legions dare against;
Whose easier business were to serve their Lord
High up in Heav'n, with songs to hymn his throne,
And practised distances to cringe, not fight.'
　　To whom the warrior angel soon replied.
'To say and straight unsay, pretending first
Wise to fly pain, professing next the spy,
Argues no leader, but a liar traced,

950　Satan, and couldst thou "faithful" add? O name,
O sacred name of faithfulness profaned!
Faithful to whom? To thy rebellious crew?
Army of fiends, fit body to fit head;
Was this your discipline and faith engaged,
Your military obedience, to dissolve
Allegiance to th' acknowledged Power Supreme?
And thou sly hypocrite, who now wouldst seem
Patron of liberty, who more than thou
Once fawned, and cringed, and servilely adored

960　Heav'n's awful Monarch? Wherefore but in hope

To dispossess him, and thyself to reign?
But mark what I aread thee now, avaunt;
Fly thither whence thou fledd'st: if from this hour
Within these hallowed limits thou appear,
Back to th' infernal pit I drag thee chained,
And seal thee so, as henceforth not to scorn
The facile gates of Hell too slightly barred.'
  So threatened he, but Satan to no threats
Gave heed, but waxing more in rage replied.
  'Then when I am thy captive talk of chains,   970
Proud limitary Cherub, but ere then
Far heavier load thyself expect to feel
From my prevailing arm, though Heaven's King
Ride on thy wings, and thou with thy compeers,
Used to the yoke, draw'st his triumphant wheels
In progress through the road of Heav'n star-paved.'
  While thus he spake, th' angelic squadron bright
Turned fiery red, sharp'ning in moonèd horns
Their phalanx, and began to hem him round
With ported spears, as thick as when a field   980
Of Ceres ripe for harvest waving bends
Her bearded grove of ears, which way the wind
Sways them; the careful ploughman doubting stands
Lest on the threshing floor his hopeful sheaves
Prove chaff. On th' other side Satan alarmed
Collecting all his might dilated stood,
Like Teneriffe or Atlas unremoved:
His stature reached the sky, and on his crest
Sat Horror plumed; nor wanted in his grasp
What seemed both spear and shield: now dreadful
                deeds   990
Might have ensued, nor only Paradise
In this commotion, but the starry cope
Of heav'n perhaps, or all the elements
At least had gone to wrack, disturbed and torn
With violence of this conflict, had not soon
Th' Eternal to prevent such horrid fray
Hung forth in heav'n his golden Scales, yet seen

Betwixt Astraea and the Scorpion sign,
Wherein all things created first he weighed,
1000   The pendulous round earth with balanced air
In counterpoise, now ponders all events,
Battles and realms: in these he put two weights
The sequel each of parting and of fight;
The latter quick up flew, and kicked the beam;
Which Gabriel spying, thus bespake the Fiend.

   'Satan, I know thy strength, and thou know'st mine,
Neither our own but giv'n; what folly then
To boast what arms can do, since thine no more
Than Heav'n permits, nor mine, though doubled now
1010   To trample thee as mire: for proof look up,
And read thy lot in yon celestial sign
Where thou art weighed, and shown how light, how
       weak,
If thou resist.' The Fiend looked up and knew
His mounted scale aloft: nor more; but fled
Murmuring, and with him fled the shades of night.

BOOK IX

No more of talk where God or angel guest
With man, as with his friend, familiar used
To sit indulgent, and with him partake
Rural repast, permitting him the while
Venial discourse unblamed: I now must change
Those notes to tragic; foul distrust, and breach
Disloyal on the part of man, revolt,
And disobedience: on the part of Heav'n
Now alienated, distance and distaste,
10   Anger and just rebuke, and judgement giv'n,
That brought into this world a world of woe,

Sin and her shadow Death, and misery
Death's harbinger: sad task, yet argument
Not less but more heroic than the wrath
Of stern Achilles on his foe pursued
Thrice fugitive about Troy wall; or rage
Of Turnus for Lavinia disespoused,
Or Neptune's ire or Juno's, that so long
Perplexed the Greek and Cytherea's son;
If answerable style I can obtain   20
Of my celestial patroness, who deigns
Her nightly visitation unimplored,
And díctates to me slumb'ring, or inspires
Easy my unpremeditated verse:
Since first this subject for heroic song
Pleased me long choosing, and beginning late;
Not sedulous by nature to indite
Wars, hitherto the only argument
Heroic deemed, chief mast'ry to dissect
With long and tedious havoc fabled knights   30
In battles feigned; the better fortitude
Of patience and heroic martyrdom
Unsung; or to describe races and games,
Or tilting furniture, emblazoned shields,
Impreses quaint, caparisons and steeds;
Bases and tinsel trappings, gorgeous knights
At joust and tournament; then marshalled feast
Served up in hall with sewers, and seneschals;
The skill of artifice or office mean,
Not that which justly gives heroic name   40
To person or to poem. Me of these
Nor skilled nor studious, higher argument
Remains, sufficient of itself to raise
That name, unless an age too late, or cold
Climate, or years damp my intended wing
Depressed, and much they may, if all be mine,
Not hers who brings it nightly to my ear.
   The sun was sunk, and after him the star
Of Hesperus, whose office is to bring

50   Twilight upon the earth, short arbiter
     'Twixt day and night, and now from end to end
     Night's hemisphere had veiled the horizon round:
     When Satan who late fled before the threats
     Of Gabriel out of Eden, now improved
     In meditated fraud and malice, bent
     On man's destruction, maugre what might hap
     Of heavier on himself, fearless returned.
     By night he fled, and at midnight returned
     From compassing the earth, cautious of day,
60   Since Uriel regent of the sun descried
     His entrance, and forewarned the Cherubim
     That kept their watch; thence full of anguish driv'n,
     The space of seven continued nights he rode
     With darkness, thrice the equinoctial line
     He circled, four times crossed the car of Night
     From pole to pole, traversing each colure;
     On the eighth returned, and on the coast averse
     From entrance or Cherubic watch, by stealth
     Found unsuspected way. There was a place,
     Now not, though sin, not time, first wrought the
70   change,
     Where Tigris at the foot of Paradise
     Into a gulf shot under ground, till part
     Rose up a fountain by the Tree of Life;
     In with the river sunk, and with it rose
     Satan involved in rising mist, then sought
     Where to lie hid; sea he had searched and land
     From Eden over Pontus, and the pool
     Maeotis, up beyond the river Ob;
     Downward as far Antarctic; and in length
80   West from Orontes to the ocean barred
     At Darien, thence to the land where flows
     Ganges and Indus: thus the orb he roamed
     With narrow search; and with inspection deep
     Considered every creature, which of all
     Most opportune might serve his wiles, and found
     The serpent subtlest beast of all the field.

Him after long debate, irresolute
Of thoughts revolved, his final sentence chose
Fit vessel, fittest imp of fraud, in whom
To enter, and his dark suggestions hide   90
From sharpest sight: for in the wily snake,
Whatever sleights none would suspicious mark,
As from his wit and native subtlety
Proceeding, which in other beasts observed
Doubt might beget of diabolic pow'r
Active within beyond the sense of brute.
Thus he resolved, but first from inward grief
His bursting passion into plaints thus poured:
   'O earth, how like to Heav'n, if not preferred
More justly, seat worthier of gods, as built   100
With second thoughts, reforming what was old!
For what god after better worse would build?
Terrestrial Heav'n, danced round by other heav'ns
That shine, yet bear their bright officious lamps,
Light above light, for thee alone, as seems,
In thee concentring all their precious beams
Of sacred influence: as God in Heav'n
Is centre, yet extends to all, so thou
Centring receiv'st from all those orbs; in thee,
Not in themselves, all their known virtue appears   110
Productive in herb, plant, and nobler birth
Of creatures animate with gradual life
Of growth, sense, reason, all summed up in man.
With what delight could I have walked thee round,
If I could joy in aught, sweet interchange
Of hill and valley, rivers, woods and plains,
Now land, now sea, and shores with forest crowned,
Rocks, dens, and caves; but I in none of these
Find place or refuge; and the more I see
Pleasures about me, so much more I feel   120
Torment within me, as from the hateful siege
Of contraries; all good to me becomes
Bane, and in Heav'n much worse would be my state.
But neither here seek I, no nor in Heav'n

To dwell, unless by mast'ring Heav'n's Supreme;
Nor hope to be myself less miserable
By what I seek, but others to make such
As I, though thereby worse to me redound:
For only in destroying I find ease
130 To my relentless thoughts; and him destroyed,
Or won to what may work his utter loss,
For whom all this was made, all this will soon
Follow, as to him linked in weal or woe;
In woe then; that destruction wide may range:
To me shall be the glory sole among
The infernal Powers, in one day to have marred
What he Almighty styled, six nights and days
Continued making, and who knows how long
Before had been contriving, though perhaps
140 Not longer than since I in one night freed
From servitude inglorious well-nigh half
Th' angelic name, and thinner left the throng
Of his adorers: he to be avenged,
And to repair his numbers thus impaired,
Whether such virtue spent of old now failed
More angels to create, if they at least
Are his created, or to spite us more,
Determined to advance into our room
A creature formed of earth, and him endow,
150 Exalted from so base original,
With Heav'nly spoils, our spoils: what he decreed
He effected; man he made, and for him built
Magnificent this world, and earth his seat,
Him lord pronounced, and, O indignity!
Subjected to his service angel wings,
And flaming ministers to watch and tend
Their earthy charge: of these the vigilance
I dread, and to elude, thus wrapped in mist
Of midnight vapour glide obscure, and pry
160 In every bush and brake, where hap may find
The serpent sleeping, in whose mazy folds
To hide me, and the dark intent I bring.

O foul descent! That I who erst contended
With Gods to sit the highest, am now constrained
Into a beast, and mixed with bestial slime,
This essence to incarnate and imbrute,
That to the heighth of Deity aspired;
But what will not ambition and revenge
Descend to? Who aspires must down as low
As high he soared, obnoxious first or last   170
To basest things. Revenge, at first though sweet,
Bitter ere long back on itself recoils;
Let it; I reck not, so it light well aimed,
Since higher I fall short, on him who next
Provokes my envy, this new favourite
Of Heav'n, this man of clay, son of despite,
Whom us the more to spite his Maker raised
From dust: spite then with spite is best repaid.'
    So saying, through each thicket dank or dry,
Like a black mist low creeping, he held on   180
His midnight search, where soonest he might find
The serpent: him fast sleeping soon he found
In labyrinth of many a round self-rolled,
His head the midst, well stored with subtle wiles:
Not yet in horrid shade or dismal den,
Not nocent yet, but on the grassy herb
Fearless unfeared he slept; in at his mouth
The Devil entered, and his brutal sense,
In heart or head, possessing soon inspired
With act intelligential; but his sleep   190
Disturbed not, waiting close th' approach of morn.
Now whenas sacred light began to dawn
In Eden on the humid flow'rs, that breathed
Their morning incense, when all things that breathe,
From th' earth's great altar send up silent praise
To the Creator, and his nostrils fill
With grateful smell, forth came the human pair
And joined their vocal worship to the choir
Of creatures wanting voice; that done, partake
The season, prime for sweetest scents and airs: 200

Then cómmune how that day they best may ply
Their growing work: for much their work outgrew
The hands' dispatch of two gard'ning so wide.
And Eve first to her husband thus began.
   'Adam, well may we labour still to dress
This garden, still to tend plant, herb and flow'r,
Our pleasant task enjoined, but till more hands
Aid us, the work under our labour grows,
Luxurious by restraint; what we by day
210 Lop overgrown, or prune, or prop, or bind,
One night or two with wanton growth derides
Tending to wild. Thou therefore now advise
Or hear what to my mind first thoughts present;
Let us divide our labours, thou where choice
Leads thee, or where most needs, whether to wind
The woodbine round this arbour, or direct
The clasping ivy where to climb, while I
In yonder spring of roses intermixed
With myrtle, find what to redress till noon:
220 For while so near each other thus all day
Our task we choose, what wonder if so near
Looks intervene and smiles, or object new
Casual discourse draw on, which intermits
Our day's work brought to little, though begun
Early, and th' hour of supper comes unearned.'
   To whom mild answer Adam thus returned.
'Sole Eve, associate sole, to me beyond
Compare above all living creatures dear,
Well hast thou motioned, well thy thoughts employed
230 How we might best fulfil the work which here
God hath assigned us, nor of me shalt pass
Unpraised: for nothing lovelier can be found
In woman, than to study household good,
And good works in her husband to promote.
Yet not so strictly hath our Lord imposed
Labour, as to debar us when we need
Refreshment, whether food, or talk between,
Food of the mind, or this sweet intercourse

Of looks and smiles, for smiles from reason flow,
To brute denied, and are of love the food,   240
Love not the lowest end of human life.
For not to irksome toil, but to delight
He made us, and delight to reason joined.
These paths and bowers doubt not but our joint hands
Will keep from wilderness with ease, as wide
As we need walk, till younger hands ere long
Assist us: but if much convérse perhaps
Thee satiate, to short absence I could yield.
For solitude sometimes is best society,
And short retirement urges sweet return.   250
But other doubt possesses me, lest harm
Befall thee severed from me; for thou know'st
What hath been warned us, what malicious Foe
Envying our happiness, and of his own
Despairing, seeks to work us woe and shame
By sly assault; and somewhere nigh at hand
Watches, no doubt, with greedy hope to find
His wish and best advantage, us asunder,
Hopeless to circumvent us joined, where each
To other speedy aid might lend at need;   260
Whether his first design be to withdraw
Our fealty from God, or to disturb
Conjugal love, than which perhaps no bliss
Enjoyed by us excites his envy more;
Or this, or worse, leave not the faithful side
That gave thee being, still shades thee and protects.
The wife, where danger or dishonour lurks,
Safest and seemliest by her husband stays,
Who guards her, or with her the worst endures.'

     To whom the virgin majesty of Eve,   270
As one who loves, and some unkindness meets,
With sweet austere composure thus replied.
     'Offspring of Heav'n and earth, and all earth's lord,
That such an Enemy we have, who seeks
Our ruin, both by thee informed I learn,

And from the parting angel overheard
As in a shady nook I stood behind,
Just then returned at shut of evening flow'rs.
But that thou shouldst my firmness therefore doubt
280   To God or thee, because we have a foe
May tempt it, I expected not to hear.
His violence thou fear'st not, being such,
As we, not capable of death or pain,
Can either not receive, or can repel.
His fraud is then thy fear, which plain infers
Thy equal fear that my firm faith and love
Can by his fraud be shaken or seduced;
Thoughts, which how found they harbour in thy
              breast,
Adam, misthought of her to thee so dear?'
290   To whom with healing words Adam replied.
'Daughter of God and man, immortal Eve,
For such thou art, from sin and blame entire:
Not diffident of thee do I dissuade
Thy absence from my sight, but to avoid
Th' attempt itself, intended by our Foe.
For he who tempts, though in vain, at least asperses
The tempted with dishonour foul, supposed
Not incorruptible of faith, not proof
Against temptation: thou thyself with scorn
300   And anger wouldst resent the offered wrong,
Though ineffectual found: misdeem not then,
If such affront I labour to avert
From thee alone, which on us both at once
The Enemy, though bold, will hardly dare,
Or daring, first on me th' assault shall light.
Nor thou his malice and false guile contemn;
Subtle he needs must be, who could seduce
Angels, nor think superfluous others' aid.
I from the influence of thy looks receive
310   Access in every virtue, in thy sight
More wise, more watchful, stronger, if need were
Of outward strength; while shame, thou looking on,

Shame to be overcome or overreached
Would utmost vigour raise, and raised unite.
Why shouldst not thou like sense within thee feel
When I am present, and thy trial choose
With me, best witness of thy virtue tried?'
    So spake domestic Adam in his care
And matrimonial love; but Eve, who thought
Less attribúted to her faith sincere,   320
Thus her reply with accent sweet renewed.
    'If this be our condition, thus to dwell
In narrow circuit straitened by a Foe,
Subtle or violent, we not endued
Single with like defence, wherever met,
How are we happy, still in fear of harm?
But harm precedes not sin: only our Foe
Tempting affronts us with his foul esteem
Of our integrity: his foul esteem
Sticks no dishonour on our front, but turns   330
Foul on himself; then wherefore shunned or feared
By us? who rather double honour gain
From his surmise proved false, find peace within,
Favour from Heav'n, our witness from th' event.
And what is faith, love, virtue unassayed
Alone, without exterior help sustained?
Let us not then suspect our happy state
Left so imperfect by the Maker wise,
As not secure to single or combined.
Frail is our happiness, if this be so,   340
And Eden were no Eden thus exposed.'
    To whom thus Adam fervently replied.
'O woman, best are all things as the will
Of God ordained them; his creating hand
Nothing imperfect or deficient left
Of all that he created, much less man,
Or aught that might his happy state secure,
Secure from outward force; within himself
The danger lies, yet lies within his power:
Against his will he can receive no harm.   350

But God left free the will, for what obeys
Reason, is free, and reason he made right,
But bid her well beware, and still erect,
Lest by some fair appearing good surprised
She dictate false, and misinform the will
To do what God expressly hath forbid.
Not then mistrust, but tender love enjoins,
That I should mind thee oft, and mind thou me.
Firm we subsist, yet possible to swerve,
360   Since reason not impossibly may meet
Some specious object by the Foe suborned,
And fall into deception unaware,
Not keeping strictest watch, as she was warned.
Seek not temptation then, which to avoid
Were better, and most likely if from me
Thou sever not: trial will come unsought.
Wouldst thou approve thy constancy, approve
First thy obedience; th' other who can know,
Not seeing thee attempted, who attest?
370   But if thou think trial unsought may find
Us both securer than thus warned thou seem'st,
Go; for thy stay, not free, absents thee more;
Go in thy native innocence, rely
On what thou hast of virtue, summon all,
For God towards thee hath done his part, do thine.'
    So spake the patriarch of mankind, but Eve
Persisted, yet submiss, though last, replied.
    'With thy permission then, and thus forewarned
Chiefly by what thy own last reasoning words
380   Touched only, that our trial, when least sought,
May find us both perhaps far less prepared,
The willinger I go, nor much expect
A Foe so proud will first the weaker seek;
So bent, the more shall shame him his repulse.'
Thus saying, from her husband's hand her hand
Soft she withdrew, and like a wood-nymph light
Oread or Dryad, or of Delia's train,
Betook her to the groves, but Delia's self

In gait surpassed and goddess-like deport,
Though not as she with bow and quiver armed,   390
But with such gard'ning tools as art yet rude,
Guiltless of fire had formed, or angels brought.
To Pales, or Pomona thus adorned,
Likeliest she seemed, Pomona when she fled
Vertumnus, or to Ceres in her prime,
Yet virgin of Proserpina from Jove.
Her long with ardent look his eye pursued
Delighted, but desiring more her stay.
Oft he to her his charge of quick return
Repeated, she to him as oft engaged   400
To be returned by noon amid the bow'r,
And all things in best order to invite
Noontide repast, or afternoon's repose.
O much deceived, much failing, hapless Eve,
Of thy presumed return! event perverse!
Thou never from that hour in Paradise
Found'st either sweet repast, or sound repose;
Such ambush hid among sweet flow'rs and shades
Waited with Hellish rancour imminent
To intercept thy way, or send thee back   410
Despoiled of innocence, of faith, of bliss.
For now, and since first break of dawn the Fiend,
Mere serpent in appearance, forth was come,
And on his quest, where likeliest he might find
The only two of mankind, but in them
The whole included race, his purposed prey.
In bow'r and field he sought, where any tuft
Of grove or garden-plot more pleasant lay,
Their tendance or plantation for delight;
By fountain or by shady rivulet   420
He sought them both, but wished his hap might find
Eve separate; he wished, but not with hope
Of what so seldom chanced, when to his wish,
Beyond his hope, Eve separate he spies,
Veiled in a cloud of fragrance, where she stood,
Half spied, so thick the roses bushing round

About her glowed, oft stooping to support
Each flow'r of slender stalk, whose head though gay
Carnation, purple, azure, or specked with gold,
430   Hung drooping unsustained; them she upstays
Gently with myrtle band, mindless the while,
Herself, though fairest unsupported flow'r,
From her best prop so far, and storm so nigh.
Nearer he drew, and many a walk traversed
Of stateliest covert, cedar, pine, or palm,
Then voluble and bold, now hid, now seen
Among thick-woven arborets and flow'rs
Embordered on each bank, the hand of Eve:
Spot more delicious than those gardens feigned
440   Or of revived Adonis, or renowned
Alcinous, host of old Laertes' son,
Or that, not mystic, where the sapient king
Held dalliance with his fair Egyptian spouse.
Much he the place admired, the person more.
As one who long in populous city pent,
Where houses thick and sewers annoy the air,
Forth issuing on a summer's morn to breathe
Among the pleasant villages and farms
Adjoined, from each thing met conceives delight,
450   The smell of grain, or tedded grass, or kine,
Or dairy, each rural sight, each rural sound;
If chance with nymph-like step fair virgin pass,
What pleasing seemed, for her now pleases more,
She most, and in her look sums all delight.
Such pleasure took the Serpent to behold
This flow'ry plat, the sweet recess of Eve
Thus early, thus alone; her Heav'nly form
Angelic, but more soft, and feminine,
Her graceful innocence, her every air
460   Of gesture or least action overawed
His malice, and with rapine sweet bereaved
His fierceness of the fierce intent it brought:
That space the Evil One abstracted stood
From his own evil, and for the time remained

Stupidly good, of enmity disarmed,
Of guile, of hate, of envy, of revenge;
But the hot Hell that always in him burns,
Though in mid-Heav'n, soon ended his delight,
And tortures him now more, the more he sees
Of pleasure not for him ordained: then soon   470
Fierce hate he recollects, and all his thoughts
Of mischief, gratulating, thus excites.
    'Thoughts, whither have ye led me? With what
        sweet
Compulsion thus transported to forget
What hither brought us? Hate, not love, nor hope
Of Paradise for Hell, hope here to taste
Of pleasure, but all pleasure to destroy,
Save what is in destroying; other joy
To me is lost. Then let me not let pass
Occasion which now smiles; behold alone   480
The woman, opportune to all attempts,
Her husband, for I view far round, not nigh,
Whose higher intellectual more I shun,
And strength, of courage haughty, and of limb
Heroic built, though of terrestrial mould,
Foe not informidable, exempt from wound,
I not; so much hath Hell debased, and pain
Enfeebled me, to what I was in Heav'n.
She fair, divinely fair, fit love for gods,
Not terrible, though terror be in love   490
And beauty, not approached by stronger hate,
Hate stronger, under show of love well-feigned,
The way which to her ruin now I tend.'
    So spake the Enemy of mankind, enclosed
In serpent, inmate bad, and toward Eve
Addressed his way, not with indented wave,
Prone on the ground, as since, but on his rear,
Circular base of rising folds, that tow'red
Fold above fold a surging maze, his head
Crested aloft, and carbuncle his eyes;   500
With burnished neck of verdant gold, erect

Amidst his circling spires, that on the grass
Floated redundant: pleasing was his shape,
And lovely, never since of serpent kind
Lovelier, not those that in Illyria changed
Hermione and Cadmus, or the god
In Epidaurus; nor to which transformed
Ammonian Jove, or Capitoline was seen,
He with Olympias, this with her who bore
510 Scipio the heighth of Rome. With tract oblique
At first, as one who sought accéss, but feared
To interrupt, sidelong he works his way.
As when a ship by skilful steersman wrought
Nigh river's mouth or foreland, where the wind
Veers oft, as oft so steers, and shifts her sail;
So varied he, and of his tortuous train
Curled many a wanton wreath in sight of Eve,
To lure her eye; she busied heard the sound
Of rustling leaves, but minded not, as used
520 To such disport before her through the field,
From every beast, more duteous at her call
Than at Circean call the herd disguised.
He bolder now, uncalled before her stood;
But as in gaze admiring: oft he bowed
His turret crest, and sleek enamelled neck,
Fawning, and licked the ground whereon she trod.
His gentle dumb expression turned at length
The eye of Eve to mark his play; he glad
Of her attention gained, with serpent tongue
530 Organic, or impúlse of vocal air,
His fraudulent temptation thus began.
    'Wonder not, sov'reign mistress, if perhaps
Thou canst, who art sole wonder, much less arm
Thy looks, the Heav'n of mildness, with disdain,
Displeased that I approach thee thus, and gaze
Insatiate, I thus single, nor have feared
Thy awful brow, more awful thus retired.
Fairest resemblance of thy Maker fair,
Thee all things living gaze on, all things thine

By gift, and thy celestial beauty adore   540
With ravishment beheld, there best beheld
Where universally admired; but here
In this enclosure wild, these beasts among,
Beholders rude, and shallow to discern
Half what in thee is fair, one man except,
Who sees thee? (and what is one?) who shouldst be
    seen
A goddess among gods, adored and served
By angels numberless, thy daily train.'
   So glozed the Tempter, and his proem tuned;
Into the heart of Eve his words made way,   550
Though at the voice much marvelling; at length
Not unamazed she thus in answer spake.
'What may this mean? Language of man pronounced
By tongue of brute, and human sense expressed?
The first at least of these I thought denied
To beasts, whom God on their Creation-day
Created mute to all articulate sound;
The latter I demur, for in their looks
Much reason, and in their actions oft appears.
Thee, serpent, subtlest beast of all the field   560
I knew, but not with human voice endued;
Redouble then this miracle, and say,
How cam'st thou speakable of mute, and how
To me so friendly grown above the rest
Of brutal kind, that daily are in sight?
Say, for such wonder claims attention due.'
   To whom the guileful Tempter thus replied.
'Empress of this fair world, resplendent Eve,
Easy to me it is to tell thee all
What thou command'st, and right thou shouldst be
    obeyed: 570
I was at first as other beasts that graze
The trodden herb, of abject thoughts and low,
As was my food, nor aught but food discerned
Or sex, and apprehended nothing high:
Till on a day roving the field, I chanced

A goodly tree far distant to behold
Loaden with fruit of fairest colours mixed,
Ruddy and gold: I nearer drew to gaze;
When from the boughs a savoury odour blown,
580   Grateful to appetite, more pleased my sense
Than smell of sweetest fennel, or the teats
Of ewe or goat dropping with milk at ev'n,
Unsucked of lamb or kid, that tend their play.
To satisfy the sharp desire I had
Of tasting those fair apples, I resolved
Not to defer; hunger and thirst at once,
Powerful persuaders, quickened at the scent
Of that alluring fruit, urged me so keen.
About the mossy trunk I wound me soon,
590   For high from ground the branches would require
Thy utmost reach or Adam's: round the tree
All other beasts that saw, with like desire
Longing and envying stood, but could not reach.
Amid the tree now got, where plenty hung
Tempting so nigh, to pluck and eat my fill
I spared not, for such pleasure till that hour
At feed or fountain never had I found.
Sated at length, ere long I might perceive
Strange alteration in me, to degree
600   Of reason in my inward powers, and speech
Wanted not long, though to this shape retained.
Thenceforth to speculations high or deep
I turned my thoughts, and with capacious mind
Considered all things visible in heav'n,
Or earth, or middle, all things fair and good;
But all that fair and good in thy divine
Semblance, and in thy beauty's Heav'nly ray
United I beheld; no fair to thine
Equivalent or second, which compelled
610   Me thus, though importune perhaps, to come
And gaze, and worship thee of right declared
Sov'reign of creatures, universal dame.'
    So talked the spirited sly snake; and Eve

Yet more amazed unwary thus replied.
   'Serpent, thy overpraising leaves in doubt
The virtue of that fruit, in thee first proved:
But say, where grows the tree, from hence how far?
For many are the trees of God that grow
In Paradise, and various, yet unknown
To us, in such abundance lies our choice,   620
As leaves a greater store of fruit untouched,
Still hanging incorruptible, till men
Grow up to their provision, and more hands
Help to disburden Nature of her bearth.'
   To whom the wily adder, blithe and glad.
'Empress, the way is ready, and not long,
Beyond a row of myrtles, on a flat,
Fast by a fountain, one small thicket past
Of blowing myrrh and balm; if thou accept
My conduct, I can bring thee thither soon.'   630
   'Lead then,' said Eve. He leading swiftly rolled
In tangles, and made intricate seem straight,
To mischief swift. Hope elevates, and joy
Brightens his crest, as when a wand'ring fire,
Compact of unctuous vapour, which the night
Condenses, and the cold environs round,
Kindled through agitation to a flame,
Which oft, they say, some evil Spirit attends
Hovering and blazing with delusive light,
Misleads th' amazed night-wanderer from his way   640
To bogs and mires, and oft through pond or pool,
There swallowed up and lost, from succour far.
So glistered the dire snake, and into fraud
Led Eve our credulous mother, to the tree
Of prohibition, root of all our woe;
Which when she saw, thus to her guide she spake.
   'Serpent, we might have spared our coming hither,
Fruitless to me, though fruit be here to excess,
The credit of whose virtue rest with thee,
Wondrous indeed, if cause of such effects.   650
But of this tree we may not taste nor touch;

God so commanded, and left that command
Sole daughter of his voice; the rest, we live
Law to ourselves, our reason is our law.'
    To whom the Tempter guilefully replied.
'Indeed? Hath God then said that of the fruit
Of all these garden trees ye shall not eat,
Yet lords declared of all in earth or air?'
    To whom thus Eve yet sinless. 'Of the fruit
660   Of each tree in the garden we may eat,
But of the fruit of this fair tree amidst
The garden, God hath said, "Ye shall not eat
Thereof, nor shall ye touch it, lest ye die."'
    She scarce had said, though brief, when now more
      bold
The Tempter, but with show of zeal and love
To man, and indignation at his wrong,
New part puts on, and as to passion moved,
Fluctuates disturbed, yet comely, and in act
Raised, as of some great matter to begin.
670   As when of old some orator renowned
In Athens or free Rome, where eloquence
Flourished, since mute, to some great cause addressed,
Stood in himself collected, while each part,
Motion, each act won audience ere the tongue,
Sometimes in heighth began, as no delay
Of preface brooking through his zeal of right.
So standing, moving, or to heighth upgrown
The Tempter all impassioned thus began.
    'O sacred, wise, and wisdom-giving plant,
680   Mother of science, now I feel thy power
Within me clear, not only to discern
Things in their causes, but to trace the ways
Of highest agents, deemed however wise.
Queen of this universe, do not believe
Those rigid threats of death; ye shall not die:
How should ye? By the fruit? It gives you life
To knowledge. By the Threat'ner? Look on me,
Me who have touched and tasted, yet both live,

And life more perfect have attained than Fate
Meant me, by vent'ring higher than my lot. 690
Shall that be shut to man, which to the beast
Is open? Or will God incense his ire
For such a petty trespass, and not praise
Rather your dauntless virtue, whom the pain
Of death denounced, whatever thing death be,
Deterred not from achieving what might lead
To happier life, knowledge of good and evil?
Of good, how just? Of evil, if what is evil
Be real, why not known, since easier shunned?
God therefore cannot hurt ye, and be just; 700
Not just, not God; not feared then, nor obeyed:
Your fear itself of death removes the fear.
Why then was this forbid? Why but to awe,
Why but to keep ye low and ignorant,
His worshippers; he knows that in the day
Ye eat thereof, your eyes that seem so clear,
Yet are but dim, shall perfectly be then
Opened and cleared, and ye shall be as gods,
Knowing both good and evil as they know.
That ye should be as gods, since I as man, 710
Internal man, is but proportion meet,
I of brute human, ye of human gods.
So ye shall die perhaps, by putting off
Human, to put on gods, death to be wished,
Though threatened, which no worse than this can bring.
And what are gods that man may not become
As they, participating godlike food?
The gods are first, and that advantage use
On our belief, that all from them proceeds;
I question it, for this fair earth I see, 720
Warmed by the sun, producing every kind,
Them nothing: if they all things, who enclosed
Knowledge of good and evil in this tree,
That whoso eats thereof, forthwith attains
Wisdom without their leave? And wherein lies
Th' offence, that man should thus attain to know?

What can your knowledge hurt him, or this tree
Impart against his will if all be his?
Or is it envy, and can envy dwell

730   In Heav'nly breasts? These, these and many more
Causes import your need of this fair fruit.
Goddess humane, reach then, and freely taste.'

   He ended, and his words replete with guile
Into her heart too easy entrance won:
Fixed on the fruit she gazed, which to behold
Might tempt alone, and in her ears the sound
Yet rung of his persuasive words, impregned
With reason, to her seeming, and with truth;
Meanwhile the hour of noon drew on, and waked

740   An eager appetite, raised by the smell
So savoury of that fruit, which with desire,
Inclinable now grown to touch or taste,
Solicited her longing eye; yet first
Pausing a while, thus to herself she mused.

   'Great are thy virtues, doubtless, best of fruits,
Though kept from man, and worthy to be admired,
Whose taste, too long forborne, at first assay
Gave elocution to the mute, and taught
The tongue not made for speech to speak thy praise:

750   Thy praise he also who forbids thy use,
Conceals not from us, naming thee the Tree
Of Knowledge, knowledge both of good and evil;
Forbids us then to taste, but his forbidding
Commends thee more, while it infers the good
By thee communicated, and our want:
For good unknown, sure is not had, or had
And yet unknown, is as not had at all.
In plain then, what forbids he but to know,
Forbids us good, forbids us to be wise?

760   Such prohibitions bind not. But if death
Bind us with after-bands, what profits then
Our inward freedom? In the day we eat
Of this fair fruit, our doom is, we shall die.
How dies the serpent? He hath eat'n and lives,

And knows, and speaks, and reasons, and discerns,
Irrational till then. For us alone
Was death invented? Or to us denied
This intellectual food, for beasts reserved?
For beasts it seems: yet that one beast which first
Hath tasted, envies not, but brings with joy   770
The good befall'n him, author unsuspect,
Friendly to man, far from deceit or guile.
What fear I then, rather what know to fear
Under this ignorance of good and evil,
Of God or death, of law or penalty?
Here grows the cure of all, this fruit divine,
Fair to the eye, inviting to the taste,
Of virtue to make wise; what hinders then
To reach, and feed at once both body and mind?'
    So saying, her rash hand in evil hour   780
Forth reaching to the fruit, she plucked, she ate:
Earth felt the wound, and Nature from her seat
Sighing through all her works gave signs of woe,
That all was lost. Back to the thicket slunk
The guilty serpent, and well might, for Eve
Intent now wholly on her taste, naught else
Regarded, such delight till then, as seemed,
In fruit she never tasted, whether true
Or fancied so, through expectation high
Of knowledge, nor was Godhead from her thought.   790
Greedily she engorged without restraint,
And knew not eating death: satiate at length,
And heightened as with wine, jocund and boon,
Thus to herself she pleasingly began.
    'O sov'reign, virtuous, precious of all trees
In Paradise, of operation blest
To sapience, hitherto obscured, infamed,
And thy fair fruit let hang, as to no end
Created; but henceforth my early care,
Not without song, each morning, and due praise   800
Shall tend thee, and the fertile burden ease
Of thy full branches offered free to all;

Till dieted by thee I grow mature
In knowledge, as the gods who all things know;
Though others envy what they cannot give;
For had the gift been theirs, it had not here
Thus grown. Experience, next to thee I owe,
Best guide; not following thee, I had remained
In ignorance; thou open'st wisdom's way,
810   And giv'st accéss, though secret she retire.
And I perhaps am secret; Heav'n is high,
High and remote to see from thence distinct
Each thing on earth; and other care perhaps
May have diverted from continual watch
Our great Forbidder, safe with all his spies
About him. But to Adam in what sort
Shall I appear? Shall I to him make known
As yet my change, and give him to partake
Full happiness with me, or rather not,
820   But keep the odds of knowledge in my power
Without copartner? So to add what wants
In female sex, the more to draw his love,
And render me more equal, and perhaps,
A thing not undesirable, sometime
Superior; for inferior who is free?
This may be well: but what if God have seen,
And death ensue? Then I shall be no more,
And Adam wedded to another Eve,
Shall live with her enjoying, I extinct;
830   A death to think. Confirmed then I resolve,
Adam shall share with me in bliss or woe:
So dear I love him, that with him all deaths
I could endure, without him live no life.'
    So saying, from the tree her step she turned,
But first low reverence done, as to the power
That dwelt within, whose presence had infused
Into the plant sciential sap, derived
From nectar, drink of gods. Adam the while
Waiting desirous her return, had wove
840   Of choicest flow'rs a garland to adorn

Her tresses, and her rural labours crown,
As reapers oft are wont their harvest queen.
Great joy he promised to his thoughts, and new
Solace in her return, so long delayed;
Yet oft his heart, divine of something ill,
Misgave him; he the falt'ring measure felt;
And forth to meet her went, the way she took
That morn when first they parted; by the Tree
Of Knowledge he must pass, there he her met,
Scarce from the tree returning; in her hand   850
A bough of fairest fruit that downy smiled,
New gathered, and ambrosial smell diffused.
To him she hasted, in her face excuse
Came prologue, and apology to prompt,
Which with bland words at will she thus addressed.
    'Hast thou not wondered, Adam, at my stay?
Thee I have missed, and thought it long, deprived
Thy presence, agony of love till now
Not felt, nor shall be twice, for never more
Mean I to try, what rash untried I sought,   860
The pain of absence from thy sight. But strange
Hath been the cause, and wonderful to hear:
This tree is not as we are told, a tree
Of danger tasted, nor to evil unknown
Op'ning the way, but of divine effect
To open eyes, and make them gods who taste;
And hath been tasted such: the serpent wise,
Or not restrained as we, or not obeying,
Hath eaten of the fruit, and is become,
Not dead, as we are threatened, but thenceforth   870
Endued with human voice and human sense,
Reasoning to admiration, and with me
Persuasively hath so prevailed, that I
Have also tasted, and have also found
Th' effects to correspond, opener mine eyes,
Dim erst, dilated spirits, ampler heart,
And growing up to godhead; which for thee
Chiefly I sought, without thee can despise.

For bliss, as thou hast part, to me is bliss,
880   Tedious, unshared with thee, and odious soon.
Thou therefore also taste, that equal lot
May join us, equal joy, as equal love;
Lest thou not tasting, different degree
Disjoin us, and I then too late renounce
Deity for thee, when Fate will not permit.'

        Thus Eve with count'nance blithe her story told;
But in her cheek distemper flushing glowed.
On th' other side, Adam, soon as he heard
The fatal trespass done by Eve, amazed,
890   Astonied stood and blank, while horror chill
Ran through his veins, and all his joints relaxed;
From his slack hand the garland wreathed for Eve
Down dropped, and all the faded roses shed:
Speechless he stood and pale, till thus at length
First to himself he inward silence broke.

        'O fairest of Creation, last and best
Of all God's works, creature in whom excelled
Whatever can to sight or thought be formed,
Holy, divine, good, amiable, or sweet!
900   How art thou lost, how on a sudden lost,
Defaced, deflow'red, and now to death devote?
Rather how hast thou yielded to transgress
The strict forbiddance, how to violate
The sacred fruit forbidd'n! Some cursèd fraud
Of Enemy hath beguiled thee, yet unknown,
And me with thee hath ruined, for with thee
Certain my resolution is to die;
How can I live without thee, how forgo
Thy sweet convérse and love so dearly joined,
910   To live again in these wild woods forlorn?
Should God create another Eve, and I
Another rib afford, yet loss of thee
Would never from my heart; no no, I feel
The link of nature draw me: flesh of flesh,
Bone of my bone thou art, and from thy state
Mine never shall be parted, bliss or woe.'

So having said, as one from sad dismay
Recomforted, and after thoughts disturbed
Submitting to what seemed remédiless,
Thus in calm mood his words to Eve he turned.   920
    'Bold deed thou hast presumed, advent'rous Eve,
And peril great provoked, who thus hath dared
Had it been only coveting to eye
That sacred fruit, sacred to abstinence,
Much more to taste it under ban to touch.
But past who can recall, or done undo?
Not God omnipotent, nor Fate; yet so
Perhaps thou shalt not die, perhaps the fact
Is not so heinous now, foretasted fruit,
Profaned first by the serpent, by him first   930
Made common and unhallowed ere our taste;
Nor yet on him found deadly; he yet lives,
Lives, as thou saidst, and gains to live as man
Higher degree of life, inducement strong
To us, as likely tasting to attain
Proportional ascent, which cannot be
But to be gods, or angels demi-gods.
Nor can I think that God, Creator wise,
Though threat'ning, will in earnest so destroy
Us his prime creatures, dignified so high,   940
Set over all his works, which in our Fall,
For us created, needs with us must fail,
Dependent made; so God shall uncreate,
Be frustrate, do, undo, and labour lose,
Not well conceived of God, who though his power
Creation could repeat, yet would be loath
Us to abolish, lest the Adversary
Triúmph and say; "Fickle their state whom God
Most favours, who can please him long? Me first
He ruined, now mankind; whom will he next?"   950
Matter of scorn, not to be given the Foe.
However, I with thee have fixed my lot,
Certain to undergo like doom; if death
Consort with thee, death is to me as life;

So forcible within my heart I feel
The bond of nature draw me to my own,
My own in thee, for what thou art is mine;
Our state cannot be severed, we are one,
One flesh; to lose thee were to lose myself.'
960 So Adam, and thus Eve to him replied.
'O glorious trial of exceeding love,
Illustrious evidence, example high!
Engaging me to emulate, but short
Of thy perfection, how shall I attain,
Adam, from whose dear side I boast me sprung,
And gladly of our union hear thee speak,
One heart, one soul in both; whereof good proof
This day affords, declaring thee resolved,
Rather than death or aught than death more dread
970 Shall separate us, linked in love so dear,
To undergo with me one guilt, one crime,
If any be, of tasting this fair fruit,
Whose virtue, for of good still good proceeds,
Direct, or by occasion hath presented
This happy trial of thy love, which else
So eminently never had been known.
Were it I thought death menaced would ensue
This my attempt, I would sustain alone
The worst, and not persuade thee, rather die
980 Deserted, than oblige thee with a fact
Pernicious to thy peace, chiefly assured
Remarkably so late of thy so true,
So faithful love unequalled; but I feel
Far otherwise th' event, not death, but life
Augmented, opened eyes, new hopes, new joys,
Taste so divine, that what of sweet before
Hath touched my sense, flat seems to this, and harsh.
On my experience, Adam, freely taste,
And fear of death deliver to the winds.'
990 So saying, she embraced him, and for joy
Tenderly wept, much won that he his love
Had so ennobled, as of choice to incur

Divine displeasure for her sake, or death.
In recompense (for such compliance bad
Such recompense best merits) from the bough
She gave him of that fair enticing fruit
With liberal hand: he scrupled not to eat
Against his better knowledge, not deceived,
But fondly overcome with female charm.
Earth trembled from her entrails, as again   1000
In pangs, and Nature gave a second groan;
Sky loured, and muttering thunder, some sad drops
Wept at completing of the mortal sin
Original; while Adam took no thought,
Eating his fill, nor Eve to iterate
Her former trespass feared, the more to soothe
Him with her loved society, that now
As with new wine intoxicated both
They swim in mirth, and fancy that they feel
Divinity within them breeding wings   1010
Wherewith to scorn the earth: but that false fruit
Far other operation first displayed,
Carnal desire inflaming; he on Eve
Began to cast lascivious eyes, she him
As wantonly repaid; in lust they burn:
Till Adam thus gan Eve to dalliance move.
     'Eve, now I see thou art exact of taste,
And elegant, of sapience no small part,
Since to each meaning savour we apply,
And palate call judicious; I the praise   1020
Yield thee, so well this day thou hast purveyed.
Much pleasure we have lost, while we abstained
From this delightful fruit, nor known till now
True relish, tasting; if such pleasure be
In things to us forbidden, it might be wished,
For this one tree had been forbidden ten.
But come, so well refreshed, now let us play,
As meet is, after such delicious fare;
For never did thy beauty since the day
I saw thee first and wedded thee, adorned   1030

With all perfections, so inflame my sense
With ardour to enjoy thee, fairer now
Than ever, bounty of this virtuous tree.'
    So said he, and forbore not glance or toy
Of amorous intent, well understood
Of Eve, whose eye darted contagious fire.
Her hand he seized, and to a shady bank,
Thick overhead with verdant roof embow'red
He led her nothing loath; flow'rs were the couch,
1040 Pansies, and violets, and asphodel,
And hyacinth, earth's freshest softest lap.
There they their fill of love and love's disport
Took largely, of their mutual guilt the seal,
The solace of their sin, till dewy sleep
Oppressed them, wearied with their amorous play.
Soon as the force of that fallacious fruit,
That with exhilarating vapour bland
About their spirits had played, and inmost powers
Made err, was now exhaled, and grosser sleep
1050 Bred of unkindly fumes, with conscious dreams
Encumbered, now had left them, up they rose
As from unrest, and each the other viewing,
Soon found their eyes how opened, and their minds
How darkened; innocence, that as a veil
Had shadowed them from knowing ill, was gone;
Just confidence, and native righteousness
And honour from about them, naked left
To guilty Shame: he covered, but his robe
Uncovered more. So rose the Danite strong
1060 Hercúlean Samson from the harlot-lap
Of Phílistéan Dálila, and waked
Shorn of his strength, they destitute and bare
Of all their virtue: silent, and in face
Confounded long they sat, as strucken mute,
Till Adam, though not less than Eve abashed,
At length gave utterance to these words constrained.
    'O Eve, in evil hour thou didst give ear
To that false worm, of whomsoever taught

To counterfeit man's voice, true in our Fall,
False in our promised rising; since our eyes   1070
Opened we find indeed, and find we know
Both good and evil, good lost, and evil got,
Bad fruit of knowledge, if this be to know,
Which leaves us naked thus, of honour void,
Of innocence, of faith, of purity,
Our wonted ornaments now soiled and stained,
And in our faces evident the signs
Of foul concupiscence; whence evil store;
Even shame, the last of evils; of the first
Be sure then. How shall I behold the face   1080
Henceforth of God or angel, erst with joy
And rapture so oft beheld? Those Heav'nly shapes
Will dazzle now this earthly, with their blaze
Insufferably bright. O might I here
In solitude live savage, in some glade
Obscured, where highest woods impenetrable
To star or sunlight, spread their umbrage broad
And brown as evening: cover me ye pines,
Ye cedars, with innumerable boughs
Hide me, where I may never see them more.   1090
But let us now, as in bad plight, devise
What best may for the present serve to hide
The parts of each from other, that seem most
To shame obnoxious, and unseemliest seen;
Some tree whose broad smooth leaves together sewed,
And girded on our loins, may cover round
Those middle parts, that this newcomer, Shame,
There sit not, and reproach us as unclean.'
    So counselled he, and both together went
Into the thickest wood; there soon they chose   1100
The fig-tree, not that kind for fruit renowned,
But such as at this day to Indians known
In Malabar or Deccan spreads her arms
Branching so broad and long, that in the ground
The bended twigs take root, and daughters grow
About the mother tree, a pillared shade

High overarched, and echoing walks between;
There oft the Indian herdsman shunning heat
Shelters in cool, and tends his pasturing herds
1110   At loopholes cut through thickest shade: those leaves
They gathered, broad as Amazonian targe,
And with what skill they had, together sewed,
To gird their waist, vain covering if to hide
Their guilt and dreaded shame; O how unlike
To that first naked glory. Such of late
Columbus found th' American so girt
With feathered cincture, naked else and wild
Among the trees on isles and woody shores.
Thus fenced, and as they thought, their shame in part
1120   Covered, but not at rest or ease of mind,
They sat them down to weep; nor only tears
Rained at their eyes, but high winds worse within
Began to rise, high passions, anger, hate,
Mistrust, suspicion, discord, and shook sore
Their inward state of mind, calm region once
And full of peace, now tossed and turbulent:
For understanding ruled not, and the will
Heard not her lore, both in subjection now
To sensual appetite, who from beneath
1130   Usurping over sov'reign reason claimed
Superior sway: from thus distempered breast,
Adam, estranged in look and altered style,
Speech intermitted thus to Eve renewed.
   'Would thou hadst hearkened to my words, and
       stayed
With me, as I besought thee, when that strange
Desire of wand'ring this unhappy morn,
I know not whence possessed thee; we had then
Remained still happy, not as now, despoiled
Of all our good, shamed, naked, miserable.
1140   Let none henceforth seek needless cause to approve
The faith they owe; when earnestly they seek
Such proof, conclude, they then begin to fail.'

To whom soon moved with touch of blame thus
    Eve.
'What words have passed thy lips, Adam severe,
Imput'st thou that to my default, or will
Of wand'ring, as thou call'st it, which who knows
But might as ill have happened thou being by,
Or to thyself perhaps: hadst thou been there,
Or here th' attempt, thou couldst not have discerned
Fraud in the serpent, speaking as he spake;   1150
No ground of enmity between us known,
Why he should mean me ill, or seek to harm.
Was I to have never parted from thy side?
As good have grown there still a lifeless rib.
Being as I am, why didst not thou the head
Command me absolutely not to go,
Going into such danger as thou saidst?
Too facile then thou didst not much gainsay,
Nay, didst permit, approve, and fair dismiss.
Hadst thou been firm and fixed in thy dissent,   1160
Neither had I transgressed, nor thou with me.'
    To whom then first incensed Adam replied.
'Is this the love, is this the recompense
Of mine to thee, ingrateful Eve, expressed
Immutable when thou wert lost, not I,
Who might have lived and joyed immortal bliss,
Yet willingly chose rather death with thee?
And am I now upbraided, as the cause
Of thy transgressing? Not enough severe,
It seems, in thy restraint: what could I more?   1170
I warned thee, I admonished thee, foretold
The danger, and the lurking Enemy
That lay in wait; beyond this had been force,
And force upon free will hath here no place.
But confidence then bore thee on, secure
Either to meet no danger, or to find
Matter of glorious trial; and perhaps
I also erred in overmuch admiring

What seemed in thee so perfect, that I thought
1180 No evil durst attempt thee, but I rue
That error now, which is become my crime,
And thou th' accuser. Thus it shall befall
Him who to worth in women overtrusting
Lets her will rule; restraint she will not brook,
And left to herself, if evil thence ensue,
She first his weak indulgence will accuse.'
    Thus they in mutual accusation spent
The fruitless hours, but neither self-condemning,
And of their vain contést appeared no end.

from PARADISE REGAINED

from THE FIRST BOOK

[Invocation]

I who erewhile the happy garden sung,
By one man's disobedience lost, now sing
Recovered Paradise to all mankind,
By one man's firm obedience fully tried
Through all temptation, and the Tempter foiled
In all his wiles, defeated and repulsed,
And Eden raised in the waste wilderness.
   Thou Spirit who led'st this glorious eremite
Into the desert, his victorious field
Against the spiritual Foe, and brought'st him thence   10
By proof th' undoubted Son of God, inspire,
As thou art wont, my prompted song else mute,
And bear through heighth or depth of Nature's bounds
With prosperous wing full-summed to tell of deeds
Above heroic, though in secret done,
And unrecorded left through many an age,
Worthy t' have not remained so long unsung.

[Satan Accosts Jesus in the Wilderness]

So spake our Morning Star then in his rise,
And looking round on every side beheld
A pathless desert, dusk with horrid shades;
The way he came not having marked, return
Was difficult, by human steps untrod;
And he still on was led, but with such thoughts
Accompanied of things past and to come
Lodged in his breast, as well might recommend
Such solitude before choicest society.
Full forty days he passed, whether on hill
Sometimes, anon in shady vale, each night
Under the covert of some ancient oak,
Or cedar, to defend him from the dew,
Or harboured in one cave, is not revealed;
Nor tasted human food, nor hunger felt
Till those days ended, hungered then at last
Among wild beasts: they at his sight grew mild,
Nor sleeping him nor waking harmed, his walk
The fiery serpent fled, and noxious worm,
The lion and fierce tiger glared aloof.
But now an agèd man in rural weeds,
Following, as seemed, the quest of some stray ewe,
Or withered sticks to gather; which might serve
Against a winter's day when winds blow keen,
To warm him wet returned from field at eve,
He saw approach, who first with curious eye
Perused him, then with words thus uttered spake.
    'Sir, what ill chance hath brought thee to this place
So far from path or road of men, who pass
In troop or caravan? For single none
Durst ever, who returned, and dropped not here
His carcass, pined with hunger and with drouth.
I ask the rather, and the more admire,
For that to me thou seem'st the man, whom late

Our new baptizing Prophet at the ford
Of Jordan honoured so, and called thee Son
Of God; I saw and heard, for we sometimes   330
Who dwell this wild, constrained by want, come forth
To town or village nigh (nighest is far)
Where aught we hear, and curious are to hear,
What happens new; fame also finds us out.'
    To whom the Son of God. 'Who brought me hither
Will bring me hence, no other guide I seek.'
    'By miracle he may,' replied the swain,
'What other way I see not, for we here
Live on tough roots and stubs, to thirst inured
More than the camel, and to drink go far,   340
Men to much misery and hardship born;
But if thou be the Son of God, command
That out of these hard stones be made thee bread;
So shalt thou save thyself and us relieve
With food, whereof we wretched seldom taste.'
    He ended, and the Son of God replied.
'Think'st thou such force in bread? Is it not written
(For I discern thee other than thou seem'st)
Man lives not by bread only, but each word
Proceeding from the mouth of God; who fed   350
Our fathers here with manna; in the mount
Moses was forty days, nor ate nor drank,
And forty days Elijah without food
Wandered this barren waste, the same I now:
Why dost thou then suggest to me distrust,
Knowing who I am, as I know who thou art?'
    Whom thus answered th' Arch Fiend now
                undisguised.
''Tis true, I am that Spirit unfortunate,
Who leagued with millions more in rash revolt
Kept not my happy station, but was driv'n   360
With them from bliss to the bottomless deep,
Yet to that hideous place not so confined
By rigour unconniving, but that oft

Leaving my dolorous prison I enjoy
Large liberty to round this globe of earth,
Or range in th' air, nor from the Heav'n of Heav'ns
Hath he excluded my resort sometimes.
I came among the sons of God, when he
Gave up into my hands Uzzéan Job
370 To prove him, and illústrate his high worth;
And when to all his angels he proposed
To draw the proud King Ahab into fraud
That he might fall in Ramoth, they demurring,
I undertook that office, and the tongues
Of all his flattering prophets glibbed with lies
To his destruction, as I had in charge.
For what he bids I do; though I have lost
Much lustre of my native brightness, lost
To be beloved of God, I have not lost
380 To love, at least contémplate and admire
What I see excellent in good, or fair,
Or virtuous; I should so have lost all sense.
What can be then less in me than desire
To see thee and approach thee, whom I know
Declared the Son of God, to hear attent
Thy wisdom, and behold thy Godlike deeds?
Men generally think me much a foe
To all mankind: why should I? They to me
Never did wrong or violence, by them
390 I lost not what I lost, rather by them
I gained what I have gained, and with them dwell
Copartner in these regions of the world,
If not disposer; lend them oft my aid,
Oft my advice by presages and signs,
And answers, oracles, portents and dreams,
Whereby they may direct their future life.
Envy they say excites me, thus to gain
Companions of my misery and woe.
At first it may be; but long since with woe
400 Nearer acquainted, now I feel by proof,
That fellowship in pain divides not smart,

Nor lightens aught each man's peculiar load.
Small consolation then, were man adjoined:
This wounds me most (what can it less) that man,
Man fall'n shall be restored, I never more.'
    To whom our Saviour sternly thus replied.
'Deservedly thou griev'st, composed of lies
From the beginning, and in lies wilt end;
Who boast'st release from Hell, and leave to come
Into the Heav'n of Heavens; thou com'st indeed,   410
As a poor miserable captive thrall
Comes to the place where he before had sat
Among the prime in splendour, now deposed,
Ejected, emptied, gazed, unpitied, shunned,
A spectacle of ruin or of scorn
To all the host of Heaven; the happy place
Imparts to thee no happiness, no joy,
Rather inflames thy torment, representing
Lost bliss, to thee no more communicable,
So never more in Hell than when in Heaven.   420
But thou art serviceable to Heaven's King.
Wilt thou impute to obedience what thy fear
Extorts, or pleasure to do ill excites?
What but thy malice moved thee to misdeem
Of righteous Job, then cruelly to afflict him
With all inflictions, but his patience won?
The other service was thy chosen task,
To be a liar in four hundred mouths;
For lying is thy sustenance, thy food.
Yet thou pretend'st to truth; all oracles   430
By thee are giv'n, and what confessed more true
Among the nations? That hath been thy craft,
By mixing somewhat true to vent more lies.
But what have been thy answers, what but dark
Ambiguous and with double sense deluding,
Which they who asked have seldom understood,
And not well understood as good not known?
Who ever by consulting at thy shrine
Returned the wiser, or the more instruct

440   To fly or follow what concerned him most,
And run not sooner to his fatal snare?
For God hath justly giv'n the nations up
To thy delusions; justly, since they fell
Idolatrous; but when his purpose is
Among them to declare his Providence
To thee not known, whence hast thou then thy truth,
But from him or his angels president
In every province, who themselves disdaining
To approach thy temples, give thee in command
450   What to the smallest tittle thou shalt say
To thy adorers; thou with trembling fear,
Or like a fawning parasite obey'st;
Then to thyself ascrib'st the truth foretold.
But this thy glory shall be soon retrenched;
No more shalt thou by oracling abuse
The Gentiles; henceforth oracles are ceased,
And thou no more with pomp and sacrifice
Shalt be inquired at Delphos or elsewhere,
At least in vain, for they shall find thee mute.
460   God hath now sent his living Oracle
Into the world, to teach his final will,
And sends his Spirit of Truth henceforth to dwell
In pious hearts, an inward oracle
To all truth requisite for men to know.'
    So spake our Saviour; but the subtle Fiend,
Though inly stung with anger and disdain,
Dissembled, and this answer smooth returned.
   'Sharply thou hast insisted on rebuke,
And urged me hard with doings, which not will
470   But misery hath wrested from me; where
Easily canst thou find one miserable,
And not enforced oft-times to part from truth,
If it may stand him more in stead to lie,
Say and unsay, feign, flatter, or abjure?
But thou art placed above me, thou art Lord;
From thee I can and must submiss endure

Check or reproof, and glad to 'scape so quit.
Hard are the ways of truth, and rough to walk,
Smooth on the tongue discoursed, pleasing to th' ear,
And tuneable as sylvan pipe or song;   480
What wonder then if I delight to hear
Her dictates from thy mouth? Most men admire
Virtue, who follow not her lore: permit me
To hear thee when I come (since no man comes)
And talk at least, though I despair to attain.
Thy Father, who is holy, wise and pure,
Suffers the hypocrite or atheous priest
To tread his sacred courts, and minister
About his altar, handling holy things,
Praying or vowing, and vouchsafed his voice   490
To Balaam reprobate, a prophet yet
Inspired; disdain not such accéss to me.'
    To whom our Saviour with unaltered brow.
'Thy coming hither, though I know thy scope,
I bid not or forbid; do as thou find'st
Permission from above; thou canst not more.'
    He added not; and Satan bowing low
His grey dissimulation, disappeared
Into thin air diffused: for now began
Night with her sullen wing to double-shade   500
The desert, fowls in their clay nests were couched;
And now wild beasts came forth the woods to roam.

from THE SECOND BOOK

[The Devils Hold a Council in the Clouds]

For Satan with sly preface to return
Had left him vacant, and with speed was gone
Up to the middle region of thick air,
Where all his Potentates in council sat;
There without sign of boast, or sign of joy,
120   Solicitous and blank he thus began.
        'Princes, Heaven's ancient sons, ethereal Thrones,
Demonian Spirits now, from the element
Each of his reign allotted, rightlier called
Powers of fire, air, water, and earth beneath,
So may we hold our place and these mild seats
Without new trouble; such an enemy
Is risen to invade us, who no less
Threatens than our expulsion down to Hell;
I, as I undertook, and with the vote
130   Consenting in full frequence was empower'd,
Have found him, viewed him, tasted him, but find
Far other labour to be undergone
Than when I dealt with Adam first of men,
Though Adam by his wife's allurement fell,
However to this man inferior far,
If he be man by his mother's side at least,
With more than human gifts from Heaven adorned,
Perfections absolute, graces divine,
And amplitude of mind to greatest deeds.
140   Therefore I am returned, lest confidence
Of my success with Eve in Paradise
Deceive ye to persuasion over-sure
Of like succeeding here; I summon all
Rather to be in readiness, with hand
Or counsel to assist; lest I who erst

Thought none my equal, now be overmatched.'
    So spake the old Serpent doubting, and from all
With clamour was assured their utmost aid
At his command; when from amidst them rose
Belial the dissolutest Spirit that fell,   150
The sensualest, and after Asmodai
The fleshliest incubus, and thus advised.
    'Set women in his eye and in his walk,
Among daughters of men the fairest found;
Many are in each region passing fair
As the noon sky; more like to goddesses
Than mortal creatures, graceful and discreet,
Expért in amorous arts, enchanting tongues
Persuasive, virgin majesty with mild
And sweet allayed, yet terrible to approach,   160
Skilled to retire, and in retiring draw
Hearts after them tangled in amorous nets.
Such object hath the power to soft'n and tame
Severest temper, smooth the rugged'st brow,
Enerve, and with voluptuous hope dissolve,
Draw out with credulous desire, and lead
At will the manliest, resolutest breast,
As the magnetic hardest iron draws.
Women, when nothing else, beguiled the heart
Of wisest Solomon, and made him build,   170
And made him bow to the gods of his wives.'
    To whom quick answer Satan thus returned.
'Belial, in much uneven scale thou weigh'st
All others by thyself; because of old
Thou thyself dot'st on womankind, admiring
Their shape, their colour, and attractive grace,
None are, thou think'st, but taken with such toys.
Before the Flood thou with thy lusty crew,
False-titled sons of God, roaming the earth
Cast wanton eyes on the daughters of men,   180
And coupled with them, and begot a race.
Have we not seen, or by relation heard,
In courts and regal chambers how thou lurk'st,

In wood or grove by mossy fountain side,
In valley or green meadow to waylay
Some beauty rare, Callisto, Clymene,
Daphne, or Semele, Antiopa,
Or Amymóne, Syrinx, many more
Too long, then lay'st thy scapes on names adored,
Apollo, Neptune, Jupiter, or Pan,
Satyr, or Faun, or Sylvan? But these haunts
Delight not all; among the sons of men,
How many have with a smile made small account
Of beauty and her lures, easily scorned
All her assaults, on worthier things intent?
Remember that Pelléan conqueror,
A youth, how all the beauties of the East
He slightly viewed, and slightly overpassed;
How he surnamed of Africa dismissed
In his prime youth the fair Iberian maid.
For Solomon he lived at ease, and full
Of honour, wealth, high fare, aimed not beyond
Higher design than to enjoy his state;
Thence to the bait of women lay exposed;
But he whom we attempt is wiser far
Than Solomon, of more exalted mind,
Made and set wholly on the accomplishment
Of greatest things; what woman will you find,
Though of this age the wonder and the fame,
On whom his leisure will vouchsafe an eye
Of fond desire? Or should she confident,
As sitting queen adored on Beauty's throne,
Descend with all her winning charms begirt
To enamour, as the zone of Venus once
Wrought that effect on Jove, so fables tell;
How would one look from his majestic brow
Seated as on the top of Virtue's hill,
Discount'nance her despised, and put to rout
All her array; her female pride deject,
Or turn to reverent awe? For Beauty stands
In the admiration only of weak minds

Led captive; cease to admire, and all her plumes
Fall flat and shrink into a trivial toy,
At every sudden slighting quite abashed:
Therefore with manlier objects we must try
His constancy, with such as have more show
Of worth, of honour, glory, and popular praise;
Rocks whereon greatest men have oftest wrecked;
Or that which only seems to satisfy
Lawful desires of nature, not beyond;   230
And now I know he hungers where no food
Is to be found, in the wide wilderness;
The rest commit to me, I shall let pass
No advantage, and his strength as oft assay.'
   He ceased, and heard their grant in loud acclaim;
Then forthwith to him takes a chosen band
Of Spirits likest to himself in guile
To be at hand, and at his beck appear,
If cause were to unfold some active scene
Of various persons each to know his part;   240
Then to the desert takes with these his flight;
Where still from shade to shade the Son of God
After forty days' fasting had remained,
Now hung'ring first . . .

[Satan Tempts Jesus with a Banquet]

   'How hast thou hunger then?' Satan replied,
'Tell me if food were now before thee set,   320
Wouldst thou not eat?' 'Thereafter as I like
The giver,' answered Jesus. 'Why should that
Cause thy refusal,' said the subtle Fiend,
'Hast thou not right to all created things,
Owe not all creatures by just right to thee
Duty and service, nor to stay till bid,
But tender all their power? Nor mention I
Meats by the Law unclean, or offered first
To idols – those young Daniel could refuse;

330   Nor proffered by an enemy, though who
       Would scruple that, with want oppressed? Behold
       Nature ashamed, or better to express,
       Troubled that thou shouldst hunger, hath purveyed
       From all the elements her choicest store
       To treat thee as beseems, and as her Lord
       With honour; only deign to sit and eat.'
          He spake no dream, for as his words had end,
       Our Saviour lifting up his eyes beheld
       In ample space under the broadest shade
340   A table richly spread, in regal mode,
       With dishes piled, and meats of noblest sort
       And savour, beasts of chase, or fowl of game,
       In pastry built, or from the spit, or boiled,
       Grisamber-steamed; all fish from sea or shore,
       Freshet, or purling brook, of shell or fin,
       And exquisitest name, for which was drained
       Pontus and Lucrine bay, and Afric coast.
       Alas how simple, to these cates compared,
       Was that crude apple that diverted Eve!
350   And at a stately sideboard by the wine
       That fragrant smell diffused, in order stood
       Tall stripling youths rich-clad, of fairer hue
       Than Ganymede or Hylas; distant more
       Under the trees now tripped, now solemn stood
       Nymphs of Diana's train, and Naiades
       With fruits and flowers from Amalthea's horn,
       And ladies of th' Hesperides, that seemed
       Fairer than feigned of old, or fabled since
       Of fairy damsels met in forest wide
360   By knights of Logres, or of Lyonesse,
       Lancelot or Pelleas, or Pellenore;
       And all the while harmonious airs were heard
       Of chiming strings, or charming pipes, and winds
       Of gentlest gale Arabian odours fanned
       From their soft wings, and Flora's earliest smells.
       Such was the splendour, and the Tempter now
       His invitation earnestly renewed.

'What doubts the Son of God to sit and eat?
These are not fruits forbidden; no interdict
Defends the touching of these viands pure;   370
Their taste no knowledge works, at least of evil,
But life preserves, destroys life's enemy,
Hunger, with sweet restorative delight.
All these are Spirits of air, and woods, and springs,
Thy gentle ministers, who come to pay
Thee homage, and acknowledge thee their Lord:
What doubt'st thou Son of God? Sit down and eat.'

from THE THIRD BOOK

[Satan Tempts Jesus with the Parthian Empire]

With that (such power was giv'n him then) he took
The Son of God up to a mountain high.
It was a mountain at whose verdant feet
A spacious plain outstretched in circuit wide
Lay pleasant; from his side two rivers flowed,
Th' one winding, the other straight, and left between
Fair champaign with less rivers interveined,
Then meeting joined their tribute to the sea:
Fertile of corn the glebe, of oil and wine,
With herds the pastures thronged, with flocks the
          hills;   260
Huge cities and high-towered, that well might seem
The seats of mightiest monarchs, and so large
The prospect was, that here and there was room
For barren desert fountainless and dry.
To this high mountain top the Tempter brought
Our Saviour, and new train of words began.
    'Well have we speeded, and o'er hill and dale,

Forest and field, and flood, temples and towers
Cut shorter many a league; here thou behold'st
270   Assyria and her empire's ancient bounds,
Araxes and the Caspian lake, thence on
As far as Indus east, Euphrates west,
And oft beyond; to south the Persian bay,
And inaccessible the Arabian drouth:
Here Nineveh, of length within her wall
Several days' journey, built by Ninus old,
Of that first golden monarchy the seat,
And seat of Salmanassar, whose success
Israel in long captivity still mourns;
280   There Babylon the wonder of all tongues,
As ancient, but rebuilt by him who twice
Judah and all thy father David's house
Led captive, and Jerusalem laid waste,
Till Cyrus set them free; Persepolis
His city there thou seest, and Bactra there;
Ecbatana her structure vast there shows,
And Hecatompylos her hundred gates,
There Susa by Choaspes, amber stream,
The drink of none but kings; of later fame
290   Built by Emathian, or by Parthian hands,
The great Seleucia, Nisibis, and there
Artaxata, Teredon, Ctesiphon,
Turning with easy eye thou may'st behold.
All these the Parthian, now some ages past,
By great Arsaces led, who founded first
That empire, under his dominion holds,
From the luxurious kings of Antioch won.
And just in time thou com'st to have a view
Of his great power; for now the Parthian king
300   In Ctesiphon hath gathered all his host
Against the Scythian, whose incursions wild
Have wasted Sogdiana; to her aid
He marches now in haste; see, though from far,
His thousands, in what martial equipage

They issue forth, steel bows, and shafts their arms
Of equal dread in flight, or in pursuit;
All horsemen, in which fight they most excel;
See how in warlike muster they appear,
In rhombs and wedges, and half moons, and wings.'
   He looked and saw what numbers numberless   310
The city gates outpoured, light-armèd troops
In coats of mail and military pride;
In mail their horses clad, yet fleet and strong,
Prancing their riders bore, the flower and choice
Of many provinces from bound to bound;
From Arachosia, from Candaor east,
And Margiana to the Hyrcanian cliffs
Of Caucasus, and dark Iberian dales,
From Atropatia and the neighbouring plains
Of Adiabéne, Media, and the south   320
Of Susiana to Balsara's hav'n.
He saw them in their forms of battle ranged,
How quick they wheeled, and flying behind them shot
Sharp sleet of arrowy showers against the face
Of their pursuers, and overcame by flight;
The field all iron cast a gleaming brown,
Nor wanted clouds of foot, nor on each horn,
Cuirassiers all in steel for standing fight;
Chariots or elephants endorsed with towers
Of archers, nor of labouring pioneers,   330
A multitude with spades and axes armed
To lay hills plain, fell woods, or valleys fill,
Or where plain was raise hill, or overlay
With bridges rivers proud, as with a yoke;
Mules after these, camels and dromedaries,
And waggons fraught with útensils of war.
Such forces met not, nor so wide a camp,
When Agrican with all his northern powers
Besieged Albracca, as romances tell;
The city of Gallaphrone, from thence to win   340
The fairest of her sex Angelica

His daughter, sought by many prowest knights,
Both paynim, and the peers of Charlemagne.
Such and so numerous was their chivalry;
At sight whereof the Fiend yet more presumed,
And to our Saviour thus his words renewed.

    'That thou may'st know I seek not to engage
Thy virtue, and not every way secure
On no slight grounds thy safety; hear, and mark
To what end I have brought thee hither and shown
All this fair sight; thy kingdom though foretold
By Prophet or by angel, unless thou
Endeavour, as thy father David did,
Thou never shalt obtain; prediction still
In all things, and all men, supposes means;
Without means used, what it predicts revokes.
But say thou wert possessed of David's throne
By free consent of all, none opposite,
Samaritan or Jew; how couldst thou hope
Long to enjoy it quiet and secure,
Between two such enclosing enemies
Roman and Parthian? Therefore one of these
Thou must make sure thy own; the Parthian first
By my advice, as nearer and of late
Found able by invasion to annoy
Thy country, and captive lead away her kings
Antigonus, and old Hyrcanus bound,
Maugre the Roman: it shall be my task
To render thee the Parthian at dispose;
Choose which thou wilt by conquest or by league.'

350

360

370

THE FOURTH BOOK

Perplexed and troubled at his bad success
The Tempter stood, nor had what to reply,
Discovered in his fraud, thrown from his hope,
So oft, and the persuasive rhetoric
That sleeked his tongue, and won so much on Eve,
So little here, nay lost; but Eve was Eve,
This far his over-match, who self-deceived
And rash, beforehand had no better weighed
The strength he was to cope with, or his own:
But as a man who had been matchless held   10
In cunning, overreached where least he thought,
To salve his credit, and for very spite
Still will be tempting him who foils him still,
And never cease, though to his shame the more;
Or as a swarm of flies in vintage-time,
About the wine-press where sweet must is poured,
Beat off, returns as oft with humming sound;
Or surging waves against a solid rock,
Though all to shivers dashed, the assault renew,
Vain battery, and in froth or bubbles end;   20
So Satan, whom repulse upon repulse
Met ever; and to shameful silence brought,
Yet gives not o'er though desperate of success,
And his vain importunity pursues.
He brought our Saviour to the western side
Of that high mountain, whence he might behold
Another plain, long but in breadth not wide;
Washed by the southern sea, and on the north
To equal length backed with a ridge of hills
That screened the fruits of the earth and seats of men   30
From cold Septentrion blasts; thence in the midst
Divided by a river, of whose banks
On each side an imperial city stood,

With towers and temples proudly elevate
On seven small hills, with palaces adorned,
Porches and theatres, baths, aqueducts,
Statues and trophies, and triumphal arcs,
Gardens and groves presented to his eyes,
Above the heighth of mountains interposed.
40   By what strange parallax or optic skill
Of vision multiplied through air, or glass
Of telescope, were curious to inquire:
And now the Tempter thus his silence broke.
        'The city which thou seest no other deem
Than great and glorious Rome, queen of the earth
So far renowned, and with the spoils enriched
Of nations; there the Capitol thou seest
Above the rest lifting his stately head
On the Tarpeian rock, her citadel
50   Impregnable, and there Mount Palatine
The imperial palace, compass huge, and high
The structure, skill of noblest architects,
With gilded battlements, conspicuous far,
Turrets and terraces, and glittering spires.
Many a fair edifice besides, more like
Houses of gods (so well I have disposed
My airy microscope) thou may'st behold
Outside and inside both, pillars and roofs
Carved work, the hand of famed artificers
60   In cedar, marble, ivory or gold.
Thence to the gates cast round thine eye, and see
What conflux issuing forth, or ent'ring in,
Praetors, proconsuls to their provinces
Hasting or on return, in robes of state;
Lictors and rods the ensigns of their power;
Legions and cohorts, turms of horse and wings:
Or embassies from regions far remote
In various habits on the Appian road,
Or on the Aemilian, some from farthest south,
70   Syene, and where the shadow both way falls,
Meroë Nilotic isle, and more to west,

The realm of Bocchus to the Blackmoor sea;
From the Asian kings and Parthian among these,
From India and the golden Chersoness,
And utmost Indian isle Tapróbanè,
Dusk faces with white silken turbans wreathed:
From Gallia, Gades, and the British west,
Germans and Scythians, and Sarmatians north
Beyond Danubius to the Tauric pool.
All nations now to Rome obedience pay,   80
To Rome's great Emperor, whose wide domain
In ample territory, wealth and power,
Civility of manners, arts, and arms,
And long renown thou justly may'st prefer
Before the Parthian; these two thrones except,
The rest are barbarous, and scarce worth the sight,
Shared among petty kings too far removed;
These having shown thee, I have shown thee all
The kingdoms of the world, and all their glory.
This Emperor hath no son, and now is old,   90
Old and lascivious, and from Rome retired
To Capreae an island small but strong
On the Campanian shore, with purpose there
His horrid lusts in private to enjoy,
Committing to a wicked favourite
All public cares, and yet of him suspicious,
Hated of all, and hating; with what ease,
Endued with regal virtues as thou art,
Appearing, and beginning noble deeds,
Might'st thou expel this monster from his throne   100
Now made a sty, and in his place ascending,
A victor-people free from servile yoke!
And with my help thou may'st; to me the power
Is given, and by that right I give it thee.
Aim therefore at no less than all the world,
Aim at the highest, without the highest attained
Will be for thee no sitting, or not long
On David's throne, be prophesied what will.'
    To whom the Son of God unmoved replied.

110   'Nor doth this grandeur and majestic show
       Of luxury, though called magnificence,
       More than of arms before, allure mine eye,
       Much less my mind; though thou shouldst add to tell
       Their sumptuous gluttonies, and gorgeous feasts
       On citron tables or Atlantic stone;
       (For I have also heard, perhaps have read)
       Their wines of Setia, Cales, and Falerne,
       Chios and Crete, and how they quaff in gold,
       Crystal and myrrhine cups embossed with gems
120   And studs of pearl, to me shouldst tell who thirst
       And hunger still: then embassies thou show'st
       From nations far and nigh; what honour that,
       But tedious waste of time to sit and hear
       So many hollow compliments and lies,
       Outlandish flatteries? Then proceed'st to talk
       Of the emperor, how easily subdued,
       How gloriously; I shall, thou say'st, expel
       A brutish monster: what if I withal
       Expel a devil who first made him such?
130   Let his tormentor Conscience find him out;
       For him I was not sent, nor yet to free
       That people victor once, now vile and base,
       Deservedly made vassal, who once just,
       Frugal, and mild, and temperate, conquered well,
       But govern ill the nations under yoke,
       Peeling their provinces, exhausted all
       By lust and rapine; first ambitious grown
       Of triumph, that insulting vanity;
       Then cruel, by their sports to blood inured
140   Of fighting beasts, and men to beasts exposed;
       Luxurious by their wealth, and greedier still,
       And from the daily scene effeminate.
       What wise and valiant man would seek to free
       These thus degenerate, by themselves enslaved,
       Or could of inward slaves make outward free?
       Know therefore when my season comes to sit
       On David's throne, it shall be like a tree

Spreading and overshadowing all the earth,
Or as a stone that shall to pieces dash
All monarchies besides throughout the world,   150
And of my kingdom there shall be no end:
Means there shall be to this, but what the means,
Is not for thee to know, nor me to tell.'
    To whom the Tempter impudent replied.
'I see all offers made by me how slight
Thou valu'st, because offered, and reject'st:
Nothing will please the difficult and nice,
Or nothing more than still to contradict:
On the other side know also thou, that I
On what I offer set as high esteem,   160
Nor what I part with mean to give for naught;
All these which in a moment thou behold'st,
The kingdoms of the world to thee I give;
For giv'n to me, I give to whom I please,
No trifle; yet with this reserve, not else,
On this condition, if thou wilt fall down,
And worship me as thy superior lord,
Easily done, and hold them all of me;
For what can less so great a gift deserve?'
    Whom thus our Saviour answered with disdain.   170
'I never liked thy talk, thy offers less,
Now both abhor, since thou hast dared to utter
The abominable terms, impious condition;
But I endure the time, till which expired,
Thou hast permission on me. It is written
The first of all commandments, "Thou shalt worship
The Lord thy God, and only him shalt serve";
And dar'st thou to the Son of God propound
To worship thee accursed, now more accursed
For this attempt bolder than that on Eve,   180
And more blasphémous? which expect to rue.
The kingdoms of the world to thee were giv'n,
Permitted rather, and by thee usurped;
Other donation none thou canst produce:
If given, by whom but by the King of kings,

God over all supreme? If given to thee,
By thee how fairly is the Giver now
Repaid? But gratitude in thee is lost
Long since. Wert thou so void of fear or shame,
As offer them to me the Son of God,   190
To me my own, on such abhorrèd pact,
That I fall down and worship thee as God?
Get thee behind me; plain thou now appear'st
That Evil One, Satan for ever damned.'
    To whom the Fiend with fear abashed replied
'Be not so sore offended, Son of God;
Though Sons of God both angels are and men,
If I to try whether in higher sort
Than these thou bear'st that title, have proposed
What both from men and angels I receive,   200
Tetrarchs of fire, air, flood, and on the earth
Nations besides from all the quartered winds,
God of this world invoked and world beneath;
Who then thou art, whose coming is foretold
To me is fatal, me it most concerns.
The trial hath endamaged thee no way,
Rather more honour left and more esteem;
Me naught advantaged, missing what I aimed.
Therefore let pass, as they are transitory,
The kingdoms of this world; I shall no more   210
Advise thee; gain them as thou canst, or not.
And thou thyself seem'st otherwise inclined
Than to a worldly crown, addicted more
To contemplation and profound dispute,
As by that early action may be judged,
When slipping from thy mother's eye thou went'st
Alone into the Temple; there wast found
Among the gravest Rabbis disputant
On points and questions fitting Moses' chair,
Teaching not taught; the childhood shows the man,   220
As morning shows the day. Be famous then
By wisdom; as thy empire must extend,
So let extend thy mind o'er all the world,

In knowledge, all things in it comprehend;
All knowledge is not couched in Moses' law,
The Pentateuch or what the Prophets wrote;
The Gentiles also know, and write, and teach
To admiration, led by Nature's light;
And with the Gentiles much thou must converse,
Ruling them by persuasion as thou mean'st;   230
Without their learning how wilt thou with them,
Or they with thee hold conversation meet?
How wilt thou reason with them, how refute
Their idolisms, traditions, paradoxes?
Error by his own arms is best evinced.
Look once more ere we leave this specular mount
Westward, much nearer by southwest, behold
Where on the Áegean shore a city stands
Built nobly, pure the air, and light the soil,
Athens the eye of Greece, mother of arts   240
And eloquence, native to famous wits
Or hospitable, in her sweet recess,
City or suburban, studious walks and shades;
See there the olive grove of Academe,
Plato's retirement, where the Attic bird
Trills her thick-warbled notes the summer long;
There flow'ry hill Hymettus with the sound
Of bees' industrious murmur oft invites
To studious musing; there Ilissus rolls
His whispering stream; within the walls then view   250
The schools of ancient sages; his who bred
Great Alexander to subdue the world,
Lyceum there, and painted Stoa next:
There thou shalt hear and learn the secret power
Of harmony in tones and numbers hit
By voice or hand, and various-measured verse,
Aeolian charms and Dorian lyric odes,
And his who gave them breath, but higher sung,
Blind Melesigenes thence Homer called,
Whose poem Phoebus challenged for his own.   260
Thence what the lofty grave tragedians taught

In chorus or iambic, teachers best
Of moral prudence, with delight received
In brief sententious precepts, while they treat
Of fate, and chance, and change in human life;
High actions, and high passions best describing:
Thence to the famous orators repair,
Those ancient, whose resistless eloquence
Wielded at will that fierce democraty,
270   Shook the Arsenal and fulmined over Greece,
To Macedon, and Artaxerxes' throne;
To sage philosophy next lend thine ear,
From heaven descended to the low-roofed house
Of Socrates, see there his tenement,
Whom well inspired the oracle pronounced
Wisest of men; from whose mouth issued forth
Mellifluous streams that watered all the schools
Of Academics old and new, with those
Surnamed Peripatetics, and the sect
280   Epicurean, and the Stoic severe;
These here revolve, or, as thou lik'st, at home,
Till time mature thee to a kingdom's weight;
These rules will render thee a king complete
Within thyself, much more with empire joined.'
     To whom our Saviour sagely thus replied.
'Think not but that I know these things, or think
I know them not; not therefore am I short
Of knowing what I ought: he who receives
Light from above, from the fountain of light,
290   No other doctrine needs, though granted true;
But these are false, or little else but dreams,
Conjectures, fancies, built on nothing firm.
The first and wisest of them all professed
To know this only, that he nothing knew;
The next to fabling fell and smooth conceits,
A third sort doubted all things, though plain sense;
Others in virtue placed felicity,
But virtue joined with riches and long life;
In corporal pleasure he, and careless ease;

The Stoic last in philosophic pride,   300
By him called virtue; and his virtuous man,
Wise, perfect in himself, and all possessing
Equal to God, oft shames not to prefer,
As fearing God nor man, contemning all
Wealth, pleasure, pain or torment, death and life,
Which when he lists, he leaves, or boasts he can,
For all his tedious talk is but vain boast,
Or subtle shifts conviction to evade.
Alas what can they teach, and not mislead:
Ignorant of themselves, of God much more,   310
And how the world began, and how man fell
Degraded by himself, on grace depending?
Much of the soul they talk, but all awry,
And in themselves seek virtue, and to themselves
All glory arrogate, to God give none;
Rather accuse him under usual names,
Fortune and Fate, as one regardless quite
Of mortal things. Who therefore seeks in these
True wisdom, finds her not, or by delusion
Far worse, her false resemblance only meets,   320
An empty cloud. However, many books,
Wise men have said, are wearisome; who reads
Incessantly, and to his reading brings not
A spirit and judgement equal or superior,
(And what he brings, what needs he elsewhere seek)
Uncertain and unsettled still remains,
Deep versed in books and shallow in himself,
Crude or intoxicate, collecting toys,
And trifles for choice matters, worth a sponge;
As children gathering pebbles on the shore.   330
Or if I would delight my private hours
With music or with poem, where so soon
As in our native language can I find
That solace? All our Law and story strewed
With hymns, our Psalms with artful terms inscribed,
Our Hebrew songs and harps in Babylon,
That pleased so well our victors' ear, declare

That rather Greece from us these arts derived;
Ill imitated, while they loudest sing
340   The vices of their deities, and their own
In fable, hymn, or song, so personating
Their gods ridiculous, and themselves past shame.
Remove their swelling epithets, thick-laid
As varnish on a harlot's cheek, the rest,
Thin-sown with aught of profit or delight,
Will far be found unworthy to compare
With Sion's songs, to all true tastes excelling,
Where God is praised aright, and Godlike men,
The Holiest of Holies, and his saints;
350   Such are from God inspired, not such from thee;
Unless where moral virtue is expressed
By light of Nature not in all quite lost.
Their orators thou then extoll'st, as those
The top of eloquence, statists indeed,
And lovers of their country, as may seem;
But herein to our Prophets far beneath,
As men divinely taught, and better teaching
The solid rules of civil government
In their majestic unaffected style
360   Than all the oratory of Greece and Rome.
In them is plainest taught, and easiest learnt,
What makes a nation happy, and keeps it so,
What ruins kingdoms, and lays cities flat;
These only with our Law best form a king.'

So spake the Son of God; but Satan now
Quite at a loss, for all his darts were spent,
Thus to our Saviour with stern brow replied.

'Since neither wealth, nor honour, arms nor arts,
Kingdom nor empire pleases thee, nor aught
370   By me proposed in life contemplative,
Or active, tended on by glory, or fame,
What dost thou in this world? The wilderness
For thee is fittest place; I found thee there,
And thither will return thee; yet remember
What I foretell thee; soon thou shalt have cause

To wish thou never hadst rejected thus
Nicely or cautiously my offered aid,
Which would have set thee in short time with ease
On David's throne; or throne of all the world,
Now at full age, fulness of time, thy season,   380
When prophecies of thee are best fulfilled.
Now contrary, if I read aught in heaven,
Or heaven write aught of Fate, by what the stars
Voluminous, or single characters,
In their conjunction met, give me to spell,
Sorrows, and labours, opposition, hate,
Attends thee, scorns, reproaches, injuries,
Violence and stripes, and lastly cruel death;
A kingdom they portend thee, but what kingdom,
Real or allegoric I discern not,   390
Nor when; eternal sure, as without end,
Without beginning; for no date prefixed
Directs me in the starry rubric set.'
    So saying he took (for still he knew his power
Not yet expired) and to the wilderness
Brought back the Son of God, and left him there,
Feigning to disappear. Darkness now rose,
As daylight sunk, and brought in louring night,
Her shadowy offspring, unsubstantial both,
Privation mere of light and absent day.   400
Our Saviour meek and with untroubled mind
After his airy jaunt, though hurried sore,
Hungry and cold betook him to his rest,
Wherever, under some concóurse of shades
Whose branching arms thick intertwined might shield
From dews and damps of night his sheltered head,
But sheltered slept in vain, for at his head
The Tempter watched, and soon with ugly dreams
Disturbed his sleep; and either tropic now
Gan thunder, and both ends of heav'n; the clouds   410
From many a horrid rift abortive poured
Fierce rain with lightning mixed, water with fire
In ruin reconciled: nor slept the winds

Within their stony caves, but rushed abroad
From the four hinges of the world, and fell
On the vexed wilderness, whose tallest pines,
Though rooted deep as high, and sturdiest oaks
Bowed their stiff necks, loaden with stormy blasts,
Or torn up sheer: ill wast thou shrouded then,
420   O patient Son of God, yet only stood'st
Unshaken; nor yet stayed the terror there;
Infernal ghosts, and Hellish Furies, round
Environed thee; some howled, some yelled, some
          shrieked,
Some bent at thee their fiery darts, while thou
Sat'st unappalled in calm and sinless peace.
Thus passed the night so foul till morning fair
Came forth with pilgrim steps in amice grey;
Who with her radiant finger stilled the roar
Of thunder, chased the clouds, and laid the winds,
430   And grisly spectres, which the Fiend had raised
To tempt the Son of God with terrors dire.
And now the sun with more effectual beams
Had cheered the face of earth, and dried the wet
From drooping plant, or dropping tree; the birds
Who all things now behold more fresh and green,
After a night of storm so ruinous,
Cleared up their choicest notes in bush and spray
To gratulate the sweet return of morn;
Nor yet amidst this joy and brightest morn
440   Was absent, after all his mischief done,
The Prince of Darkness; glad would also seem
Of this fair change, and to our Saviour came,
Yet with no new device, they all were spent;
Rather by this his last affront resolved,
Desperate of better course, to vent his rage
And mad despite to be so oft repelled.
Him walking on a sunny hill he found,
Backed on the north and west by a thick wood;
Out of the wood he starts in wonted shape;
450   And in a careless mood thus to him said.

'Fair morning yet betides thee Son of God,
After a dismal night; I heard the rack
As earth and sky would mingle; but myself
Was distant; and these flaws, though mortals fear
     them
As dangerous to the pillared frame of heaven,
Or to the earth's dark basis underneath,
Are to the main as inconsiderable,
And harmless, if not wholesome, as a sneeze
To man's less universe, and soon are gone;
Yet as being ofttimes noxious where they light   460
On man, beast, plant, wasteful and turbulent,
Like turbulencies in the affairs of men,
Over whose heads they roar, and seem to point,
They oft fore-signify and threaten ill:
This tempest at this desert most was bent;
Of men at thee, for only thou here dwell'st.
Did I not tell thee, if thou didst reject
The perfect season offered with my aid
To win thy destined seat, but wilt prolong
All to the push of Fate, pursue thy way   470
Of gaining David's throne no man knows when,
For both the when and how is nowhere told,
Thou shalt be what thou art ordained, no doubt;
For angels have proclaimed it, but concealing
The time and means: each act is rightliest done,
Not when it must, but when it may be best.
If thou observe not this, be sure to find,
What I foretold thee, many a hard assay
Of dangers, and adversities and pains,
Ere thou of Israel's sceptre get fast hold;   480
Whereof this ominous night that closed thee round,
So many terrors, voices, prodigies
May warn thee, as a sure foregoing sign.'
   So talked he, while the Son of God went on
And stayed not, but in brief him answered thus.
   'Me worse than wet thou find'st not; other harm
Those terrors which thou speak'st of, did me none;

I never feared they could, though noising loud
And threat'ning nigh; what they can do as signs
490 Betok'ning, or ill boding, I contemn
As false portents, not sent from God, but thee;
Who knowing I shall reign past thy preventing,
Obtrud'st thy offered aid, that I accepting
At least might seem to hold all power of thee,
Ambitious Spirit, and wouldst be thought my God,
And storm'st refused, thinking to terrify
Me to thy will; desist, thou art discerned
And toil'st in vain, nor me in vain molest.'
　　　To whom the Fiend now swoll'n with rage replied:
500 'Then hear, O Son of David, virgin-born,
For Son of God to me is yet in doubt;
Of the Messiah I have heard foretold
By all the Prophets; of thy birth at length
Announced by Gabriel with the first I knew,
And of the angelic song in Bethlehem field,
On thy birth-night, that sung thee Saviour born.
From that time seldom have I ceased to eye
Thy infancy, thy childhood, and thy youth,
Thy manhood last, though yet in private bred;
510 Till at the ford of Jordan whither all
Flocked to the Baptist, I among the rest,
Though not to be baptized, by voice from Heav'n
Heard thee pronounced the Son of God beloved.
Thenceforth I thought thee worth my nearer view
And narrower scrutiny, that I might learn
In what degree or meaning thou art called
The Son of God, which bears no single sense;
The Son of God I also am, or was,
And if I was, I am; relation stands;
520 All men are Sons of God; yet thee I thought
In some respect far higher so declared.
Therefore I watched thy footsteps from that hour,
And followed thee still on to this waste wild;
Where by all best conjectures I collect
Thou art to be my fatal enemy.

Good reason then, if I beforehand seek
To understand my adversary, who
And what he is; his wisdom, power, intent,
By parle, or composition, truce, or league
To win him, or win from him what I can.   530
And opportunity I here have had
To try thee, sift thee, and confess have found thee
Proof against all temptation as a rock
Of adamant, and as a centre, firm
To the utmost of mere man both wise and good,
Not more; for honours, riches, kingdoms, glory
Have been before contemned, and may again:
Therefore to know what more thou art than man,
Worth naming Son of God by voice from Heav'n,
Another method I must now begin.'   540
    So saying he caught him up, and without wing
Of hippogriff bore through the air sublime
Over the wilderness and o'er the plain;
Till underneath them fair Jerusalem,
The holy city lifted high her towers,
And higher yet the glorious Temple reared
Her pile, far off appearing like a mount
Of alabaster, topped with golden spires:
There on the highest pinnacle he set
The Son of God; and added thus in scorn: 550
    'There stand, if thou wilt stand; to stand upright
Will ask thee skill; I to thy Father's house
Have brought thee, and highest placed; highest is best;
Now show thy progeny; if not to stand,
Cast thyself down; safely if Son of God:
For it is written, "He will give command
Concerning thee to his angels, in their hands
They shall uplift thee, lest at any time
Thou chance to dash thy foot against a stone."'
    To whom thus Jesus: 'Also it is written,   560
"Tempt not the Lord thy God,"' he said and stood.
But Satan smitten with amazement fell
As when Earth's son Antaeus (to compare

Small things with greatest) in Irassa strove
With Jove's Alcides, and oft foiled still rose,
Receiving from his mother Earth new strength,
Fresh from his fall, and fiercer grapple joined,
Throttled at length in the air, expired and fell;
So after many a foil the Tempter proud,
570   Renewing fresh assaults, amidst his pride
Fell whence he stood to see his victor fall.
And as that Theban monster that proposed
Her riddle, and him, who solved it not, devoured;
That once found out and solved, for grief and spite
Cast herself headlong from th' Ismenian steep,
So struck with dread and anguish fell the Fiend,
And to his crew, that sat consulting, brought
Joyless triumphals of his hoped success,
Ruin, and desperation, and dismay,
580   Who durst so proudly tempt the Son of God.
So Satan fell and straight a fiery globe
Of angels on full sail of wing flew nigh,
Who on their plumy vans received him soft
From his uneasy station, and upbore
As on a floating couch through the blithe air,
Then in a flow'ry valley set him down
On a green bank, and set before him spread
A table of celestial food, divine,
Ambrosial, fruits fetched from the Tree of Life,
590   And from the Fount of Life ambrosial drink,
That soon refreshed him wearied, and repaired
What hunger, if aught hunger had impaired,
Or thirst; and as he fed, angelic choirs
Sung Heavenly anthems of his victory
Over temptation, and the Tempter proud.
   'True image of the Father whether throned
In the bosom of bliss, and light of light
Conceiving, or remote from Heaven, enshrined
In fleshly tabernacle, and human form,
600   Wand'ring the wilderness, whatever place,
Habit, or state, or motion, still expressing

The Son of God, with Godlike force endued
Against th' attempter of thy Father's throne,
And thief of Paradise; him long of old
Thou didst debel, and down from Heav'n cast
With all his army; now thou hast avenged
Supplanted Adam, and by vanquishing
Temptation, hast regained lost Paradise,
And frustrated the conquest fraudulent:
He never more henceforth will dare set foot   610
In Paradise to tempt; his snares are broke:
For though that seat of earthly bliss be failed,
A fairer Paradise is founded now
For Adam and his chosen sons, whom thou
A Saviour art come down to re-install.
Where they shall dwell secure, when time shall be
Of Tempter and temptation without fear.
But thou, Infernal Serpent, shalt not long
Rule in the clouds; like an autumnal star
Or lightning thou shalt fall from heav'n trod down   620
Under his feet: for proof, ere this thou feel'st
Thy wound, yet not thy last and deadliest wound
By this repulse received, and hold'st in Hell
No triumph; in all her gates Abaddon rues
Thy bold attempt; hereafter learn with awe
To dread the Son of God: he all unarmed
Shall chase thee with the terror of his voice
From thy demoniac holds, possession foul,
Thee and thy legions; yelling they shall fly,
And beg to hide them in a herd of swine,   630
Lest he command them down into the deep
Bound, and to torment sent before their time.
Hail Son of the Most High, heir of both worlds,
Queller of Satan, on thy glorious work
Now enter, and begin to save mankind.'
    Thus they the Son of God our Saviour meek
Sung victor, and from Heavenly feast refreshed
Brought on his way with joy; he unobserved
Home to his mother's house private returned.

SAMSON AGONISTES

Of that Sort of Dramatic Poem which is Called Tragedy

Tragedy, as it was anciently composed, hath been ever held
the gravest, moralest, and most profitable of all other poems:
therefore said by Aristotle to be of power by raising pity and
fear, or terror, to purge the mind of those and such like passions,
that is to temper and reduce them to just measure with a kind
of delight, stirred up by reading or seeing those passions well
imitated. Nor is nature wanting in her own effects to make
good his assertion: for so in physic things of melancholic hue
and quality are used against melancholy, sour against sour, salt
to remove salt humours. Hence philosophers and other gravest
writers, as Cicero, Plutarch and others, frequently cite out of
tragic poets, both to adorn and illustrate their discourse. The
Apostle Paul himself thought it not unworthy to insert a verse
of Euripides into the text of Holy Scripture, I Cor. 15. 33, and
Paraeus commenting on the *Revelation*, divides the whole book
as a tragedy, into acts, distinguished each by a chorus of
Heavenly harpings and song between. Heretofore men in high-
est dignity have laboured not a little to be thought able to
compose a tragedy. Of that honour Dionysius the elder was no
less ambitious, than before of his attaining to the tyranny.
Augustus Caesar also had begun his *Ajax*, but unable to please
his own judgement with what he had begun, left it unfinished.
Seneca the philosopher is by some thought the author of those
tragedies (at least the best of them) that go under that name.
Gregory Nazianzen, a Father of the Church, thought it not
unbeseeming the sanctity of his person to write a tragedy, which

he entitled *Christ Suffering*. This is mentioned to vindicate
tragedy from the small esteem, or rather infamy, which in the
account of many it undergoes at this day with other common
interludes; happening through the poet's error of intermixing   30
comic stuff with tragic sadness and gravity; or introducing
trivial and vulgar persons, which by all judicious hath been
counted absurd; and brought in without discretion, corruptly
to gratify the people. And though ancient tragedy use no pro-
logue, yet using sometimes, in case of self-defence, or expla-
nation, that which Martial calls an epistle; in behalf of this
tragedy, coming forth after the ancient manner, much different
from what among us passes for best, thus much beforehand
may be epistled: that chorus is here introduced after the Greek
manner, not ancient only, but modern, and still in use among   40
the Italians. In the modelling therefore of this poem, with good
reason, the ancients and Italians are rather followed, as of much
more authority and fame. The measure of verse used in the
chorus is of all sorts, called by the Greeks *monostrophic*, or
rather *apolelymenon*, without regard had to *strophe*, *antis-
trophe*, or *epode*, which were a kind of stanzas framed only for
the music, then used with the chorus that sung; not essential to
the poem, and therefore not material; or being divided into
stanzas or pauses, they may be called *alloeostropha*. Division
into act and scene referring chiefly to the stage (to which this   50
work was never intended) is here omitted.

It suffices if the whole drama be found not produced beyond
the fifth act. Of the style and uniformity, and that commonly
called the plot, whether intricate or explicit, which is nothing
indeed but such economy, or disposition of the fable as may
stand best with verisimilitude and decorum; they only will best
judge who are not unacquainted with Aeschylus, Sophocles,
and Euripides, the three tragic poets unequalled yet by any,
and the best rule to all who endeavour to write tragedy. The
circumscription of time wherein the whole drama begins and   60
ends, is according to ancient rule, and best example, within the
space of twenty-four hours.

The Argument

Samson made captive, blind, and now in the prison at Gaza,
there to labour as in a common workhouse, on a festival day,
in the general cessation from labour, comes forth into the open
air, to a place nigh, somewhat retired, there to sit a while and
bemoan his condition. Where he happens at length to be visited
by certain friends and equals of his tribe, which make the
chorus, who seek to comfort him what they can; then by his
old father Manoa, who endeavours the like, and withal tells
him his purpose to procure his liberty by ransom; lastly, that
10   this feast was proclaimed by the Philistines as a day of thanks-
giving for their deliverance from the hands of Samson, which
yet more troubles him. Manoa then departs to prosecute his
endeavour with the Philistian lords for Samson's redemption;
who in the meanwhile is visited by other persons; and lastly by
a public officer to require his coming to the feast before the
lords and people, to play or show his strength in their presence;
he at first refuses, dismissing the public officer with absolute
denial to come; at length persuaded inwardly that this was from
God, he yields to go along with him, who came now the second
20   time with great threatenings to fetch him; the chorus yet remain-
ing on the place, Manoa returns full of joyful hope, to procure
ere long his son's deliverance: in the midst of which discourse
an Hebrew comes in haste confusedly at first; and afterward
more distinctly relating the catastrophe, what Samson had done
to the Philistines, and by accident to himself; wherewith the
tragedy ends.

The Persons

Samson
Manoa, the father of Samson
Dalila his wife
Harapha of Gath
Public Officer
Messenger
Chorus of Danites

The Scene before the Prison in Gaza

Samson. A little onward lend thy guiding hand
To these dark steps, a little further on;
For yonder bank hath choice of sun or shade;
There I am wont to sit, when any chance
Relieves me from my task of servile toil,
Daily in the common prison else enjoined me,
Where I a prisoner chained, scarce freely draw
The air imprisoned also, close and damp,
Unwholesome draught: but here I feel amends,
The breath of heav'n fresh blowing, pure and sweet,   10
With day-spring born; here leave me to respire.
This day a solemn feast the people hold
To Dagon their sea-idol, and forbid
Laborious works; unwillingly this rest
Their superstition yields me; hence with leave
Retiring from the popular noise, I seek
This unfrequented place to find some ease.
Ease to the body some, none to the mind
From restless thoughts, that like a deadly swarm
Of hornets armed, no sooner found alone,   20
But rush upon me thronging, and present
Times past, what once I was, and what am now.
O wherefore was my birth from Heaven foretold
Twice by an angel, who at last in sight
Of both my parents all in flames ascended
From off the altar, where an off'ring burned,
As in a fiery column charioting
His godlike presence, and from some great act
Or benefit revealed to Abraham's race?
Why was my breeding ordered and prescribed   30
As of a person separate to God,
Designed for great explóits; if I must die
Betrayed, captíved, and both my eyes put out,
Made of my enemies the scorn and gaze;
To grind in brazen fetters under task
With this Heav'n-gifted strength? O glorious strength

Put to the labour of a beast, debased
Lower than bond-slave! Promise was that I
Should Israel from Philistian yoke deliver;
40   Ask for this great deliverer now, and find him
Eyeless in Gaza at the mill with slaves,
Himself in bonds under Philistian yoke;
Yet stay, let me not rashly call in doubt
Divine prediction; what if all foretold
Had been fulfilled but through mine own default,
Whom have I to complain of but myself?
Who this high gift of strength committed to me,
In what part lodged, how easily bereft me,
Under the seal of silence could not keep,
50   But weakly to a woman must reveal it,
O'ercome with importunity and tears.
O impotence of mind, in body strong!
But what is strength without a double share
Of wisdom? Vast, unwieldy, burdensome,
Proudly secure, yet liable to fall
By weakest subtleties, not made to rule,
But to subserve where wisdom bears command.
God, when he gave me strength, to show withal
How slight the gift was, hung it in my hair.
60   But peace, I must not quarrel with the will
Of highest dispensation, which herein
Haply had ends above my reach to know:
Suffices that to me strength is my bane,
And proves the source of all my miseries;
So many, and so huge, that each apart
Would ask a life to wail, but chief of all,
O loss of sight, of thee I most complain!
Blind among enemies, O worse than chains,
Dungeon, or beggary, or decrepit age!
70   Light the prime work of God to me is extinct,
And all her various objects of delight
Annulled, which might in part my grief have eased;
Inferior to the vilest now become
Of man or worm; the vilest here excel me,

They creep, yet see; I dark in light exposed
To daily fraud, contempt, abuse and wrong,
Within doors, or without, still as a fool,
In power of others, never in my own;
Scarce half I seem to live, dead more than half.
O dark, dark, dark, amid the blaze of noon,   80
Irrecoverably dark, total eclipse
Without all hope of day!
O first-created beam, and thou great Word,
'Let there be light, and light was over all';
Why am I thus bereaved thy prime decree?
The sun to me is dark
And silent as the moon,
When she deserts the night
Hid in her vacant interlunar cave.
Since light so necessary is to life,   90
And almost life itself, if it be true
That light is in the soul,
She all in every part, why was the sight
To such a tender ball as th' eye confined?
So obvious and so easy to be quenched,
And not, as feeling, through all parts diffused,
That she might look at will through every pore?
Then had I not been thus exiled from light;
As in the land of darkness yet in light,
To live a life half dead, a living death,   100
And buried; but O yet more miserable!
Myself my sepulchre, a moving grave,
Buried, yet not exempt
By privilege of death and burial
From worst of other evils, pains and wrongs,
But made hereby obnoxious more
To all the miseries of life,
Life in captivity
Among inhuman foes.
But who are these? For with joint pace I hear   110
The tread of many feet steering this way;
Perhaps my enemies who come to stare

At my affliction, and perhaps to insult,
Their daily practice to afflict me more.
Chorus. This, this is he; softly a while,
Let us not break in upon him;
O change beyond report, thought, or belief!
See how he lies at random, carelessly diffused,
With languished head unpropped,
As one past hope, abandoned,
And by himself given over;
In slavish habit, ill-fitted weeds
O'erworn and soiled;
Or do my eyes misrepresent? Can this be he,
That heroic, that renowned,
Irresistible Samson? whom unarmed
No strength of man, or fiercest wild beast could
        withstand;
Who tore the lion, as the lion tears the kid,
Ran on embattled armies clad in iron,
And weaponless himself,
Made arms ridiculous, useless the forgery
Of brazen shield and spear, the hammered cuirass,
Chalybean-tempered steel, and frock of mail
Adamantean proof;
But safest he who stood aloof,
When insupportably his foot advanced,
In scorn of their proud arms and warlike tools,
Spurned them to death by troops. The bold Ascalonite
Fled from his lion ramp, old warriors turned
Their plated backs under his heel;
Or grovelling soiled their crested helmets in the dust.
Then with what trivial weapon came to hand,
The jaw of a dead ass, his sword of bone,
A thousand foreskins fell, the flower of Palestine
In Ramath-lechi famous to this day:
Then by main force pulled up, and on his shoulders
        bore
The gates of Azza, post and massy bar,
Up to the hill by Hebron, seat of giants old,

120

130

140

No journey of a sabbath day, and loaded so,
Like whom the Gentiles feign to bear up heaven.   150
Which shall I first bewail,
Thy bondage or lost sight,
Prison within prison
Inseparably dark?
Thou art become (O worst imprisonment!)
The dungeon of thyself; thy soul
(Which men enjoying sight oft without cause complain)
Imprisoned now indeed,
In real darkness of the body dwells,
Shut up from outward light   160
To incorporate with gloomy night;
For inward light alas
Puts forth no visual beam.
O mirror of our fickle state,
Since man on earth unparalleled!
The rarer thy example stands,
By how much from the top of wondrous glory,
Strongest of mortal men,
To lowest pitch of abject fortune thou art fall'n.
For him I reckon not in high estate   170
Whom long descent of birth
Or the sphere of fortune raises;
But thee whose strength, while virtue was her mate,
Might have subdued the earth,
Universally crowned with highest praises.
Samson. I hear the sound of words, their sense the air
Dissolves unjointed ere it reach my ear.
Chorus. He speaks, let us draw nigh. Matchless in might,
The glory late of Israel, now the grief;
We come thy friends and neighbours not unknown   180
From Eshtaol and Zora's fruitful vale
To visit or bewail thee, or if better,
Counsel or consolation we may bring,
Salve to thy sores; apt words have power to swage
The tumours of a troubled mind,
And are as balm to festered wounds.

Samson. Your coming, friends, revives me, for I learn
Now of my own experience, not by talk,
How counterfeit a coin they are who 'friends'
190   Bear in their superscription (of the most
I would be understood); in prosperous days
They swarm, but in adverse withdraw their head
Not to be found, though sought. Ye see, O friends,
How many evils have enclosed me round;
Yet that which was the worst now least afflicts me,
Blindness; for had I sight, confused with shame,
How could I once look up, or heave the head,
Who like a foolish pilot have shipwrecked
My vessel trusted to me from above,
200   Gloriously rigged; and for a word, a tear,
Fool, have divulged the secret gift of God
To a deceitful woman? Tell me friends,
Am I not sung and proverbed for a fool
In every street, do they not say, 'How well
Are come upon him his deserts'? Yet why?
Immeasurable strength they might behold
In me, of wisdom nothing more than mean;
This with the other should, at least, have paired,
These two proportioned ill drove me transverse.
210   *Chorus.* Tax not divine disposal; wisest men
Have erred, and by bad women been deceived;
And shall again, pretend they ne'er so wise.
Deject not then so overmuch thyself,
Who hast of sorrow thy full load besides;
Yet truth to say, I oft have heard men wonder
Why thou shouldst wed Philistian women rather
Than of thine own tribe fairer, or as fair,
At least of thy own nation, and as noble.
Samson. The first I saw at Timna, and she pleased
220   Me, not my parents, that I sought to wed,
The daughter of an infidel: they knew not
That what I motioned was of God; I knew
From intimate impúlse, and therefore urged
The marriage on; that by occasion hence

I might begin Israel's deliverance,
The work to which I was divinely called;
She proving false, the next I took to wife
(O that I never had! fond wish too late)
Was in the vale of Sorec, Dálila,
That specious monster, my accomplished snare.   230
I thought it lawful from my former act,
And the same end; still watching to oppress
Israel's oppressors: of what now I suffer
She was not the prime cause, but I myself,
Who vanquished with a peal of words (O weakness!)
Gave up my fort of silence to a woman.
Chorus. In seeking just occasion to provoke
The Philistine, thy country's enemy,
Thou never wast remiss, I bear thee witness:
Yet Israel still serves with all his sons.   240
Samson. That fault I take not on me, but transfer
On Israel's governors and heads of tribes,
Who seeing those great acts which God had done
Singly by me against their conquerors,
Acknowledged not, or not at all considered
Deliverance offered: I on th' other side
Used no ambition to commend my deeds;
The deeds themselves, though mute, spoke loud
        the doer;
But they persisted deaf, and would not seem
To count them things worth notice, till at length   250
Their lords the Philistines with gathered powers
Entered Judea seeking me, who then
Safe to the rock of Etham was retired,
Not flying, but forecasting in what place
To set upon them, what advantaged best;
Meanwhile the men of Judah to prevent
The harass of their land, beset me round;
I willingly on some conditions came
Into their hands, and they as gladly yield me
To the uncircumcised a welcome prey,   260
Bound with two cords; but cords to me were threads

Touched with the flame: on their whole host I flew
Unarmed, and with a trivial weapon felled
Their choicest youth; they only lived who fled.
Had Judah that day joined, or one whole tribe,
They had by this possessed the towers of Gath,
And lorded over them whom now they serve;
But what more oft in nations grown corrupt,
And by their vices brought to servitude,
270 Than to love bondage more than liberty,
Bondage with ease than strenuous liberty;
And to despise, or envy, or suspect
Whom God hath of his special favour raised
As their deliverer; if he aught begin,
How frequent to desert him, and at last
To heap ingratitude on worthiest deeds?
Chorus. Thy words to my remembrance bring
How Succoth and the fort of Penuel
Their great deliverer contemned,
280 The matchless Gideon in pursuit
Of Madian and her vanquished kings:
And how ingrateful Ephraim
Had dealt with Jephtha, who by argument,
Not worse than by his shield and spear
Defended Israel from the Ammonite,
Had not his prowess quelled their pride
In that sore battle when so many died
Without reprieve adjudged to death,
For want of well pronouncing *Shibboleth.*
290 *Samson.* Of such examples add me to the roll;
Me easily indeed mine may neglect,
But God's proposed deliverance not so.
Chorus. Just are the ways of God,
And justifiable to men;
Unless there be who think not God at all;
If any be, they walk obscure;
For of such doctrine never was there school,
But the heart of the fool,
And no man therein doctor but himself.

Yet more there be who doubt his ways not just,   300
As to his own edícts, found contradicting,
Then give the reins to wand'ring thought,
Regardless of his glory's diminution;
Till by their own perplexities involved
They ravel more, still less resolved,
But never find self-satisfying solution.

    As if they would confine th' Interminable,
And tie him to his own prescript,
Who made our laws to bind us, not himself,
And hath full right to exempt   310
Whom so it pleases him by choice
From national obstriction, without taint
Of sin, or legal debt;
For with his own laws he can best dispense.

    He would not else who never wanted means,
Nor in respect of th' enemy just cause
To set his people free,
Have prompted this heroic Nazarite,
Against his vow of strictest purity,
To seek in marriage that fallacious bride,   320
Unclean, unchaste.

    Down Reason then, at least vain reasonings
       down,
Though Reason here aver
That moral verdict quits her of unclean:
Unchaste was subsequent; her stain, not his.

    But see here comes thy reverend sire
With careful step, locks white as down,
Old Mánoa: advise
Forthwith how thou ought'st to receive him.
Samson. Ay me, another inward grief awaked,   330
With mention of that name renews th' assault.
Manoa. Brethren and men of Dan, for such ye seem,
Though in this uncouth place; if old respect,
As I suppose, towards your once gloried friend,
My son now captive, hither hath informed
Your younger feet, while mine cast back with age

Came lagging after; say if he be here.
Chorus. As signal now in low dejected state,
As erst in highest, behold him where he lies.
340 *Manoa.* O miserable change! Is this the man,
That invincible Samson, far renowned,
The dread of Israel's foes, who with a strength
Equivalent to angels' walked their streets,
None offering fight; who single combatant
Duelled their armies ranked in proud array,
Himself an army, now unequal match
To save himself against a coward armed
At one spear's length. O ever-failing trust
In mortal strength! And O what not in man
350 Deceivable and vain! Nay what thing good
Prayed for, but often proves our woe, our bane?
I prayed for children, and thought barrenness
In wedlock a reproach; I gained a son,
And such a son as all men hailed me happy;
Who would be now a father in my stead?
O wherefore did God grant me my request,
And as a blessing with such pomp adorned?
Why are his gifts desirable, to tempt
Our earnest prayers, then giv'n with solemn hand
360 As graces, draw a scorpion's tail behind?
For this did the angel twice descend? For this
Ordained thy nurture holy, as of a plant;
Select and sacred, glorious for a while,
The miracle of men: then in an hour
Ensnared, assaulted, overcome, led bound,
Thy foes' derision, captive, poor, and blind
Into a dungeon thrust, to work with slaves?
Alas methinks whom God hath chosen once
To worthiest deeds, if he through frailty err,
370 He should not so o'erwhelm, and as a thrall
Subject him to so foul indignities,
Be it but for honour's sake of former deeds.
Samson. Appoint not Heavenly disposition, father,
Nothing of all these evils hath befall'n me

But justly; I myself have brought them on,
Sole author I, sole cause: if aught seem vile,
As vile hath been my folly, who have profaned
The mystery of God giv'n me under pledge
Of vow, and have betrayed it to a woman,
A Canaanite, my faithless enemy.   380
This well I knew, nor was at all surprised,
But warned by oft experience: did not she
Of Timna first betray me, and reveal
The secret wrested from me in her heighth
Of nuptial love professed, carrying it straight
To them who had corrupted her, my spies,
And rivals? In this other was there found
More faith? who also in her prime of love,
Spousal embraces, vitiated with gold,
Though offered only, by the scent conceived   390
Her spurious first-born, treason against me?
Thrice she assayed with flattering prayers and sighs,
And amorous reproaches to win from me
My capital secret, in what part my strength
Lay stored, in what part summed, that she might
      know:
Thrice I deluded her, and turned to sport
Her importunity, each time perceiving
How openly, and with what impudence
She purposed to betray me, and (which was worse
Than undissembled hate) with what contempt   400
She sought to make me traitor to myself;
Yet the fourth time, when must'ring all her wiles,
With blandished parleys, feminine assaults,
Tongue-batteries, she surceased not day nor night
To storm me over-watched, and wearied out.
At times when men seek most repose and rest,
I yielded, and unlocked her all my heart,
Who with a grain of manhood well resolved
Might easily have shook off all her snares:
But foul effeminacy held me yoked   410
Her bond-slave; O indignity, O blot

To honour and religion! Servile mind
Rewarded well with servile punishment!
The base degree to which I now am fall'n,
These rags, this grinding, is not yet so base
As was my former servitude, ignoble,
Unmanly, ignominious, infamous,
True slavery, and that blindness worse than this,
That saw not how degenerately I served.
420 *Manoa.* I cannot praise thy marriage choices, son,
Rather approved them not; but thou didst plead
Divine impulsion prompting how thou might'st
Find some occasion to infest our foes.
I state not that; this I am sure; our foes
Found soon occasion thereby to make thee
Their captive, and their triumph; thou the sooner
Temptation found'st, or over-potent charms
To violate the sacred trust of silence
Deposited within thee; which to have kept
430 Tacit was in thy power; true; and thou bear'st
Enough, and more, the burden of that fault;
Bitterly hast thou paid, and still art paying
That rigid score. A worse thing yet remains:
This day the Philistines a popular feast
Here celebrate in Gaza; and proclaim
Great pomp, and sacrifice, and praises loud
To Dagon, as their god who hath delivered
Thee Samson bound and blind into their hands,
Them out of thine, who slew'st them many a slain.
440 So Dagon shall be magnified, and God,
Besides whom is no God, compared with idols,
Disglorified, blasphemed, and had in scorn
By th' idolatrous rout amidst their wine;
Which to have come to pass by means of thee,
Samson, of all thy sufferings think the heaviest,
Of all reproach the most with shame that ever
Could have befall'n thee and thy father's house.
Samson. Father, I do acknowledge and confess
That I this honour, I this pomp have brought

To Dagon, and advanced his praises high   450
Among the heathen round; to God have brought
Dishonour, obloquy, and oped the mouths
Of idolists and atheists; have brought scandal
To Israel, diffidence of God, and doubt
In feeble hearts, propense enough before
To waver, or fall off and join with idols;
Which is my chief affliction, shame and sorrow,
The anguish of my soul, that suffers not
Mine eye to harbour sleep, or thoughts to rest.
This only hope relieves me, that the strife   460
With me hath end; all the contést is now
'Twixt God and Dagon; Dagon hath presumed,
Me overthrown, to enter lists with God,
His deity comparing and preferring
Before the God of Abraham. He, be sure,
Will not connive, or linger, thus provoked,
But will arise and his great name assert:
Dagon must stoop, and shall ere long receive
Such a discomfit, as shall quite despoil him
Of all these boasted trophies won on me,   470
And with confusion blank his worshippers.
Manoa. With cause this hope relieves thee, and
        these words
I as a prophecy receive: for God,
Nothing more certain, will not long defer
To vindicate the glory of his name
Against all competition, nor will long
Endure it doubtful whether God be Lord,
Or Dagon. But for thee what shall be done?
Thou must not in the meanwhile here forgot
Lie in this miserable loathsome plight   480
Neglected. I already have made way
To some Philistian lords, with whom to treat
About thy ransom: well they may by this
Have satisfied their utmost of revenge
By pains and slaveries, worse than death inflicted
On thee, who now no more canst do them harm.

Samson. Spare that proposal, father, spare the trouble
Of that solicitation; let me here,
As I deserve, pay on my punishment;
490 And expiate, if possible, my crime,
Shameful garrulity. To have revealed
Secrets of men, the secrets of a friend,
How heinous had the fact been, how deserving
Contempt, and scorn of all, to be excluded
All friendship, and avoided as a blab,
The mark of fool set on his front!
But I God's counsel have not kept, his holy secret
Presumptuously have published, impiously,
Weakly at least, and shamefully: a sin
500 That Gentiles in their parables condemn
To their abyss and horrid pains confined.
Manoa. Be penitent and for thy fault contrite,
But act not in thy own affliction, son;
Repent the sin, but if the punishment
Thou canst avoid, self-preservation bids;
Or th' execution leave to high disposal,
And let another hand, not thine, exact
Thy penal forfeit from thyself; perhaps
God will relent, and quit thee all his debt;
510 Who evermore approves and more accepts
(Best pleased with humble and filial submission)
Him who imploring mercy sues for life,
Than who self-rigorous chooses death as due;
Which argues over-just, and self-displeased
For self-offence, more than for God offended.
Reject not then what offered means, who knows
But God hath set before us, to return thee
Home to thy country and his sacred house,
Where thou mayst bring thy off'rings, to avert
520 His further ire, with prayers and vows renewed.
Samson. His pardon I implore; but as for life,
To what end should I seek it? When in strength
All mortals I excelled, and great in hopes
With youthful courage and magnanimous thoughts

Of birth from Heav'n foretold and high explóits,
Full of divine instínct, after some proof
Of acts indeed heroic, far beyond
The sons of Anak, famous now and blazed,
Fearless of danger, like a petty god
I walked about admired of all and dreaded   530
On hostile ground, none daring my affront.
Then swoll'n with pride into the snare I fell
Of fair fallacious looks, venereal trains,
Softened with pleasure and voluptuous life;
At length to lay my head and hallowed pledge
Of all my strength in the lascivious lap
Of a deceitful concubine who shore me
Like a tame wether, all my precious fleece,
Then turned me out ridiculous, despoiled,
Shav'n, and disarmed among my enemies.   540
Chorus. Desire of wine and all delicious drinks,
Which many a famous warrior overturns,
Thou couldst repress, nor did the dancing ruby
Sparkling, out-poured, the flavour, or the smell,
Or taste that cheers the heart of gods and men,
Allure thee from the cool crystálline stream.
Samson. Wherever fountain or fresh current flowed
Against the eastern ray, translucent, pure
With touch ethereal of heaven's fiery rod
I drank, from the clear milky juice allaying   550
Thirst, and refreshed; nor envied them the grape
Whose heads that turbulent liquor fills with fumes.
Chorus. O madness, to think use of strongest wines
And strongest drinks our chief support of health,
When God with these forbidd'n made choice to rear
His mighty champion, strong above compare,
Whose drink was only from the liquid brook.
Samson. But what availed this temperance, not
    complete
Against another object more enticing?
What boots it at one gate to make defence,   560
And at another to let in the foe,

Effeminately vanquished? By which means,
Now blind, disheartened, shamed, dishonoured,
     quelled,
To what can I be useful, wherein serve
My nation, and the work from Heav'n imposed,
But to sit idle on the household hearth,
A burdenous drone; to visitants a gaze,
Or pitied object, these redundant locks
Robustious to no purpose clust'ring down,
570   Vain monument of strength; till length of years
And sedentary numbness craze my limbs
To a contemptible old age obscure.
Here rather let me drudge and earn my bread,
Till vermin or the draff of servile food
Consume me, and oft-invocated death
Hasten the welcome end of all my pains.
     Manoa. Wilt thou then serve the Philistines with that
          gift
Which was expressly giv'n thee to annoy them?
Better at home lie bed-rid, not only idle,
580   Inglorious, unemployed, with age outworn.
But God who caused a fountain at thy prayer
From the dry ground to spring, thy thirst to allay
After the brunt of battle, can as easy
Cause light again within thy eyes to spring,
Wherewith to serve him better than thou hast;
And I persuade me so; why else this strength
Miraculous yet remaining in those locks?
His might continues in thee not for naught,
Nor shall his wondrous gifts be frustrate thus.
590   *Samson.* All otherwise to me my thoughts portend,
That these dark orbs no more shall treat with light,
Nor th' other light of life continue long,
But yield to double darkness nigh at hand:
So much I feel my genial spirits droop,
My hopes all flat, nature within me seems
In all her functions weary of herself;
My race of glory run, and race of shame,

And I shall shortly be with them that rest.
Manoa. Believe not these suggestions, which proceed
From anguish of the mind and humours black,   600
That mingle with thy fancy. I however
Must not omit a father's timely care
To prosecute the means of thy deliverance
By ransom or how else: meanwhile be calm,
And healing words from these thy friends admit.
Samson. O that torment should not be confined
To the body's wounds and sores
With maladies innumerable
In heart, head, breast, and reins;
But must secret passage find   610
To th' inmost mind,
There exercise all his fierce accidents,
And on her purest spirits prey,
As on entrails, joints, and limbs,
With answerable pains, but more intense,
Though void of corporal sense.
    My griefs not only pain me
As a ling'ring disease,
But finding no redress, ferment and rage,
Nor less than wounds immedicable   620
Rankle, and fester, and gangrene,
To black mortification.
Thoughts, my tormentors, armed with deadly stings
Mangle my apprehensive tenderest parts,
Exasperate, exulcerate, and raise
Dire inflammation which no cooling herb
Or med'cinal liquor can assuage,
Nor breath of vernal air from snowy alp.
Sleep hath forsook and giv'n me o'er
To death's benumbing opium as my only cure.   630
Thence faintings, swoonings of despair,
And sense of Heav'n's desertion.
    I was his nursling once and choice delight,
His destined from the womb,
Promised by Heavenly message twice descending.

Under his special eye
Abstemious I grew up and thrived amain;
He led me on to mightiest deeds
Above the nerve of mortal arm
640   Against the uncircumcised, our enemies.
But now hath cast me off as never known,
And to those cruel enemies,
Whom I by his appointment had provoked,
Left me all helpless with th' irreparable loss
Of sight, reserved alive to be repeated
The subject of their cruelty or scorn.
Nor am I in the list of them that hope;
Hopeless are all my evils, all remédiless;
This one prayer yet remains, might I be heard,
650   No long petition, speedy death,
The close of all my miseries, and the balm.
Chorus. Many are the sayings of the wise
In ancient and in modern books enrolled,
Extolling patience as the truest fortitude;
And to the bearing well of all calamities,
All chances incident to man's frail life;
Consolatories writ
With studied argument, and much persuasion sought,
Lenient of grief and anxious thought;
660   But with th' afflicted in his pangs their sound
Little prevails, or rather seems a tune
Harsh, and of dissonant mood from his complaint,
Unless he feel within
Some source of consolation from above;
Secret refreshings, that repair his strength,
And fainting spirits uphold.
    God of our fathers, what is man!
That thou towards him with hand so various,
Or might I say contrarious,
670   Temper'st thy providence through his short course,
Not evenly, as thou rul'st
The angelic orders and inferior creatures mute,
Irrational and brute.

Nor do I name of men the common rout,
That wand'ring loose about
Grow up and perish, as the summer fly,
Heads without name, no more remembered;
But such as thou hast solemnly elected,
With gifts and graces eminently adorned
To some great work, thy glory,   680
And people's safety, which in part they effect:
Yet toward these thus dignified, thou oft
Amidst their heighth of noon,
Changest thy countenance and thy hand, with no regard
Of highest favours past
From thee on them, or them to thee of service.
   Nor only dost degrade them, or remit
To life obscured, which were a fair dismission,
But throw'st them lower than thou didst exalt them
       high,
Unseemly falls in human eye,   690
Too grievous for the trespass or omission;
Oft leav'st them to the hostile sword
Of heathen and profane, their carcasses
To dogs and fowls a prey, or else captíved:
Or to th' unjust tribunals, under change of times,
And condemnation of the ingrateful multitude.
If these they 'scape, perhaps in poverty
With sickness and disease thou bow'st them down,
Painful diseases and deformed,
In crude old age;   700
Though not disordinate, yet causeless suff'ring
The punishment of dissolute days; in fine,
Just or unjust, alike seem miserable,
For oft alike, both come to evil end.
   So deal not with this once thy glorious champion,
The image of thy strength, and mighty minister.
What do I beg? How hast thou dealt already?
Behold him in this state calamitous, and turn
His labours, for thou canst, to peaceful end.
   But who is this, what thing of sea or land?   710

Female of sex it seems,
That so bedecked, ornate, and gay,
Comes this way sailing
Like a stately ship
Of Tarsus, bound for th' isles
Of Javan or Gadire
With all her bravery on, and tackle trim,
Sails filled, and streamers waving,
Courted by all the winds that hold them play,
720   An amber scent of odorous perfume
Her harbinger, a damsel train behind;
Some rich Philistian matron she may seem,
And now at nearer view, no other certain
Than Dálila thy wife.
Samson. My wife, my traitress, let her not come
    near me.
Chorus. Yet on she moves, now stands and eyes thee
    fixed,
About t' have spoke, but now, with head declined
Like a fair flower surcharged with dew, she weeps,
And words addressed seem into tears dissolved,
730   Wetting the borders of her silken veil:
But now again she makes address to speak.
Dalila. With doubtful feet and wavering resolution
I came, still dreading thy displeasure, Samson,
Which to have merited, without excuse,
I cannot but acknowledge; yet if tears
May expiate (though the fact more evil drew
In the perverse event than I foresaw),
My penance hath not slackened, though my pardon
No way assured. But conjugal affection,
740   Prevailing over fear and timorous doubt,
Hath led me on desirous to behold
Once more thy face, and know of thy estate.
If aught in my ability may serve
To lighten what thou suffer'st, and appease
Thy mind with what amends is in my power,
Though late, yet in some part to recompense

My rash but more unfortunate misdeed.
Samson. Out, out hyena; these are thy wonted arts,
And arts of every woman false like thee,
To break all faith, all vows, deceive, betray,   750
Then as repentant to submit, beseech,
And reconcilement move with feigned remorse,
Confess, and promise wonders in her change,
Not truly penitent, but chief to try
Her husband, how far urged his patience bears,
His virtue or weakness which way to assail:
Then with more cautious and instructed skill
Again transgresses, and again submits;
That wisest and best men, full oft beguiled,
With goodness principled not to reject   760
The penitent, but ever to forgive,
Are drawn to wear out miserable days,
Entangled with a poisonous bosom snake,
If not by quick destruction soon cut off
As I by thee, to ages an example.
Dalila. Yet hear me Samson; not that I endeavour
To lessen or extenuate my offence,
But that on th' other side if it be weighed
By itself, with aggravations not surcharged,
Or else with just allowance counterpoised,   770
I may, if possible, thy pardon find
The easier towards me, or thy hatred less.
First granting, as I do, it was a weakness
In me, but incident to all our sex,
Curiosity, inquisitive, importune
Of secrets, then with like infirmity
To publish them, both common female faults;
Was it not weakness also to make known
For importunity, that is for naught,
Wherein consisted all thy strength and safety?   780
To what I did thou show'dst me first the way.
But I to enemies revealed, and should not.
Nor shouldst thou have trusted that to woman's frailty:
Ere I to thee, thou to thyself wast cruel.

Let weakness then with weakness come to parle,
So near related, or the same of kind;
Thine forgive mine, that men may censure thine
The gentler, if severely thou exact not
More strength from me than in thyself was found.
790 And what if love, which thou interpret'st hate,
The jealousy of love, powerful of sway
In human hearts, nor less in mine towards thee,
Caused what I did? I saw thee mutable
Of fancy, feared lest one day thou wouldst leave me
As her at Timna, sought by all means therefore
How to endear, and hold thee to me firmest:
No better way I saw than by importuning
To learn thy secrets, get into my power
Thy key of strength and safety: thou wilt say,
800 'Why then revealed?' I was assured by those
Who tempted me, that nothing was designed
Against thee but safe custody and hold:
That made for me; I knew that liberty
Would draw thee forth to perilous enterprises,
While I at home sat full of cares and fears
Wailing thy absence in my widowed bed;
Here I should still enjoy thee day and night,
Mine and love's prisoner, not the Philistines',
Whole to myself, unhazarded abroad,
810 Fearless at home of partners in my love.
These reasons in love's law have passed for good,
Though fond and reasonless to some perhaps;
And love hath oft, well meaning, wrought much woe,
Yet always pity or pardon hath obtained.
Be not unlike all others, not austere
As thou art strong, inflexible as steel.
If thou in strength all mortals dost exceed,
In uncompassionate anger do not so.
Samson. How cunningly the sorceress displays
820 Her own transgressions, to upbraid me mine!
That malice not repentance brought thee hither,
By this appears: I gave, thou say'st, th' example,

I led the way; bitter reproach, but true,
I to myself was false ere thou to me;
Such pardon therefore as I give my folly,
Take to thy wicked deed: which when thou seest
Impartial, self-severe, inexorable,
Thou wilt renounce thy seeking, and much rather
Confess it feigned; weakness is thy excuse,
And I believe it, weakness to resist   830
Philistian gold: if weakness may excuse,
What murderer, what traitor, parricide,
Incestuous, sacrilegious, but may plead it?
All wickedness is weakness: that plea therefore
With God or man will gain thee no remission.
But love constrained thee; call it furious rage
To satisfy thy lust: love seeks to have love;
My love how couldst thou hope, who took'st the way
To raise in me inexpiable hate,
Knowing, as needs I must, by thee betrayed?   840
In vain thou striv'st to cover shame with shame,
Or by evasions thy crime uncover'st more.
Dalila. Since thou determin'st weakness for no plea
In man or woman, though to thy own condemning,
Hear what assaults I had, what snares besides,
What sieges girt me round, ere I consented;
Which might have awed the best-resolved of men,
The constantest to have yielded without blame.
It was not gold, as to my charge thou lay'st,
That wrought with me: thou know'st the magistrates   850
And princes of my country came in person,
Solicited, commanded, threatened, urged,
Adjured by all the bonds of civil duty
And of religion, pressed how just it was,
How honourable, how glorious to entrap
A common enemy, who had destroyed
Such numbers of our nation: and the priest
Was not behind, but ever at my ear,
Preaching how meritorious with the gods
It would be to ensnare an irreligious   860

Dishonourer of Dagon: what had I
To oppose against such powerful arguments?
Only my love of thee held long debate;
And combated in silence all these reasons
With hard contést: at length that grounded maxim
So rife and celebrated in the mouths
Of wisest men; that to the public good
Private respects must yield; with grave authority
Took full possession of me and prevailed;
870   Virtue, as I thought, truth, duty so enjoining.
    Samson. I thought where all thy circling wiles
        would end;
In feigned religion, smooth hypocrisy.
But had thy love, still odiously pretended,
Been, as it ought, sincere, it would have taught thee
Far other reasonings, brought forth other deeds.
I before all the daughters of my tribe
And of my nation chose thee from among
My enemies, loved thee, as too well thou knew'st,
Too well; unbosomed all my secrets to thee,
880   Not out of levity, but overpow'red
By thy request, who could deny thee nothing;
Yet now am judged an enemy. Why then
Didst thou at first receive me for thy husband?
Then, as since then, thy country's foe professed:
Being once a wife, for me thou wast to leave
Parents and country; nor was I their subject,
Nor under their protection but my own;
Thou mine, not theirs: if aught against my life
Thy country sought of thee, it sought unjustly,
890   Against the law of nature, law of nations,
No more thy country, but an impious crew
Of men conspiring to uphold their state
By worse than hostile deeds, violating the ends
For which our country is a name so dear;
Not therefore to be obeyed. But zeal moved thee;
To please thy gods thou didst it; gods unable
To acquit themselves and prosecute their foes

But by ungodly deeds, the contradiction
Of their own deity, gods cannot be:
Less therefore to be pleased, obeyed, or feared;   900
These false pretéxts and varnished colours failing,
Bare in thy guilt how foul must thou appear!
Dalila. In argument with men a woman ever
Goes by the worse, whatever be her cause.
Samson. For want of words no doubt, or lack of breath;
Witness when I was worried with thy peals.
Dalila. I was a fool, too rash, and quite mistaken
In what I thought would have succeeded best.
Let me obtain forgiveness of thee, Samson,
Afford me place to show what recompense   910
Towards thee I intend for what I have misdone,
Misguided; only what remains past cure
Bear not too sensibly, nor still insist
To afflict thyself in vain: though sight be lost,
Life yet hath many solaces, enjoyed
Where other senses want not their delights
At home in leisure and domestic ease,
Exempt from many a care and chance to which
Eyesight exposes daily men abroad.
I to the lords will intercede, not doubting   920
Their favourable ear, that I may fetch thee
From forth this loathsome prison-house, to abide
With me, where my redoubled love and care
With nursing diligence, to me glad office,
May ever tend about thee to old age
With all things grateful cheered, and so supplied,
That what by me thou hast lost thou least shalt miss.
Samson. No, no, of my condition take no care;
It fits not; thou and I long since are twain;
Nor think me so unwary or accursed   930
To bring my feet again into the snare
Where once I have been caught; I know thy trains
Though dearly to my cost, thy gins, and toils;
Thy fair enchanted cup, and warbling charms
No more on me have power, their force is nulled,

So much of adder's wisdom I have learnt
To fence my ear against thy sorceries.
If in my flower of youth and strength, when all men
Loved, honoured, feared me, thou alone could hate me
940   Thy husband, slight me, sell me, and forgo me;
How wouldst thou use me now, blind, and thereby
Deceivable, in most things as a child
Helpless, thence easily contemned, and scorned,
And last neglected? How wouldst thou insult
When I must live uxorious to thy will
In perfect thraldom, how again betray me,
Bearing my words and doings to the lords
To gloss upon, and censuring, frown or smile?
This jail I count the house of liberty
950   To thine whose doors my feet shall never enter.
Dalila. Let me approach at least, and touch thy hand.
Samson. Not for thy life, lest fierce remembrance wake
My sudden rage to tear thee joint by joint.
At distance I forgive thee, go with that;
Bewail thy falsehood, and the pious works
It hath brought forth to make thee memorable
Among illustrious women, faithful wives:
Cherish thy hastened widowhood with the gold
Of matrimonial treason: so farewell.
960   *Dalila.* I see thou art implacable, more deaf
To prayers than winds and seas; yet winds to seas
Are reconciled at length, and sea to shore:
Thy anger, unappeasable, still rages,
Eternal tempest never to be calmed.
Why do I humble thus myself, and suing
For peace, reap nothing but repulse and hate?
Bid go with evil omen and the brand
Of infamy upon my name denounced?
To mix with thy concernments I desist
970   Henceforth, nor too much disapprove my own.
Fame, if not double-faced, is double-mouthed,
And with contráry blast proclaims most deeds;
On both his wings, one black, th' other white,

Bears greatest names in his wild airy flight.
My name perhaps among the circumcised
In Dan, in Judah, and the bordering tribes,
To all posterity may stand defamed,
With malediction mentioned, and the blot
Of falsehood most unconjugal traduced.
But in my country where I most desire,   980
In Ecron, Gaza, Asdod, and in Gath
I shall be named among the famousest
Of women, sung at solemn festivals,
Living and dead recorded, who to save
Her country from a fierce destroyer chose
Above the faith of wedlock-bands; my tomb
With odours visited and annual flowers.
Not less renowned than in Mount Ephraim,
Jael, who with inhospitable guile
Smote Sisera sleeping, through the temples nailed.   990
Nor shall I count it heinous to enjoy
The public marks of honour and reward
Conferred upon me for the piety
Which to my country I was judged to have shown.
At this whoever envies or repines,
I leave him to his lot, and like my own.
Chorus. She's gone, a manifest serpent by her sting
Discovered in the end, till now concealed.
Samson. So let her go, God sent her to debase me,
And aggravate my folly who committed   1000
To such a viper his most sacred trust
Of secrecy, my safety, and my life.
Chorus. Yet beauty, though injurious, hath strange
        power,
After offence returning, to regain
Love once possessed, nor can be easily
Repulsed, without much inward passion felt
And secret sting of amorous remorse.
Samson. Love-quarrels oft in pleasing concord end,
Not wedlock-treachery endangering life.
Chorus. It is not virtue, wisdom, valour, wit,   1010

Strength, comeliness of shape, or amplest merit
That woman's love can win or long inherit;
But what it is, hard is to say,
Harder to hit,
(Which way soever men refer it)
Much like thy riddle, Samson, in one day
Or seven, though one should musing sit;
    If any of these or all, the Timnian bride
Had not so soon preferred
1020 Thy paranymph, worthless to thee compared,
Successor in thy bed,
Nor both so loosely disallied
Their nuptials, nor this last so treacherously
Had shorn the fatal harvest of thy head.
Is it for that such outward ornament
Was lavished on their sex, that inward gifts
Were left for haste unfinished, judgement scant,
Capacity not raised to apprehend
Or value what is best
1030 In choice, but oftest to affect the wrong?
Or was too much of self-love mixed,
Of constancy no root infixed,
That either they love nothing, or not long?
    Whate'er it be, to wisest men and best
Seeming at first all Heavenly under virgin veil,
Soft, modest, meek, demure,
Once joined, the contrary she proves, a thorn
Intestine, far within defensive arms
A cleaving mischief, in his way to virtue
1040 Adverse and turbulent; or by her charms
Draws him awry enslaved
With dotage, and his sense depraved
To folly and shameful deeds which ruin ends.
What pilot so expért but needs must wreck
Embarked with such a steers-mate at the helm?
    Favoured of Heav'n who finds
One virtuous rarely found,
That in domestic good combines:

Happy that house! His way to peace is smooth:
But virtue which breaks through all opposition,   1050
And all temptation can remove,
Most shines and most is ácceptáble above.
     Therefore God's universal law
Gave to the man despotic power
Over his female in due awe,
Nor from that right to part an hour,
Smile she or lour:
So shall he least confusion draw
On his whole life, not swayed
By female usurpation, nor dismayed.   1060
     But had we best retire? I see a storm.
Samson. Fair days have oft contracted wind and rain.
Chorus. But this another kind of tempest brings.
Samson. Be less abstruse, my riddling days are past.
Chorus. Look now for no enchanting voice, nor fear
The bait of honeyed words; a rougher tongue
Draws hitherward; I know him by his stride,
The giant Hárapha of Gath, his look
Haughty as is his pile high-built and proud.
Comes he in peace? What wind hath blown him
          hither   1070
I less conjecture than when first I saw
The sumptuous Dálila floating this way:
His habit carries peace, his brow defiance.
Samson. Or peace or not, alike to me he comes.
Chorus. His fraught we soon shall know, he now
          arrives.
Harapha. I come not Samson, to condole thy chance,
As these perhaps, yet wish it had not been,
Though for no friendly intent. I am of Gath,
Men call me Hárapha, of stock renowned
As Og or Anak and the Emims old   1080
That Kiriathaim held; thou know'st me now
If thou at all art known. Much I have heard
Of thy prodigious might and feats performed
Incredible to me, in this displeased,

That I was never present on the place
Of those encounters, where we might have tried
Each other's force in camp or listed field:
And now am come to see of whom such noise
Hath walked about, and each limb to survey,
1090 If thy appearance answer loud report.
Samson. The way to know were not to see but taste.
Harapha. Dost thou already single me? I thought
Gyves and the mill had tamed thee. O that fortune
Had brought me to the field where thou art famed
To have wrought such wonders with an ass's jaw;
I should have forced thee soon wish other arms,
Or left thy carcass where the ass lay thrown:
So had the glory of prowess been recovered
To Palestine, won by a Philistine
1100 From the unforeskinned race, of whom thou bear'st
The highest name for valiant acts; that honour
Certain to have won by mortal duel from thee,
I lose, prevented by thy eyes put out.
Samson. Boast not of what thou wouldst have done,
        but do
What then thou wouldst; thou seest it in thy hand.
Harapha. To combat with a blind man I disdain,
And thou hast need much washing to be touched.
Samson. Such usage as your honourable lords
Afford me assassinated and betrayed,
1110 Who durst not with their whole united powers
In fight withstand me single and unarmed,
Nor in the house with chamber ambushes
Close-banded durst attack me, no not sleeping,
Till they had hired a woman with their gold
Breaking her marriage faith to circumvent me.
Therefore without feigned shifts let be assigned
Some narrow place enclosed, where sight may give
        thee,
Or rather flight, no great advantage on me;
Then put on all thy gorgeous arms, thy helmet
1120 And brigandine of brass, thy broad habergeon,

Vant-brace and greaves, and gauntlet, add thy spear
A weaver's beam, and seven-times-folded shield,
I only with an oaken staff will meet thee,
And raise such outcries on thy clattered iron,
Which long shall not withhold me from thy head,
That in a little time while breath remains thee,
Thou oft shalt wish thyself at Gath to boast
Again in safety what thou wouldst have done
To Samson, but shalt never see Gath more.
Harapha. Thou durst not thus disparage glorious
    arms   1130
Which greatest heroes have in battle worn,
Their ornament and safety, had not spells
And black enchantments, some magician's art,
Armed thee or charmed thee strong, which thou from
    Heaven
Feign'dst at thy birth was giv'n thee in thy hair,
Where strength can least abide, though all thy hairs
Were bristles ranged like those that ridge the back
Of chafed wild boars or ruffled porcupines.
Samson. I know no spells, use no forbidden arts;
My trust is in the living God who gave me   1140
At my nativity this strength, diffused
No less through all my sinews, joints and bones,
Than thine, while I preserved these locks unshorn,
The pledge of my unviolated vow.
For proof hereof, if Dagon be thy god,
Go to his temple, invocate his aid
With solemnest devotion, spread before him
How highly it concerns his glory now
To frustrate and dissolve these magic spells,
Which I to be the power of Israel's God   1150
Avow, and challenge Dagon to the test,
Offering to combat thee his champion bold,
With th' utmost of his godhead seconded:
Then thou shalt see, or rather to thy sorrow
Soon feel, whose God is strongest, thine or mine.
Harapha. Presume not on thy God, whate'er he be,

Thee he regards not, owns not, hath cut off
Quite from his people, and delivered up
Into thy enemies' hand, permitted them
1160 To put out both thine eyes, and fettered send thee
Into the common prison, there to grind
Among the slaves and asses thy comrádes,
As good for nothing else; no better service
With those thy boist'rous locks, no worthy match
For valour to assail, nor by the sword
Of noble warrior, so to stain his honour,
But by the barber's razor best subdued.
Samson. All these indignities, for such they are
From thine, these evils I deserve and more,
1170 Acknowledge them from God inflicted on me
Justly, yet despair not of his final pardon
Whose ear is ever open; and his eye
Gracious to re-admit the suppliant;
In confidence whereof I once again
Defy thee to the trial of mortal fight,
By combat to decide whose god is God,
Thine or whom I with Israel's sons adore.
Harapha. Fair honour that thou dost thy God, in
      trusting
He will accept thee to defend his cause,
1180 A murderer, a revolter, and a robber.
Samson. Tongue-doughty giant, how dost thou
      prove me these?
Harapha. Is not thy nation subject to our lords?
Their magistrates confessed it, when they took thee
As a league-breaker and delivered bound
Into our hands: for hadst thou not committed
Notorious murder on those thirty men
At Ascalon, who never did thee harm,
Then like a robber stripp'dst them of their robes?
The Philistines, when thou hadst broke the league,
1190 Went up with armèd powers thee only seeking,
To others did no violence nor spoil.
Samson. Among the daughters of the Philistines

I chose a wife, which argued me no foe;
And in your city held my nuptial feast:
But your ill-meaning politician lords,
Under pretence of bridal friends and guests,
Appointed to await me thirty spies,
Who threat'ning cruel death constrained the bride
To wring from me and tell to them my secret,
That solved the riddle which I had proposed.   1200
When I perceived all set on enmity,
As on my enemies, wherever chanced,
I used hostility, and took their spoil
To pay my underminers in their coin.
My nation was subjected to your lords.
It was the force of conquest; force with force
Is well ejected when the conquered can.
But I a private person, whom my country
As a league-breaker gave up bound, presumed
Single rebellion and did hostile acts.   1210
I was no private but a person raised
With strength sufficient and command from Heav'n
To free my country; if their servile minds
Me their deliverer sent would not receive,
But to their masters gave me up for nought,
Th' unworthier they; whence to this day they serve.
I was to do my part from Heav'n assigned,
And had performed it if my known offence
Had not disabled me, not all your force:
These shifts refuted, answer thy appellant,   1220
Though by his blindness maimed for high attempts,
Who now defies thee thrice to single fight,
As a petty enterprise of small enforce.
Harapha. With thee a man condemned, a slave
      enrolled,
Due by the law to capital punishment?
To fight with thee no man of arms will deign.
Samson. Cam'st thou for this, vain boaster, to
      survey me,
To descant on my strength, and give thy verdict?

Come nearer, part not hence so slight informed;
1230 But take good heed my hand survey not thee.
Harapha. O Baäl-zebub! Can my ears unused
Hear these dishonours, and not render death?
Samson. No man withholds thee, nothing from thy
          hand
Fear I incurable; bring up thy van,
My heels are fettered, but my fist is free.
Harapha. This insolence other kind of answer fits.
Samson. Go baffled coward, lest I run upon thee,
Though in these chains, bulk without spirit vast,
And with one buffet lay thy structure low,
1240 Or swing thee in the air, then dash thee down
To the hazard of thy brains and shattered sides.
Harapha. By Astaroth ere long thou shalt lament
These braveries in irons loaden on thee.
Chorus. His giantship is gone somewhat crestfall'n,
Stalking with less unconscionable strides,
And lower looks, but in a sultry chafe.
Samson. I dread him not, nor all his giant brood,
Though fame divulge him father of five sons
All of gigantic size, Goliah chief.
1250 *Chorus.* He will directly to the lords, I fear,
And with malicious counsel stir them up
Some way or other yet further to afflict thee.
Samson. He must allege some cause, and offered fight
Will not dare mention, lest a question rise
Whether he durst accept the offer or not,
And that he durst not plain enough appeared.
Much more affliction than already felt
They cannot well impose, nor I sustain;
If they intend advantage of my labours,
1260 The work of many hands, which earns my keeping
With no small profit daily to my owners.
But come what will, my deadliest foe will prove
My speediest friend, by death to rid me hence,
The worst that he can give, to me the best.
Yet so it may fall out, because their end

Is hate, not help to me, it may with mine
Draw their own ruin who attempt the deed.
Chorus. O how comely it is and how reviving
To the spirits of just men long oppressed!
When God into the hands of their deliverer   1270
Puts invincible might
To quell the mighty of the earth, th' oppressor,
The brute and boist'rous force of violent men
Hardy and industrious to support
Tyrannic power, but raging to pursue
The righteous and all such as honour truth;
He all their ammunition
And feats of war defeats
With plain heroic magnitude of mind
And celestial vigour armed;   1280
Their armouries and magazines contemns,
Renders them useless, while
With wingèd expedition
Swift as the lightning glance he executes
His errand on the wicked, who surprised
Lose their defence distracted and amazed.
    But patience is more oft the exercise
Of saints, the trial of their fortitude,
Making them each his own deliverer,
And victor over all   1290
That tyranny or fortune can inflict;
Either of these is in thy lot,
Samson, with might endued
Above the sons of men; but sight bereaved
May chance to number thee with those
Whom patience finally must crown.
This idol's day hath been to thee no day of rest,
    Labouring thy mind
More than the working day thy hands,
And yet perhaps more trouble is behind.   1300
For I descry this way
Some other tending, in his hand
A sceptre or quaint staff he bears,

Comes on amain, speed in his look.
By his habit I discern him now
A public officer, and now at hand.
His message will be short and voluble.
Officer. Hebrews, the prisoner Samson here I seek.
Chorus. His manacles remark him, there he sits.
1310   *Officer.* Samson, to thee our lords thus bid me say;
This day to Dagon is a solemn feast,
With sacrifices, triumph, pomp, and games;
Thy strength they know surpassing human rate,
And now some public proof thereof require
To honour this great feast, and great assembly;
Rise therefore with all speed and come along,
Where I will see thee heartened and fresh clad
To appear as fits before th' illustrious lords.
Samson. Thou know'st I am an Hebrew, therefore tell
    them,
1320   Our Law forbids at their religious rites
My presence; for that cause I cannot come.
Officer. This answer, be assured, will not content
    them.
Samson. Have they not sword-players, and every sort
Of gymnic artists, wrestlers, riders, runners,
Jugglers and dancers, antics, mummers, mimics,
But they must pick me out with shackles tired,
And over-laboured at their public mill,
To make them sport with blind activity?
Do they not seek occasion of new quarrels
1330   On my refusal to distress me more,
Or make a game of my calamities?
Return the way thou cam'st, I will not come.
Officer. Regard thyself, this will offend them highly.
Samson. Myself? My conscience and internal peace.
Can they think me so broken, so debased
With corporal servitude, that my mind ever
Will condescend to such absurd commands?
Although their drudge, to be their fool or jester,
And in my midst of sorrow and heart-grief

To show them feats, and play before their god,   1340
The worst of all indignities, yet on me
Joined with extreme contempt? I will not come.
Officer. My message was imposed on me with speed,
Brooks no delay: is this thy resolution?
Samson. So take it with what speed thy message
     needs.
Officer. I am sorry what this stoutness will produce.
Samson. Perhaps thou shalt have cause to sorrow
     indeed.
Chorus. Consider, Samson; matters now are strained
Up to the heighth, whether to hold or break;
He's gone, and who knows how he may report   1350
Thy words by adding fuel to the flame?
Expect another message more imperious,
More lordly thund'ring than thou well wilt bear.
Samson. Shall I abuse this consecrated gift
Of strength, again returning with my hair
After my great transgression, so requite
Favour renewed, and add a greater sin
By prostituting holy things to idols;
A Nazarite in place abominable
Vaunting my strength in honour to their Dagon?   1360
Besides, how vile, contemptible, ridiculous,
What act more execrably unclean, profane?
Chorus. Yet with this strength thou serv'st the
     Philistines,
Idolatrous, uncircumcised, unclean.
Samson. Not in their idol-worship, but by labour
Honest and lawful to deserve my food
Of those who have me in their civil power.
Chorus. Where the heart joins not, outward acts defile
     not.
Samson. Where outward force constrains, the sentence
     holds;
But who constrains me to the temple of Dagon,   1370
Not dragging? The Philistian lords command.
Commands are no constraints. If I obey them,

I do it freely; venturing to displease
God for the fear of man, and man prefer,
Set God behind: which in his jealousy
Shall never, unrepented, find forgiveness.
Yet that he may dispense with me or thee
Present in temples at idolatrous rites
For some important cause, thou need'st not doubt.
Chorus. How thou wilt here come off surmounts my
1380   reach.
Samson. Be of good courage, I begin to feel
Some rousing motions in me which dispose
To something extraordinary my thoughts.
I with this messenger will go along,
Nothing to do, be sure, that may dishonour
Our Law, or stain my vow of Nazarite.
If there be aught of presage in the mind,
This day will be remarkable in my life
By some great act, or of my days the last.
1390 *Chorus.* In time thou hast resolved, the man returns.
Officer. Samson, this second message from our lords
To thee I am bid say. Art thou our slave,
Our captive, at the public mill our drudge,
And dar'st thou at our sending and command
Dispute thy coming? Come without delay;
Or we shall find such engines to assail
And hamper thee, as thou shalt come of force,
Though thou wert firmlier fastened than a rock.
Samson. I could be well content to try their art,
1400 Which to no few of them would prove pernicious.
Yet knowing their advantages too many,
Because they shall not trail me through their streets
Like a wild beast, I am content to go.
Masters' commands come with a power resistless
To such as owe them absolute subjection;
And for a life who will not change his purpose?
(So mutable are all the ways of men)
Yet this be sure, in nothing to comply
Scandalous or forbidden in our Law.

Officer. I praise thy resolution, doff these links: 1410
By this compliance thou wilt win the lords
To favour, and perhaps to set thee free.
Samson. Brethren farewell, your company along
I will not wish, lest it perhaps offend them
To see me girt with friends; and how the sight
Of me as of a common enemy,
So dreaded once, may now exasperate them
I know not. Lords are lordliest in their wine;
And the well-feasted priest then soonest fired
With zeal, if aught religion seem concerned: 1420
No less the people on their holy-days
Impetuous, insolent, unquenchable;
Happen what may, of me expect to hear
Nothing dishonourable, impure, unworthy
Our God, our Law, my nation, or myself;
The last of me or no I cannot warrant.
Chorus. Go, and the Holy One
Of Israel be thy guide
To what may serve his glory best, and spread his
          name
Great among the heathen round: 1430
Send thee the angel of thy birth, to stand
Fast by thy side, who from thy father's field
Rode up in flames after his message told
Of thy conception, and be now a shield
Of fire; that Spirit that first rushed on thee
In the camp of Dan
Be efficacious in thee now at need.
For never was from Heaven imparted
Measure of strength so great to mortal seed,
As in thy wondrous actions hath been seen.   1440
But wherefore comes old Mánoa in such haste
With youthful steps? Much livelier than erewhile
He seems: supposing here to find his son,
Or of him bringing to us some glad news?
Manoa. Peace with you brethren; my inducement hither
Was not at present here to find my son,

By order of the lords new parted hence
To come and play before them at their feast.
I heard all as I came; the city rings,
1450   And numbers thither flock; I had no will,
Lest I should see him forced to things unseemly.
But that which moved my coming now, was chiefly
To give ye part with me what hope I have
With good success to work his liberty.
Chorus. That hope would much rejoice us to partake
With thee; say reverend sire, we thirst to hear.
Manoa. I have attempted one by one the lords
Either at home, or through the high street passing,
With supplication prone and father's tears
1460   To accept of ransom for my son their prisoner;
Some much averse I found and wondrous harsh,
Contemptuous, proud, set on revenge and spite;
That part most reverenced Dagon and his priests;
Others more moderate seeming, but their aim
Private reward, for which both god and state
They easily would set to sale; a third
More generous far and civil, who confessed
They had enough revenged, having reduced
Their foe to misery beneath their fears,
1470   The rest was magnanimity to remit,
If some convenient ransom were proposed.
What noise or shout was that? It tore the sky.
Chorus. Doubtless the people shouting to behold
Their once great dread, captive, and blind before them,
Or at some proof of strength before them shown.
Manoa. His ransom, if my whole inheritance
May compass it, shall willingly be paid
And numbered down: much rather I shall choose
To live the poorest in my tribe, than richest,
1480   And he in that calamitous prison left.
No, I am fixed not to part hence without him.
For his redemption all my patrimony,
If need be, I am ready to forgo
And quit: not wanting him, I shall want nothing.

Chorus. Fathers are wont to lay up for their sons,
Thou for thy son art bent to lay out all;
Sons wont to nurse their parents in old age,
Thou in old age car'st how to nurse thy son,
Made older than thy age through eyesight lost.
Manoa. It shall be my delight to tend his eyes,   1490
And view him sitting in the house, ennobled
With all those high explóits by him achieved,
And on his shoulders waving down those locks,
That of a nation armed the strength contained:
And I persuade me God had not permitted
His strength again to grow up with his hair
Garrisoned round about him like a camp
Of faithful soldiery, were not his purpose
To use him further yet in some great service,
Not to sit idle with so great a gift   1500
Useless, and thence ridiculous about him.
And since his strength with eyesight was not lost,
God will restore him eyesight to his strength.
Chorus. Thy hopes are not ill-founded nor seem vain
Of his delivery, and thy joy thereon
Conceived, agreeable to a father's love,
In both which we, as next, participate.
Manoa. I know your friendly minds and – O what
     noise!
Mercy of Heav'n what hideous noise was that?
Horribly loud unlike the former shout.   1510
Chorus. Noise call you it or universal groan
As if the whole inhabitation perished;
Blood, death, and deathful deeds are in that noise,
Ruin, destruction at the utmost point.
Manoa. Of ruin indeed methought I heard the noise,
O it continues, they have slain my son.
Chorus. Thy son is rather slaying them; that outcry
From slaughter of one foe could not ascend.
Manoa. Some dismal accident it needs must be;
What shall we do, stay here or run and see?   1520
Chorus. Best keep together here, lest running thither

We unawares run into danger's mouth.
This evil on the Philistines is fall'n,
From whom could else a general cry be heard?
The sufferers then will scarce molest us here;
From other hands we need not much to fear.
What if his eyesight (for to Israel's God
Nothing is hard) by miracle restored,
He now be dealing dole among his foes,
1530 And over heaps of slaughtered walk his way?
Manoa. That were a joy presumptuous to be thought.
Chorus. Yet God hath wrought things as incredible
For his people of old; what hinders now?
Manoa. He can I know, but doubt to think he will;
Yet hope would fain subscribe, and tempts belief.
A little stay will bring some notice hither.
Chorus. Of good or bad so great, of bad the sooner;
For evil news rides post, while good news baits.
And to our wish I see one hither speeding,
1540 An Hebrew, as I guess, and of our tribe.
Messenger. O whither shall I run, or which way fly
The sight of this so horrid spectacle
Which erst my eyes beheld and yet behold?
For dire imagination still pursues me.
But providence or instinct of nature seems,
Or reason though disturbed, and scarce consulted,
To have guided me aright, I know not how,
To thee first reverend Mánoa, and to these
My countrymen, whom here I knew remaining,
1550 As at some distance from the place of horror,
So in the sad event too much concerned.
Manoa. The accident was loud, and here before thee
With rueful cry, yet what it was we hear not;
No preface needs, thou seest we long to know.
Messenger. It would burst forth, but I recover breath
And sense distract, to know well what I utter.
Manoa. Tell us the sum, the circumstance defer.
Messenger. Gaza yet stands, but all her sons are fall'n,
All in a moment overwhelmed and fall'n.

Manoa. Sad, but thou know'st to Israelites not
    saddest   1560
The desolation of a hostile city.
Messenger. Feed on that first, there may in grief be
    surfeit.
Manoa. Relate by whom.
Messenger.   By Samson.
Manoa.   That still lessens
The sorrow, and converts it nigh to joy.
Messenger. Ah Mánoa I refrain, too suddenly
To utter what will come at last too soon;
Lest evil tidings with too rude irruption
Hitting thy agèd ear should pierce too deep.
Manoa. Suspense in news is torture, speak them out.
Messenger. Then take the worst in brief, Samson is
    dead.   1570
Manoa. The worst indeed, O all my hope's defeated
To free him hence! But death who sets all free
Hath paid his ransom now and full discharge.
What windy joy this day had I conceived
Hopeful of his delivery, which now proves
Abortive as the first-born bloom of spring
Nipped with the lagging rear of winter's frost.
Yet ere I give the reins to grief, say first,
How died he? Death to life is crown or shame.
All by him fell thou say'st; by whom fell he,   1580
What glorious hand gave Samson his death's
    wound?
Messenger. Unwounded of his enemies he fell.
Manoa. Wearied with slaughter then or how? Explain.
Messenger. By his own hands.
Manoa.   Self-violence? What cause
Brought him so soon at variance with himself
Among his foes?
Messenger.   Inevitable cause
At once both to destroy and be destroyed;
The edifice where all were met to see him
Upon their heads and on his own he pulled.

1590   *Manoa.* O lastly over-strong against thyself!
       A dreadful way thou took'st to thy revenge.
       More than enough we know; but while things yet
       Are in confusion, give us if thou canst,
       Eye-witness of what first or last was done,
       Relation more particular and distinct.
       Messenger. Occasions drew me early to this city,
       And as the gates I entered with sunrise,
       The morning trumpets festival proclaimed
       Through each high street; little I had dispatched
1600   When all abroad was rumoured that this day
       Samson should be brought forth to show the people
       Proof of his mighty strength in feats and games;
       I sorrowed at his captive state, but minded
       Not to be absent at that spectacle.
       The building was a spacious theatre
       Half round on two main pillars vaulted high,
       With seats where all the lords and each degree
       Of sort, might sit in order to behold;
       The other side was open, where the throng
1610   On banks and scaffolds under sky might stand;
       I among these aloof obscurely stood.
       The feast and noon grew high, and sacrifice
       Had filled their hearts with mirth, high cheer, and
            wine,
       When to their sports they turned. Immediately
       Was Samson as a public servant brought,
       In their state livery clad; before him pipes
       And timbrels; on each side went armèd guards,
       Both horse and foot before him and behind
       Archers, and slingers, cataphracts and spears.
1620   At sight of him the people with a shout
       Rifted the air clamouring their god with praise,
       Who had made their dreadful enemy their thrall.
       He patient but undaunted where they led him,
       Came to the place, and what was set before him
       Which without help of eye might be assayed,
       To heave, pull, draw, or break, he still performed

All with incredible, stupendious force,
None daring to appear antagonist.
At length for intermission sake they led him
Between the pillars; he his guide requested   1630
(For so from such as nearer stood we heard)
As over-tired to let him lean a while
With both his arms on those two massy pillars
That to the archèd roof gave main support.
He unsuspicious led him; which when Samson
Felt in his arms, with head a while inclined,
And eyes fast fixed he stood, as one who prayed,
Or some great matter in his mind revolved.
At last with head erect thus cried aloud,
'Hitherto, lords, what your commands imposed   1640
I have performed, as reason was, obeying,
Not without wonder or delight beheld.
Now of my own accord such other trial
I mean to show you of my strength, yet greater;
As with amaze shall strike all who behold.'
This uttered, straining all his nerves he bowed;
As with the force of winds and waters pent,
When mountains tremble, those two massy pillars
With horrible convulsion to and fro,
He tugged, he shook, till down they came and drew   1650
The whole roof after them, with burst of thunder
Upon the heads of all who sat beneath,
Lords, ladies, captains, counsellors, or priests,
Their choice nobility and flower, not only
Of this but each Philistian city round
Met from all parts to solemnize this feast.
Samson with these immixed, inevitably
Pulled down the same destruction on himself;
The vulgar only 'scaped who stood without.
Chrous. O dearly-bought revenge, yet glorious!   1660
Living or dying thou hast fulfilled
The work for which thou wast foretold
To Israel, and now li'st victorious
Among thy slain self-killed,

Not willingly, but tangled in the fold
Of dire Necessity, whose law in death conjoined
Thee with thy slaughtered foes in number more
Than all thy life had slain before.
Semichorus. While their hearts were jocund and
    sublime,
1670   Drunk with idolatry, drunk with wine,
And fat regorged of bulls and goats,
Chanting their idol, and preferring
Before our living Dread who dwells
In Silo his bright sanctuary:
Among them he a spirit of frenzy sent,
Who hurt their minds,
And urged them on with mad desire
To call in haste for their destroyer;
They only set on sport and play
1680   Unweetingly importuned
Their own destruction to come speedy upon them.
So fond are mortal men
Fall'n into wrath divine,
As their own ruin on themselves to invite,
Insensate left, or to sense reprobate,
And with blindness internal struck.
Semichorus. But he though blind of sight,
Despised and thought extinguished quite,
With inward eyes illuminated,
1690   His fiery virtue roused
From under ashes into sudden flame,
And as an evening dragon came,
Assailant on the perchèd roosts,
And nests in order ranged
Of tame villatic fowl; but as an eagle
His cloudless thunder bolted on their heads.
So virtue giv'n for lost,
Depressed, and overthrown, as seemed,
Like that self-begotten bird
1700   In the Arabian woods embossed,
That no second knows nor third,

And lay erewhile a holocaust,
From out her ashy womb now teemed,
Revives, reflourishes, then vigorous most
When most unactive deemed,
And though her body die, her fame survives,
A secular bird ages of lives.
Manoa. Come, come, no time for lamentation now,
Nor much more cause; Samson hath quit himself
Like Samson, and heroically hath finished   1710
A life heroic, on his enemies
Fully revenged, hath left them years of mourning,
And lamentation to the sons of Caphtor
Through all Philistian bounds. To Israel
Honour hath left, and freedom, let but them
Find courage to lay hold on this occasion;
To himself and father's house eternal fame;
And which is best and happiest yet, all this
With God not parted from him, as was feared,
But favouring and assisting to the end.   1720
Nothing is here for tears, nothing to wail
Or knock the breast, no weakness, no contempt,
Dispraise, or blame, nothing but well and fair,
And what may quiet us in a death so noble.
Let us go find the body where it lies
Soaked in his enemies' blood, and from the stream
With lavers pure and cleansing herbs wash off
The clotted gore. I with what speed the while
(Gaza is not in plight to say us nay)
Will send for all my kindred, all my friends,   1730
To fetch him hence and solemnly attend
With silent obsequy and funeral train
Home to his father's house: there will I build him
A monument, and plant it round with shade
Of laurel ever green, and branching palm,
With all his trophies hung, and acts enrolled
In copious legend, or sweet lyric song.
Thither shall all the valiant youth resort,
And from his memory inflame their breasts

1740 To matchless valour and adventures high:
The virgins also shall on feastful days
Visit his tomb with flowers, only bewailing
His lot unfortunate in nuptial choice,
From whence captivity and loss of eyes.
Chorus. All is best, though we oft doubt,
What th' unsearchable dispose
Of highest wisdom brings about,
And ever best found in the close.
Oft he seems to hide his face,
1750 But unexpectedly returns
And to his faithful champion hath in place
Bore witness gloriously; whence Gaza mourns
And all that band them to resist
His uncontrollable intent;
His servants he with new acquist
Of true experience from this great event
With peace and consolation hath dismissed,
And calm of mind all passion spent.

Notes

Abbreviations

I have used the following abbreviations of specific manuscripts and editions of Milton's works:

BMS	Bridgewater Manuscript of *A Masque*
1667	*Paradise Lost* (first edition)
1674	*Paradise Lost* (second edition)
MS	The Manuscript of *Paradise Lost*, Book I
TMS	The Trinity Manuscript
1637	*A Maske Presented at Ludlow Castle* (1637)
1638	*Justa Edouardo King naufrago* (1638)
1645	*Poems of Mr John Milton* (1645)
1671	*Paradise Regain'd. A Poem in IV Books. To which is added Samson Agonistes* (1671)
1673	*Poems, &c. Upon Several Occasions* (1673)

The following abbreviations are used for titles of works by Milton.

Nativity	*On the Morning of Christ's Nativity*
PL	*Paradise Lost*
PR	*Paradise Regained*
SA	*Samson Agonistes*

Unless otherwise stated, all biblical citations are from the Authorized King James version.

POEMS 1645

'On the Morning of Christ's Nativity. Composed 1629.'

Milton began this poem before dawn on Christmas Day, 1629. It is placed first in both *1645* and *1673*.

5.   *holy sages*: Hebrew prophets.
6.   *deadly forfeit*: Sentence of death (for Adam's Fall).
23.   *star-led wizards*: The Magi.
24.   *prevent*: Come before.
48.   *turning sphere*: Outermost of the revolving Ptolemaic spheres surrounding our universe.
49.   *harbinger*: (1) Forerunner; (2) one sent before a lord to commandeer a lodging.
50.   *turtle*: Turtle-dove. Like the *myrtle* (51), an attribute of Venus.
53.   *No war*: Peace prevailed over the Roman world at the time of Christ's birth.
56.   *hookèd*: Scythed.
64.   *whist*: Silent, still.
68.   *birds of calm*: Halcyons (kingfishers). The sea was thought to remain calm during their winter nesting period.
71.   *influence*: Ethereal fluid thought to stream from the stars and affect humankind.
74.   *Lucifer*: Venus, the morning star (with a glance at Satan, the other Lucifer).
83.   *Sun*: The pun on 'Son' had biblical justification in Malachi 4:2.
84.   *axle-tree*: Axle of the sun's chariot.
86.   *Or ere*: Before.
89.   *Pan*: Greek god of shepherds, glossed as Christ in Spenser's *Shepheardes Calender*.
90.   *kindly*: (1) Lovingly; (2) as one of their kind.
92.   *silly*: Simple, rustic.
100. *close*: End of a musical phrase.
103. *Cynthia*: The moon. The *airy region* beneath her *hollow round* (sphere) is the sublunary world of *Nature*, subject to decay. The Music of the Spheres should be audible only above the moon; hence Nature's surprise at hearing it. See ll. 125–32.
104. *won*: (1) Persuaded; (2) rescued, redeemed.
116. *unexpressive*: Inexpressible.
122. *hinges*: Poles of the earth's axis.
140. *peering*: (1) Looking narrowly; (2) just appearing.
142. *return*: Astraea, goddess of Justice, fled the earth after the Golden

Age. Virgil announces her return in his 'Messianic' eclogue, which Christians read as a prophecy of Christ's birth.

146. *tissued*: Woven with gold or silver thread.

149. *Fate*: That which God has spoken (Latin *fari*, 'to speak').

151. *infancy*: Including the Latin sense 'unspeaking' (*fari*, 'to speak').

168. *Th' old Dragon*: 'The dragon, that old serpent, which is the Devil, and Satan' (Rev. 20:2).

172. *Swinges*: Lashes.

173. *The oracles are dumb*: Ancient tradition held that the pagan oracles had ceased with Christ.

186. *Genius*: Local deity.

191. *lars and lemures*: Gods and ancestral spirits of the Roman household.

194. *flamens*: Roman priests.

197. *Peor and Baälim*: Canaanite sun-gods (Baälim being the plural form of Baal).

199. *twice-battered god*: Dagon, the Philistine god whose idol was twice thrown down by God.

200. *Ashtaroth*: Plural form of Ashtoreth (Astarte), the Phoenician moon-goddess.

203. *Hammon*: Ammon, an Egyptian god depicted as a ram (hence *horn*).

204. *Thammuz*: The Phoenician Adonis, lover of Astarte (Venus).

205. *Moloch*: Ammonite god, supposedly worshipped with human sacrifice. See *PL*, I, 392–403.

217. *sacred chest*: Osiris's image was carried around in a small casket.

218. *shroud*: (1) Winding sheet; (2) place of shelter.

220. *ark*: Chest (parodying the ark of the covenant).

223. *eyn*: Eyes (archaic plural).

226. *Typhon*: (1) In Egyptian myth, the murderer of Osiris; (2) in Greek myth, a terrifying serpent.

228. *swaddling bands*: Alluding to the infant Hercules, who strangled snakes in his cradle.

'On Time'

Date unknown (though usually dated 1633). In *TMS* Milton wrote (and deleted) the subtitle: 'to be set on a clock case'.

1. *Fly*: (1) Pass rapidly; (2) flee.

3. *plummet*: A lead weight whose slow descent impels a clock.

4. *womb*: Stomach. Chronos (Time) was identified with Cronos, who devoured his children.

12. *individual*: (1) Inseparable; (2) peculiar to a particular person.

14. *sincerely*: Purely.
18. *happy-making sight*: Beatific vision.
21. *Attired*: Crowned (a common confusion with 'tiara').

'At a Solemn Music'

Date unknown (usually dated 1633, with 'On Time', but conjectures range from 1631 to 1637). The modern equivalent of the title would be 'At a Sacred Concert'.

1. *Sirens*: Plato imagines eight celestial Sirens who create the Music of the Spheres (*Republic*, X).
     pledges: (1) Assurances; (2) offspring.
2. *Sphere-borne*: In TMS (all three drafts); 'Sphere-born' in 1645 and 1673. 'Born' is supported by *pledges*, but *borne* points more clearly to Plato's Sirens, who are carried by the spheres.
6. *concent*: Harmony.
7. *Ay*: For all eternity.
22. *swayed*: Ruled (but *motion swayed ... stood* also suggests the precariousness of innocence).
23. *diapason*: Harmony of the octave (associated with Pythagoras and the Music of the Spheres).
27. *consort*: (1) Harmony; (2) company of musicians; (3) spouse (the Church as Bride of Christ).

'Song. On May Morning'

Dated variously between 1629 and 1631 (probably written on May Day). May is both the month and the May Queen presiding over the May Day dance.

'On Shakespeare. 1630'

Milton's first published English poem; it appeared anonymously in the Second Folio of Shakespeare (1632) and with Milton's initials in *Poems: Written by Wil. Shakespeare, Gent.* (1640). The present title is from *1645* and *1673*.

4. *ypointing*: The 'y' is an archaism, here used inaccurately, since the Middle English prefix was used before the past (not present) participle.
5. *son of Memory*: The nine Muses were daughters of Memory (Mnemosyne).
10. *easy numbers*: Inspired verses.
11. *unvalued*: Invaluable. See note to *PL* IV, 493.
12. *Delphic lines*: Apollo, god of poetry, had his oracle at Delphi.

'On the University Carrier'

Thomas Hobson died on 1 January 1631, aged eighty-six, having carried passengers between London and Cambridge for sixty years. His insistence that customers take the horse nearest the door gave rise to the phrase 'Hobson's choice'.

1. *girt*: A leather belt securing a saddle to a horse.
5. *shifter*: (1) Trickster; (2) mover.
8. *Bull*: Bull Inn, Bishopsgate (Hobson's London terminus).
11. *lately*: The plague closed the university in 1630.
14. *chamberlain*: Attendant in charge of bedchambers at an inn.

'L'Allegro'

'The cheerful man'. The title designates the state of mind invoked in the poem. The same is true of 'Il Penseroso' ('The contemplative man'). The date of the companion poems is unknown. They may have been written while Milton was in Hammersmith (1632–5) or Horton (1635–8).

1. *Melancholy*: In Galenic medicine, a physiological condition caused by an excess of bile. It could lead to depression.
2. *Cerberus*: The many-headed hound of Hades. His name means 'heart-eating'.
5. *uncouth cell*: Desolate cave or den of a wild beast.
8. *low-browed*: Beetling.
10. *Cimmerian*: Homer's Cimmerians live in a land of perpetual night.
12. *yclept*: Named. *Euphrosyne*: 'Mirth' (one of the three Graces).
19. *playing*: Having sex. Zephyr is the west wind, Aurora the dawn.
24. *buxom*: Jolly, well-favoured.
27. *Cranks*: Verbal tricks.
28. *Becks*: Beckonings, 'come-ons'.
29. *Hebe*: Goddess of youth.
34. *fantastic*: Making elaborate movements.
40. *unreprovèd*: Irreproachable. See note to *PL*, IV, 493.
45. *in spite of sorrow*: In defiance of sorrow (not 'despite an existing sorrow').
55. *hoar*: Grey with mist.
60. *state*: Stately progress (as of a monarch).
62. *dight*: Dressed.
67. *tells his tale*: (1) Counts his sheep; (2) tells his story.
75. *pied*: Parti-coloured.
80. *Cynosure*: Centre of attraction (originally, a name for the Pole Star).

83–8. *Where Corydon ... the sheaves*: Milton's rustics all have stock pastoral names. *Corydon* and *Thyrsis* are men, *Phyllis* and *Thestylis* are women.

91. *secure*: Carefree.

94. *rebecks*: Fiddles (an early form, with three strings).

102. *Mab*: Queen of the fairies; *junkets*: cream cheeses.

104. *friar's lantern*: Will-o'-the-wisp.

105. *drudging goblin*: Robin Goodfellow. The *cream-bowl* (106) is his traditional reward for household chores.

109. *end*: Put (corn) into a barn.

110. *lubber*: Drudge, scullion (with a play on Robin's other name, 'Lob-lie-by-the-fire').

111. *chimney*: Fireplace.

113. *crop-full*: Filled to repletion.

120. *weeds*: Clothes.

122. *Rain influence*: The ladies' eyes are imagined as stars. See note to 'Nativity', 71.

125. *Hymen*: God of marriage. His *clear* (bright) torch is a good omen.

132. *sock*: Slipper worn by the Greek comic actor, here a metonymy for comedy.

136. *Lydian*: A musical mode deemed relaxing (by Horace) and morally lax (by Plato).

139. *bout*: Circuit.

145–50. *That Orpheus' self ... Eurydice*: Eurydice was killed by a snake on her wedding day. Orpheus sought her in Hades and so moved Pluto with his song that Pluto agreed to release her on condition that Orpheus not look back until he reached the upper world. Orpheus looked back and so lost her again.

'Il Penseroso'

See headnote to 'L'Allegro'.

3. *bestead*: Help.

6. *fond*: Foolish.

10. *pensioners*: Attendants.

14. *hit*: Suit, fit.

18. *Memnon's sister*: Memnon was a black Ethiopian king who fought for Troy. Later myth gave him a sister, Himera.

19. *queen*: Cassiopeia, stellified when she boasted of being more beautiful than the Nereids.

23. *Vesta*: Virgin goddess of the hearth.

29–30. *Ida's ... Jove*: Saturn ruled the world from Mount Ida in

Crete. The Golden Age ended when he was overthrown by his
son Jove.

33. *grain*: Dye.

35. *cypress lawn*: Fine black material used for mourning clothes.

43. *cast*: Glance, expression.

44. *fast*: fixedly.

48. *Ay*: For all eternity.

55. *hist*: An exclamation used to enjoin silence.

56. *Philomel*: The nightingale (Philomela was turned into a nightin-
gale after Tereus raped her).

59. *Cynthia*: The moon; *dragon yoke*: Diana, goddess of the moon,
was sometimes identified with Hecate, goddess of witchcraft,
who drove a chariot drawn by dragons.

73. *plat*: Plot, patch.

74. *curfew*: Bell rung at 8 or 9 p.m. as a sign to extinguish fires.

76. *sullen*: Of a deep or mournful tone.

77. *air*: Weather.

83. *bellman's drowsy charm*: Nightwatchman's drowsy incantation.

87. *outwatch the Bear*: Stay up all night. Ursa Major never sets.

88. *thrice-great Hermes*: Hermes Trismegistus, supposed author of
ancient mystical writings translated by Marsilio Ficino in 1463.

88-9. *unsphere . . . Plato*: Summon Plato from his celestial sphere.

93. *daemons*: Spirits (not necessarily evil) presiding over the
elements.

98. *pall*: (1) Royal mantle; (2) the tragic actor's robe (Latin *palla*).

99. *Thebes*: The scene of tragedies about Oedipus and his descen-
dants.

   Pelops' line: The royal house of Mycenae, including Agamem-
non, Orestes and Electra.

102. *buskined*: The buskin was a high boot worn by Greek tragic
actors.

104. *Musaeus*: Mythical Greek poet, son of Orpheus.

109. *him*: Chaucer, whose Squire's Tale is unfinished.

113. *virtuous*: Magical.

120. *more is meant than meets the ear*: OED's earliest instance of the
phrase (which here refers to allegory).

122. *civil-suited*: Soberly dressed.

123. *tricked and frounced*: Adorned and curly-headed.

124. *Attic boy*: Cephalus, lover of Aurora, goddess of the dawn.

127. *still*: Gentle.

134. *Sylvan*: Silvanus, Roman god of woods.

145. *consort*: Harmony.
154. *Genius*: Local deity.
156. *pale*: Enclosure.
157. *embowèd roof*: Vaulted roof of a chapel.
158. *antique*: (1) Venerable; (2) grotesque; *massy proof*: Massive strength.
159. *dight*: Decorated.
170–71. *spell / Of*: Study (with a suggestion of magic spells).

Sonnet I ('O nightingale')

Usually dated *c.* 1628–30.
4.   *Hours*: The Horae, goddesses of the seasons.
5–7. *Thy liquid notes ... love*: Tradition held that it was lucky to hear the nightingale before the cuckoo (which was associated with cuckoldry).
6.   *shallow*: Shrill.
9.   *rude*: Unmusical.

Sonnet VII ('How soon hath Time')

Line 2 suggests that the poem was composed on or soon after Milton's twenty-third birthday (9 December 1631), but most critics now date the poem to 9 December 1632 (when Milton ceased being twenty-three).
2.   *Stol'n*: Including the intransitive sense – 'stolen (himself) away'.
3.   *full career*: Full speed.
4.   *bud or blossom*: A common metaphor for poetry (from Latin *flos*).
5.   *deceive*: Misrepresent.
10–11. *even / To*: (1) Level with, no less and no more; (2) all the way to (as in Latin *usque ad* and Shakespeare, Sonnet 116: 'even to the edge of doom'). The latter sense hints at *high* aspirations.

Sonnet VIII ('Captain or colonel')

Date could be November 1642. After the battle of Edgehill (23 October 1642), the Parliamentarian army retreated, leaving the road to London undefended. Charles advanced as far as Turnham Green (a few miles from Milton's house on Aldersgate Street), but retreated when the London trained bands assembled to meet him (13 November). The title 'When the assault was intended to the city' appears only in *TMS*, not the printed editions.
10. *Emathian conqueror*: Alexander the Great. When he sacked

Thebes in 335 BC, he spared only the house where Pindar had lived. *Emathia* was the Homeric name for Macedonia.

13. *Electra's poet*: Euripides. When Sparta defeated Athens in 404 BC, the Thebans urged the Spartans to destroy the city and enslave its people. Athens was saved when a man from Phocis moved the conquerors to compassion by singing a chorus from Euripides' *Electra*.

Sonnet IX ('Lady that in the prime')

Dated to *c.* 1642–5. The subject's identity is unknown.

2. *broad way*: 'Broad is the way, that leadeth to destruction' (Matt. 7: 13).

5. *better part with Mary and with Ruth*: Mary sat at Jesus's feet while her sister Martha served. When Martha complained, Jesus said: 'Mary hath chosen that good part' (Luke 10:42). Ruth chose to abandon her home in Moab and live with Naomi, her Hebrew mother-in-law.

6. *overween*: Are presumptuous.

7. *fret their spleen*: Consume themselves with spite.

9–14. *Thy care is fixed . . . wise and pure*: Alluding to the parable of the wise and foolish virgins (Matt. 25: 1–13).

Sonnet X ('Daughter to that good Earl')

Dated *c.* 1642–5. The fair copy in *TMS* (but not the printed versions) is entitled 'To the Lady Margaret Ley'. Edward Phillips, Milton's nephew and biographer, reports that Lady Margaret and her husband were Milton's near neighbours and close friends in the 1640s, after his wife had left him.

1. *Earl*: James Ley (1550–1629), Earl of Marlborough from 1626.

3. *fee*: Bribe.

5. *sad breaking of that Parliament*: Charles I dissolved Parliament amid much tumult on 10 March 1629. The Earl died four days later, aged seventy-nine. Charles ruled without Parliament for the next eleven years.

7. *Chaeronea*: Where Philip of Macedon defeated Athens and Thebes in 338 BC, thus ending Greek liberty.

8. *old man eloquent*: The Athenian orator Isocrates. He died (aged ninety-eight) soon after Chaeronea, supposedly of grief on hearing the news.

'Lycidas'

Dated November 1637 (in *TMS*). On 10 August 1637, Edward King, a Fellow of Christ's College, Cambridge (and a former classmate of Milton), drowned in the Irish Sea, aged twenty-five. His body was not recovered. *Lycidas* was first published in a commemorative volume of Latin, Greek and English poems by King's Cambridge contemporaries entitled *Justa Edouardo King naufrago* (1638). Milton's poem was placed last in the volume. 'Lycidas' is a stock name in pastoral.

1. *laurels*: An emblem of poetry, sacred to Apollo.
2. *myrtles brown, with ivy*: Myrtles were an emblem of love, sacred to Venus. Ivy was an emblem of immortality and learning, sacred to Bacchus.
3. *crude*: Unripe.
13. *welter*: Of a dead body: to be tossed on the waves (*OED*).
14. *meed of some melodious tear*: The reward for an elegy (a common metonymy).
15. *Sisters*: The Muses. The *well* is their sacred fountain (either Aganippe or the Pierian spring).
29. *Batt'ning*: Feeding.
33. *Tempered*: (1) Attuned; (2) restrained within bounds.
36. *Damoetas*: A stock pastoral name (here, probably a Cambridge tutor, perhaps the quasi-anagrammatic Joseph Mead).
40. *gadding*: Straggling.
46. *taint-worm*: An intestinal parasite fatal to *weanling* (newly weaned) calves.
48. *whitethorn blows*: Hawthorn blossoms.
52. *steep*: Bardsey Island.
54. *Mona*: Anglesey.
55. *Deva*: the Dee (*wizard* because it was anciently credited with powers of divination).
58–63. *What could the Muse ... Lesbian shore*: Orpheus was torn to pieces by female worshippers of Bacchus after he rejected their sexual advances.
68–9. *Amaryllis ... Neaera*: Stock pastoral names for nymphs or shepherdesses.
73. *guerdon*: Reward.
75. *Fury*: Atropos, the Fate who cuts the thread of life.
77. *Phoebus*: Apollo, god of poetry.
79. *foil*: Thin leaf of metal placed under a gem to set off its brilliancy.
85. *Arethuse*: A spring in Sicily, here representing Sicilian Greek pastoral poetry. See below, note to 132.

86. *Mincius*: A river near Mantua, Virgil's birthplace, here representing Latin pastoral poetry.

88. *Oat*: The 'oaten flute' (33) of pastoral.

89. *herald*: Triton. He comes to gather evidence for Neptune's court (hence *plea* at 90).

96. *Hippotades*: Aeolus, god of the winds.

99. *Panope*: One of fifty Nereids (sea-nymphs).

103. *Camus*: The river Cam representing the University of Cambridge.

106. *sanguine flower*: The hyacinth, sprung from the blood of Hyacinthus, a youth accidentally killed by Apollo, who *inscribed* the flower *AI AI* ('alas, alas').

107. *pledge*: Child.

109. *pilot*: St Peter. His *keys* open and shut the gates of Heaven (Matt. 16: 19).

111. *amain*: With full force.

112. *mitred*: St Peter was the first bishop and so wears a bishop's mitre.

114. *Enow*: plural of 'enough'.

119. *Blind mouths*: Ruskin comments: 'A "Bishop" means "a person who sees". A "Pastor" means "a person who feeds". The most unbishoply character a man can have is therefore to be blind. The most unpastoral is, instead of feeding, to want to be fed' (*Sesame and Lilies*, I, 22).

122. *sped*: Satisfied.

123. *list*: (1) Choose (to play pipes); (2) listen (to the resulting cacophony).

124. *scrannel*: Harsh, unmelodious.

130. *two-handed engine*: A famous crux. Many interpretations have been offered. *At the door* means 'at hand' and probably refers to the Last Judgement (see Matt. 24: 33).

132. *Alpheus*: A river in Arcadia, here representing Greek pastoral. The river-god pursued the nymph Arethusa under the Adriatic to Sicily, where she rose as a spring (see above, note to 85).

136. *use*: Haunt, frequent.

138. *swart star*: Sirius, the Dog Star, associated with summer heat.

142. *rathe*: Blooming early.

149. *amaranthus*: A mythical flower that never fades – but it might for Lycidas.

160. *Bellerus*: A hero invented by Milton to explain 'Bellerium', the Latin name for Land's End.

161. *mount*: St Michael's Mount, Cornwall. St Michael supposedly appeared to fishermen there in 495 (hence *great vision*).

162. *Namancos and Bayona*: A region and fortress in north-western Spain. St Michael looks south from Cornwall, guarding England against Spanish Catholicism.

164. *waft*: Convey safely to land. Dolphins were thought to escort living and dead humans.

168. *day-star*: Either the sun or the morning star (both symbols of resurrection).

170. *tricks*: Adorns.

176. *unexpressive nuptial song*: Inexpressible marriage-song of the Lamb (Rev. 19).

178. *entertain*: Receive.

183. *Genius*: Local guardian spirit.

186. *uncouth*: (1) Rustic; (2) unknown. In *1638* Milton signed 'Lycidas' only with his initials.

188. *tender stops*: Responsive finger-holes.

189. *Doric*: The dialect of Greek pastoral poets.

A Masque Presented at Ludlow Castle ['Comus']

Popularly known as *Comus* since the late seventeenth century, *A Masque* was performed on 29 September 1634 at Ludlow Castle in Shropshire to celebrate the Earl of Bridgewater's appointment as Lord President of Wales. The Earl's three children were among the performers: Lady Alice Egerton, aged fifteen, played the Lady, and her brothers John, Viscount Brackley, aged eleven, and Lord Thomas Egerton, aged nine, played the two brothers. Henry Lawes, who was the children's music tutor, composed the music for the songs and played the part of the Attendant Spirit. It was probably Lawes who invited Milton to compose the text. Lawes published the poem in 1637.

The text survives in various versions, reflecting several stages of composition. *TMS* has many corrections and revisions, some added after the performance. Other versions are the Bridgewater manuscript (*BMS*), the first printed edition (issued anonymously in 1637), the printed text of 1645 (followed here), and that of 1673, which differs significantly from 1645 in only one passage (166–9).

3. *live insphered*: Inhabit one of the celestial spheres.

4. *sérene*: Bright (Latin *serenus*).

7. *pestered in this pinfold*: Crowded or plagued in this cattle-pen, hence 'place of confinement'.

16. *weeds*: Clothes.

20. *nether Jove*: Pluto.

30. *this tract*: Wales and the Marches.

31. *peer*: The Earl of Bridgewater.
37. *pérplexed*: Entangled.
50. *Circe*: The enchantress who turned Odysseus's men into swine.
58. *Comus*: The name means 'revelry' (Greek *komos*).
66. *drouth of Phoebus*: Thirst caused by the hot sun.
71. *ounce*: Lynx.
83. *Iris' woof*: Rainbow-coloured thread.
92. *viewless*: Invisible.
110. *saws*: Maxims.
129. *Cotytto*: Thracian goddess worshipped with nocturnal torchlit orgies.
135. *Hecat'*: Hecate, goddess of witchcraft.
151. *trains*: Tricks, baits.
157. *quaint habits*: Strange, foppish clothes.
161. *glozing*: Flattering.
167. *gear*: Doings, business.
174. *hinds*: Rustics.
189. *palmer's weed*: Pilgrim's attire.
197. *dark lantern*: A lantern with a shutter, often used by high-waymen.
230. *Echo*: A talkative nymph condemned by Juno to repeat whatever she heard.
232. *Meander*: A winding river in Phrygia.
253. *Sirens*: Sea-nymphs who lured sailors to destruction with their songs.
254. *Naiades*: Freshwater nymphs.
257. *Scylla*: A nymph transformed into a monster by Circe.
268. *Sylvan*: Roman wood-god.
290. *Hebe*: Goddess of youth.
293. *swinked*: Tired.
312. *Dingle*: Wooded hollow.
313. *bosky bourn*: Bushy stream.
318. *thatched pallet*: Straw nest.
332. *benison*: Blessing.
335. *shades*: Trees.
338. *rush-candle*: Candle made by dipping rush in tallow (which gave a weak light).
341. *star of Arcady*: Arcturus, the star by which Greek navigators steered.
342. *Cynosure*: The Pole Star, by which the Phoenicians steered.
360. *cast*: Forecast.
380. *to-ruffled*: Ruffled up.

382. *centre*: Of the earth.

393. *Hesperian tree*: A tree bearing golden apples, traditionally associated with female beauty.

407. *unownèd*: Lost (*OED*'s sole instance in this sense).

423. *unharboured*: Offering no shelter.

442. *silver-shafted*: (1) Armed with silver arrows; (2) shining with shafts of moonlight.

447. *Gorgon shield*: The virgin goddess Minerva wore on her shield the face of the Gorgon Medusa, with which she froze her enemies to stone.

480. *crude*: Indigestible.

494. *Thyrsis*: A common name in pastoral poetry.

495. *huddling*: Hurrying in disorder.

499. *wether*: Castrated ram.

517. *Chimeras*: Fire-breathing monsters.

542. *besprent*: Sprinkled.

545. *flaunting*: Waving like a plume.

560. *Still*: (1) Silent; (2) always.

599. *stubble*: Stalks of grain left after reaping (a biblical symbol of a poor foundation).

605. *Harpies*: Taloned bird-women; *Hydras*: fifty-headed serpents.

610. *emprise*: Chivalric prowess.

626. *scrip*: Small bag.

627. *simples*: Medicinal herbs.

635. *clouted shoon*: Shoes studded with nails.

636. *Moly*: Mythical herb that protected Odysseus from Circe's spells.

638. *haemony*: Various explanations have been offered. The name could suggest Thessaly (Haemonia), famous for witchcraft, or Greek *haimonios*, 'blood red'.

646. *lime-twigs*: Twigs smeared with bird lime to catch birds.

660. *nerves*: Sinews (thought to be the source of strength).

672. *julep*: A sweet drink.

675. *Nepenthes*: A drug given to Helen on her way home from Troy by Polydamna of Egypt.

700. *lickerish*: (1) Tempting to the palate; (2) lustful.

707. *budge*: Solemn.

707–8. *Stoic . . . Cynic*: Ascetic schools of philosophy.

722. *frieze*: Coarse woollen cloth.

733–6. *the forehead . . . shameless brows*: The *deep* is the centre of the earth, the *forehead* the roof of the underworld, and *they below* its inhabitants.

750. *grain*: Colour.

751. *tease*: Comb in preparation for spinning.

757. *juggler*: (1) Sorcerer; (2) trickster.

760. *bolt*: (1) Utter hastily; (2) sift, select.

793. *uncontrolled*: Indisputable.

805. *Saturn's crew*: The Titans, imprisoned in Hell (*Erebus*) by Jove.

808. *canon laws*: Rules (with a glance at ecclesiastical 'Canon Law', casting Comus as priest).

809. *lees*: Sediment (of the melancholic humour).

822. *Meliboeus*: Probably Spenser, who told Sabrina's story in *The Faerie Queene*, II, x, 14–19.

826. *Sabrina*: Goddess of the Severn. Milton's version of her myth emphasizes her virginity.

828. *Brute*: Brutus, great-grandson of Aeneas and legendary founder of Britain.

835. *Nereus*: Greek sea-deity, father of the fifty Nereids (sea-nymphs).

838. *lavers*: Basins. The flower *asphodel* symbolizes immortality.

845. *urchin blasts*: Infections caused by mischievous elves.

852. *swain*: Meliboeus.

863. *amber*: Ambergris (a perfume derived from the dung of the sperm whale).

868. *Oceanus*: A Titan, the father of the rivers.

870. *Tethys*: Wife of Oceanus and mother of the rivers.

872. *Carpathian wizard*: Proteus, the shepherd (hence *hook*) of the seals.

873. *Triton*: Neptune's herald.

874. *Glaucus*: A fisherman transformed into an oracular sea-god.

875. *Leucothea*: Ino, transformed into a sea-goddess after she leapt into the sea to escape Juno.

876. *her son*: Melicertes, transformed into Palaemon, god of harbours, after Ino leapt into the sea.

877. *Thetis*: A Nereid, the mother of Achilles.

879. *Parthenope*: One of the Sirens. She drowned herself after Odysseus escaped her song.

880. *Ligea*: Another Siren.

921. *Amphitrite*: A Nereid, wife of Neptune.

923. *Anchises*: Father of Aeneas and ancestor of Sabrina.

964. *mincing*: Dancing in double time. *Dryades* are tree-nymphs.

991. *Nard and cassia*: Aromatic plants.

992. *Iris*: Goddess of the rainbow.

995. *purfled*: Variegated.

999. *Adonis*: A youthful hunter loved by Venus and slain by a boar.

1004–8. *Celestial Cupid . . . eternal bride*: The mortal woman *Psyche* ('soul') endured many trials to be reunited with *Cupid*.

1004. *advanced*: Raised on high.

1015. *welkin*: Sky.

1017. *corners*: Horns.

1021. *sphery chime*: The music of the spheres.

ENGLISH POEMS ADDED IN 1673

Sonnet XI ('A book was writ of late')

Dated late 1645 or early 1646. This and the next sonnet are Milton's response to the attacks he suffered after the publication of his divorce tracts, *The Doctrine and Discipline of Divorce* (1643, 1644), *The Judgment of Martin Bucer* (1644), *Tetrachordon* and *Colasterion* (1645). The title 'On the detraction which followed upon my writing certain treatises' appears only in *TMS*, where it covers both sonnets. Sonnet XI follows Sonnet XII in *TMS*, and it is generally agreed that Sonnet XII was written first. Sonnet XI is more cool and detached in tone, using colloquialisms and comic rhymes to express contempt for an unlearned age.

1. *Tetrachordon*: Greek, 'four-stringed'. The tract's title refers to Milton's attempt to harmonize four key biblical passages on marriage and divorce.

7. *spelling false*: (1) Misspelling (the title); (2) misunderstanding (the argument).

8–9. *Gordon . . . Galasp*: The Scottish names are chosen partly for their harsh sound (which Milton's English readers accept even as they baulk at *Tetrachordon*) and partly to excite anti-Scottish feeling harmful to the Presbyterians. The names have been plausibly attached to three Royalists and one member of the Westminster Assembly (George Gillespie).

11. *Quintilian*: A Roman rhetorician who condemned the use of foreign words.

12. *Sir John Cheke*: King Edward VI's tutor and the first Professor of Greek at Cambridge.

Sonnet XII ('I did but prompt the age')

For date see previous headnote.

1. *quit their clogs*: Throw off their shackles.

4. *owls and cuckoos, asses, apes and dogs*: Symbols respectively of ignorance, ingratitude, stupidity, mockery and quarrelsomeness.

5–7. *As when those hinds ... moon*: Latona turned two peasants
     (*hinds*) into frogs when they prevented her infants, Apollo and
     Diana, from drinking from a pool. Milton had his own *twin-born
     progeny*, as *Tetrachordon* and *Colasterion* were published on
     the same day, 4 March 1645.

7.   *fee*: Absolute and rightful possession.

8.   *casting pearl to hogs*: Matt. 7:6.

10.   *revolt*: Draw back from a course of action (*OED*, 2b). Milton's
     Presbyterian detractors 'revolt' by backsliding into conservative
     traditions when they should be pushing the Reformation
     forward.

11.   *Licence*: (1) Licentiousness; (2) licence to print.

13.   *mark ... rove*: Shoot wide of the target (a metaphor from
     archery).

Sonnet XIII. 'To Mr H. Lawes, on his Airs'

A draft in *TMS* is dated 9 February 1645 (i.e. 1646). Henry Lawes, a
member of the King's Music, had long been Milton's friend, and in
1634 had written the music for *A Masque (Comus)*. Lawes was a
Royalist, and the present sonnet was first published in his *Choice
Psalmes* (1648), which was dedicated to the imprisoned Charles I, and
commemorated Henry's brother William, who had died fighting for
the king.

4.   *Midas' ears*: Midas was given ass's ears for preferring Pan's music
     to Apollo's; *committing*: misjoining.

10.   *Phoebus' choir*: The Muses.

12–14. *Dante ... Purgatory*: In *Purgatorio*, ii, Dante meets the shade
     of Casella the musician, and asks him to sing. Casella sings his
     setting of one of Dante's *canzoni*.

Sonnet XIV ('When Faith and Love which parted from thee never')

Dated December 1646. Catharine Thomason was the wife of the
London bookseller George Thomason, whose collection of over
22,000 Civil War pamphlets ('the Thomason tracts') still exists in the
British Library.

Sonnet XV. On the Late Massacre in Piedmont

On 24 April 1655, the Duke of Savoy sent French, Irish and Piedmon-
tese troops to remove the sect known as the Vaudois or Waldensians
from their Alpine villages. Over 1,700 Vaudois were massacred. The
sect had been persecuted since its foundation in the twelfth century.

Protestants in Milton's time believed that the Vaudois were a living link between the Reformation and Apostolic purity. Cromwell voiced his protest in several letters (which Milton composed).

4.   *stocks and stones*: Idols made of wood and stone.
11. *sway*: (1) Rule; (2) swing precariously. The pun implies 'tyranny *and* instability' (Christopher Hill, *Milton and the English Revolution*, London: Faber and Faber, 1977, p. 209).
12. *triple Tyrant*: The Pope with his three-tiered crown.
14. *Babylonian*: Protestants identified the Babylon of Revelation with papal Rome.

Sonnet XVI ('When I consider how my light is spent')

Date unknown, but it obviously postdates Milton's loss of sight in 1652.

1.   *light*: Eyesight (*OED*, 4).
2.   *Ere half my days*: Milton was forty-three in 1652. He may have expected to live as long as his father, who lived to be eighty-four.
3.   *talent*: Literary talent, with an allusion to the parable of the talents (Matt. 25: 14–30).
4.   *useless*: (1) Futile; (2) without usury (as in the parable of the talents).
8.   *fondly*: Foolishly.
12. *Thousands*: The angels.
14. *wait*: (1) Stand ready to receive orders; (2) place hope in God.

Sonnet XVII ('Lawrence of virtuous father virtuous son')

Edward Lawrence (1633–57) was the elder son of Henry Lawrence (1600–64), who became President of Cromwell's Council of State in 1654. Edward began visiting Milton in 1651, and the sonnet could have been written in any winter between 1651 and 1657, when he died, aged twenty-four.

6.   *Favonius*: Zephyrus, the west wind.
8.   *lily . . . spun*: Matt. 6: 28–9.
10.   *Attic taste*: The simple and refined elegance of the Athenians.
12.   *Tuscan air*: Italian song.
13–14. *spare / To interpose*: A famous crux. Some take *spare* to mean 'forbear', and so infer that Milton is advising Lawrence to enjoy himself sparingly. Others take *spare* to mean 'spare time for', and so infer that Milton is advocating frequent delights.

Sonnet XVIII ('Cyriack, whose grandsire on the Royal Bench')

Dated possibly to 1655. Cyriack Skinner (1627-1700) was Milton's close friend in the 1650s, and may have been his pupil before that. His political views accorded with Milton's, and he is the probable author of the anonymous early life of Milton that Helen Darbishire attributed to John Phillips.

1. *grandsire*: Sir Edward Coke (1552-1634), the most celebrated lawyer of his age and a defender of Parliament's privileges.
2. *Themis*: Greek goddess of Justice.
3. *volumes*: These include *Institutes of the Laws of England*.
8. *Swede ... French*: Referring to Skinner's interest in topical international politics.

Sonnet XIX ('Methought I saw my late espousèd saint')

Critics debate whether the subject of this sonnet is Milton's first wife, Mary Powell, who died in May 1652, three days after giving birth to their daughter Deborah, or his second wife, Katherine Woodcock, who died in February 1658 after giving birth in October 1657. The blind Milton had never seen Katherine. A likely pun on 'Katherine' (see note to 9) supports her candidacy.

2. *Alcestis*: The loyal wife who chose to die in place of her husband Admetus. Hercules (*Jove's great son*) rescued her from Death, and restored her, veiled, to Admetus.
6. *old Law*: The Mosaic law prescribing purification of women after childbirth (Lev. 12: 4-8).
9. *pure*: Perhaps a pun on 'Katherine' (Greek *katharos*, 'pure').

'On the New Forcers of Conscience under the Long Parliament'

Dated summer 1646. The 'New Forcers' are the Presbyterians, Milton's old allies against Laudian episcopacy. In 1643 Parliament had established the Westminster Assembly to reorganize the Church, and on 28 August 1646 Parliament established the ordination of ministers by Classical Presbyteries. Milton's poem was probably written in anticipation of that event. The poem is a 'tailed sonnet', Milton's only example of the form.

3. *Plurality*: The practice of holding more than one living.
4. *abhorred*: Playing on *whore* (3).
7. *ride*: Tyrannize over; *classic*: Refers to the *classis*, a body of elders acting as a disciplinary court in the Presbyterian system.

8.   *A. S.*: Adam Stewart, a Scottish Presbyterian resident in London
      in the 1640s; *Rutherford*: Samuel Rutherford, a Scottish member
      of the Westminster Assembly, who argued against toleration.

12.   *Edwards*: Thomas Edwards, a Presbyterian who had attacked
      Milton's divorce pamphlets.

14.   *packing*: (1) Packed votes; (2) fraudulent dealing.
         Trent: the Council of Trent (1545–63), 'packed' in Rome's
      interests.

17.   *phylacteries*: Small boxes worn on the forehead by pious Jews;
      here a metaphor for self-righteous ostentation. *TMS* at first read:
      'Clip ye as close as marginal P—'s ears,' alluding more clearly
      to William Prynne, a Presbyterian whose ears had twice been
      cropped.

20.   *New Presbyter . . . old Priest*: Etymologically *Priest* is a contrac-
      ted form of *Presbyter*.

UNCOLLECTED ENGLISH SONNETS

These four sonnets were omitted from *1673*, probably due to the
political views they express. The present text follows *TMS*.

'On the Lord General Fairfax at the Siege of Colchester'

Sir Thomas Fairfax was commander-in-chief of the New Model Army,
in which role he had crushed the king's forces at Naseby (June 1645).
He laid siege to Colchester on 13 June 1648, and the city fell on
27 August. Milton's sonnet was evidently written after the Scots
invaded England (8 July).

5.   *virtue*: (1) Moral worth; (2) martial valour.

7.   *Hydra*: Mythical serpent with regenerating heads.

8.   *broken league*: The Solemn League and Covenant (1643), which
      the Scots (*false North*) violated when they invaded England; *imp*:
      Engraft new feathers on to a bird's wing.

12.   *public faith*: A topical catchphrase. Parliament had borrowed
      money from private creditors (including Milton) 'on the public
      faith'.

'To the Lord General Cromwell, May 1652'

On 10 February 1652 Parliament had appointed a Committee for the
Propagation of the Gospel to settle the state of religion in England.
The Committee proposed limited toleration and a stipendiary clergy.

Milton here urges Cromwell, as a member of the Committee, to defend liberty and make no provision for a paid clergy.

5.   *neck . . . crownèd*: Alluding to the beheading of King Charles I.

7–9. *Darwen . . . Dunbar . . . Worcester*: Sites of Cromwell's victories over the Scottish Covenanters in 1648, 1650 and 1651.

12.   *secular chains*: Alludes to the Committee's proposal that the state should limit toleration.

14.   *hireling wolves*: Stipendiary clergy; *maw*: Belly, mouth, appetite.

'To Sir Henry Vane the Younger'

Sir Henry Vane (1613–62) championed toleration and the Puritan cause in Parliament. He disapproved of the king's execution, but joined the Council of State soon afterwards. In July 1652, when Milton sent him this sonnet, he was a member of the Council concerned with foreign affairs. He broke with Cromwell when the latter dissolved the Rump (April 1653). Although not a regicide, he was executed in 1662.

3.   *gowns*: Senatorial togas.

4.   *Epirot . . . African*: Pyrrhus and Hannibal. Both failed to break the Romans' spirit.

6.   *drift of hollow states . . . spelled*: Plots of untrustworthy nations (with puns on 'Holland' and 'States-General') discovered.

8.   *nerves*: Sinews (the supposed source of strength).

12.   *either sword*: Spiritual and civil (see 9).

'To Mr Cyriack Skinner upon his Blindness'

Dated 1655 (see 1).

1.   *this three years' day*: For the past three years. Milton became totally blind in 1652.

7.   *bate a jot*: Lose the least part.

8.   *bear up*: (1) Keep up courage; (2) sail against the wind.

10.   *overplied*: (1) Overworked; (2) sailed against the wind.

13.   *masque*: (1) Masquerade, false show; (2) theatrical masque.

PARADISE LOST

Milton's great epic is the culmination of two ambitions. He had wanted to write an epic since his youth, but his plan had been to write an Arthuriad. He had also planned to write a tragedy about the Fall of man. The title 'Paradise Lost' first appears in draft outlines for such a tragedy in *TMS*, written about 1640. Milton's nephew Edward Phillips reports that part of Satan's address to the sun (IV, 32–41) was shown to him 'several Years before the Poem was begun', when it was intended to be 'the very beginning' of a tragedy (Helen Darbishire (ed.), *The Early Lives of Milton*, London: Constable, p. 72). John Aubrey (1626–97) reports that Milton began writing *PL* in earnest in about 1658 and finished in about 1663 (Darbishire (ed.), *Early Lives of Milton*, p. 13).

BOOK I

1. *fruit*: (1) The apple; (2) the consequences of eating it.
4. *greater man*: Christ, the Second Adam.
8. *That shepherd*: Moses (the supposed author of Genesis).
11. *Siloa's brook*: Near the Temple on Mount Zion. Jesus cured a blind man with its waters.
15. *Aonian mount*: Helicon, sacred to the Muses.
25. *assert*: Maintain the cause of, defend.
29. *grand*: (1) Original; (2) all-inclusive (as in 'grand total').
30. *fall off*: (1) Of friends – to become estranged; (2) of subjects – to revolt.
46. *ruin*: Falling (Latin *ruina*); *combustion*: (1) Conflagration (2) tumult.
48. *adamantine*: Made of adamant, a mythical substance of unbreakable hardness.
56. *baleful*: (1) Malign; (2) mournful.
57. *witnessed*. (1) Bore witness to (his *affliction*); (2) beheld (his followers).
59. *ken*: Range of sight.
72. *utter*: (1) Total; (2) outer.
74. *centre . . . pole*: Earth . . . celestial pole (outermost point of the universe).
82. *thence in Heav'n called Satan*: The name means 'enemy'.
109. *And . . . overcome*: 'What else does "not being overcome" mean?'
128. *Powers*: One of nine angelic orders, the others being Seraphim, Cherubim, Thrones, Dominations, Virtues, Principalities, Archangels and Angels.
168. *destined*: Intended (but the other sense tells against Satan's boast).
178. *slip*: Let slip.
186. *afflicted powers*: (1) Overthrown armies; (2) spiritless faculties.
187. *offend*: (1) Take the offensive against; (2) sin against.
196. *rood*: A measure of land, about a quarter of an acre.

198–9. *Titanian . . . Typhon*: Titans (including *Briareos*) and *Earth-born* giants (including *Typhon*) fought against Jove and were imprisoned in Tartarus or beneath volcanoes.

201. *Leviathan*: Biblical sea-monster, here a whale. The story of the illusory island appears in medieval bestiaries, which draw a parallel with Satan's deceptions.

224. *horrid*: (1) Dreadful; (2) bristling (with *spires*).

226. *incumbent*: Pressing down.

230–37. *as when the force . . . and smoke*: Earthquakes were thought to be caused by *subterranean wind*. *Pelorus* is a promontory near Mount Etna in Sicily. *Sublimed* means 'vaporized'.

239. *Stygian*: Black as Styx, one of the four rivers of the classical underworld.

266. *astonished on th' oblivious pool*: Stunned on the pool that causes oblivion.

276. *edge*: (1) Line of battle; (2) critical moment.

285. *Ethereal temper*: Tempered in Heavenly fire (Greek *aithein*, 'to burn').

288. *Tuscan artist*: Galileo.

294. *ammiral*: Flagship.

296. *marl*: Soil.

299. *Nathless*: Nevertheless.

303. *Vallombrosa*: Tuscan 'shady valley', evoking 'valley of the shadow of death' (Psalm 23).

307. *Busiris*: Mythical Egyptian tyrant, here identified with the Pharaoh who *pursued* Moses.

312. *Abject*: Cast down (both literally and metaphorically).

339. *Amram's son*: Moses.

341. *warping*: Swarming, whirling through the air.

345. *cope*: Sky.

353. *Rhene . . . Danaw*: The Rhine and the Danube.

372. *gay religions*: Showy rites.

401–16. *Solomon . . . hill of scandal*: Solomon built temples for Moloch (god of the Ammonites) and Chemos (god of the Moabites) on the Mount of Olives (*that opprobrious hill, that hill of scandal*) directly opposite (*right against*) God's Temple on Mount Zion.

411. *Asphaltic pool*: The Dead Sea, which has deposits of bitumen, or asphalt.

417. *lust hard by hate*: (1) Chemos's temple abutting Moloch's; (2) priapically erect with hate.

422. *Baälim and Ashtaroth*: Plural forms of 'Baal' and 'Ashtoreth', the

chief male and female deities of the Phoenicians and Canaanites.

441. *Sidonian*: Of Sidon, the Phoenician city.

444. *uxorious king*: Solomon built a temple to Astarte on the Mount of Olives to please his wives.

446. *Thammuz*: Syrian counterpart to Adonis, slain by a boar.

450. *Adonis*: A river in Lebanon, associated with Thammuz because it turned blood-red each July.

460. *grunsel*: Groundsel, threshold.

467. *Rimmon*: Syrian god. The Syrian Naaman was cured of leprosy when he renounced Rimmon for God; but King Ahaz of Judah converted to Rimmon's worship.

484. *rebel king*: Jeroboam became King of Israel after seceding from Solomon's son Rehoboam.

485. *Doubled*: (1) Repeated; (2) made twice as many. Aaron made one calf; Jeroboam, two.

487. *one night*: The Passover.

490. *Belial*: An abstract noun (Hebrew 'worthlessness'), not a proper name, but the Old Testament phrase 'sons of Belial' encouraged the notion that 'Belial' was a devil.

498. *luxurious*: Lustful.

502. *flown*: In flood (used figuratively for excess of any kind).

504–5. *when ... rape*: Following *1674*. *MS* and *1667* read: 'hospitable doors / Yielded their matrons to prevent [*MS* avoid] worse rape'. Both versions allude to Gen. 19 and Judges 19, but *1674* gives priority to Judges. No rape took place in Genesis (though Lot offered his daughters to the Sodomites). In Judges, a Levite escaped sodomitical rape by surrendering his concubine, who was raped and killed.

508. *Javan*: Noah's grandson, ancestor of the Ionians (Greeks).

509. *Heav'n and Earth*: Uranus and Gaea, progenitors of the gods.

510. *Titan, Heav'n's First-born*: Titan deposed his father Uranus, only to be deposed by his younger brother Saturn, who was in turn deposed by his son Jove.

534. *Azazel*: A fallen angel in cabbalistic lore, one of four standard-bearers in Satan's army.

550. *phalanx*: Greek battle line; *Dorian mood*: The gravest of the Greek musical modes, said to inspire courage. The Dorian Spartans marched to the sound of *flutes*.

556. *swage*: Assuage.

563. *horrid*: (1) Terrifying; (2) bristling (with spears).

573. *since created man*: Since man was created (Latin idiom).

575. *small infantry*: The pygmies (with a contemptuous pun on 'infants'). Homer describes their war with the *cranes*.

577. *Phlegra*: Where the gods fought the Giants.

579. *auxiliar*: (1) Helpfully assisting; (2) serving as auxiliaries (inferior troops). The latter sense belittles pagan epics.

580. *Uther's son*: King Arthur.

581. *Armoric*: Breton.

583–5. *Aspramont ... Biserta*: Place-names associated with chivalric epics.

586–7. *Charlemagne ... Fontarabbia*: Charlemagne's paladin Roland made a famous last stand at Roncesvalles, some forty miles from *Fontarabbia*, but there is no known source for Milton's story that *Charlemagne ... fell*.

594–9. *as when the sun ... Perplexes monarchs*: Charles II's censor objected to these lines, perhaps suspecting an allusion to the *eclipse* of 29 May 1630 (the day of Charles's birth).

595. *horizontal*: On the horizon.

597. *disastrous*: Ill-starred (from Latin *astrum*).

603. *considerate*: Deliberate, as in 'considerate murderer' (1597, OED).

609. *amerced Of*: (1) Deprived of (a Grecism, as Carter and Stella Revard point out in *Milton Quarterly* 12, 1978, pp. 105–6); (2) at the mercy of (from French *amercié*).

624. *event*: Outcome.

636. *different*: Wavering.

651. *fame*: Rumour.

656. *eruption*: (1) Break-out; (2) Titanic volcanic eruption. See above, note to 198–9.

672. *scurf*: Sulphurous crust (suggesting also a diseased body).

676. *pioneers*: Military engineers.

678. *Mammon*: The Aramaic word for 'riches', frequently personified and associated with Plutus, god of wealth, and Pluto, god of the underworld.

679. *erected*: (1) High-souled; (2) upright in posture.

684. *vision beatific*: Blessed experience of seeing God.

690. *ribs*: Veins of ore; *admire*: Marvel.

694. *Memphian*: Egyptian.

703. *founded*: Melted.

704. *scummed the bullion dross*: Skimmed off the boiling impurities.

716. *bossy*: Carved in relief.

717. *fretted*: Carved into decorative patterns.

720. *Belus or Serapis*: Baal had a magnificent temple in *Babylon*; *Serapis* had one at Cairo (*Alcairo*).

728. *cressets*: Iron baskets hung from the ceiling as lanterns.

739. *Ausonian land*: Italy.

740. *Mulciber*: Vulcan, god of fire and smithery.

750. *engines*: (1) Tricks; (2) mechanical contrivances.

756. *Pandaemonium*: In Greek, 'all the devils'. Milton's coinage.

765. *paynim*: Pagan.

766. *career*: Gallop (at a tournament).

774. *expatiate*: (1) Wander at will; (2) talk at length.

785. *arbitress*: Judge. The etymology (*ad + bito*, 'go to see') suggests that the moon leaves her orbit to come *nearer to the earth*.

790. *at large*: Christopher Ricks notes the 'superbly contemptuous pun' (see *Milton's Grand Style*, p. 15).

795. *conclave*: Secret assembly (especially an assembly of cardinals met to elect a Pope).

797. *Frequent*: Crowded.

BOOK II

2. *Ormus*: Hormuz, an island in the Persian Gulf, famous for jewels.

9. *success*: Outcome (with a wry pun on the modern sense).

50. *thereafter*: Accordingly.

65. *engine*: Machine of war.

69. *Tartarean*: Of Tartarus, the classical Hell.

79. *Insulting*: (1) Triumphing; (2) making sudden attacks.

82. *event*: Outcome.

89. *exercise*: (1) Afflict; (2) subject to religious discipline (notice *scourge* and *penance*).

97. *essential*: Essence.

100–101. *And cannot cease . . . this side nothing*: 'We are already in the worst state possible, short of annihilation'.

104. *fatal*: (1) Upheld by Fate; (2) deadly.

106. *denounced*: Portended.

110. *person*: (1) Bodily figure; (2) semblance (Latin *persona*, 'a mask'). Notice *false and hollow*.

124. *fact*: Feat of valour.

127. *scope*: Target.

156. *Belike*: 'No doubt' (sarcastic).

165. *What when*: 'What about when?'; *amain*: (1) At full speed; (2) in full force of numbers.

182. *racking*: (1) Torturing; (2) driving (as the wind drives clouds).

184. *converse*: (1) Dwell; (2) talk by means of; (3) turn to and fro (Latin *convertere*).

212. *mind*: (1) Care about; (2) be aware of.

216. *inured*: (1) Accustomed; (2) burned away (Latin *inurere*, 'remove by burning').

218 (and 277). *temper*: (1) Humoral mixture; (2) resiliency (as of tempered steel).

220. *light*: (1) Luminous; (2) easy to bear.

224. *For happy*: So far as happiness is concerned.

243. *Forced*: (1) Extorted; (2) produced with effort, strained.

275. *our elements*: (1) Elements composing our bodies; (2) fire (the devils' natural abode).

278. *The sensible*: That which feels sensations.

288. *o'erwatched*: Exhausted from lack of sleep.

297. *policy*: Statecraft, including the bad sense of 'cunning'.

302. *front*: Forehead or face.

306. *Atlantean*: Atlas carried the world on his shoulders.

329. *What*: Why.

330. *determined us*: (1) Decided our course; (2) brought us to this end.

336. *to*: To the limit of.

337. *reluctance*: Resistance, struggling.

355. *mould*: (1) Bodily form; (2) earth as material of the human body.

367. *puny*: (1) Weak; (2) born since us (*puis né*).

374. *partake with us*: (1) Share our fate; (2) join our side.

375. *original*: (1) Progenitor (Adam); (2) parentage (Adam and Eve); (3) archetype (God's image).

383. *one root*: Adam, but glancing also at the forbidden tree, 'root of all our woe' (Book IX, 645).

387. *States*: Lords (one of the 'estates' of Parliament).

391. *Synod*: Assembly (usually of clergy, so *Synod of gods* is satirical).

404. *tempt*: Risk the perils of (with a glance at satanic temptation).

407. *uncouth*: Unknown.

439. *unessential*: Having no essence.

441. *abortive*: Chaos is a 'womb' (II, 911) full of 'embryon atoms' (II, 900).

457. *intend*: (1) Spread (yourselves) out; (2) turn (your thoughts) to.

478. *reverence prone*: Low bow.

485. *close*: Secret.

490. *louring element*: Threatening sky.

513. *horrent*: Bristling.

517. *sounding alchemy*: Brass trumpets.

528. *sublime*: (1) Aloft; (2) elated.

530. *Pythian*: The Pythian Games, held at Delphi in honour of Apollo.

531. *shun the goal*: Swing tight around the turning-pole in a chariot race.

538. *welkin*: Sky.

539. *Typhoean*: For Typhon see note to 198–9. His name (associated with 'typhoon') means 'whirlwind' (see 541).

540. *ride*: (1) Torment; (2) fly through.

542–6. *As when Alcides … Euboic Sea*: Dying in agony from the corrosive touch of a poisoned robe, Hercules (*Alcides*) threw his friend *Lichas* (who had innocently brought the robe) from Mount Oeta into the Euboean Sea.

550. *complain*: (1) Compose a musical lament; (2) express a sense of injury.

552. *partial*: (1) Polyphonic; (2) prejudiced.

554. *Suspended*: (1) Enraptured (the audience); (2) put a temporary stop to (Hell's torments).

564. *apathy*: The Stoic virtue of freedom from passion.

568. *obdurèd*: (1) Unyielding; (2) hardened in sin.

591. *pile*: Massive building.

592. *Serbonian bog*: Lake Serbonis, famous for quicksands, near the mouth of the Nile.

595. *frore*: Frosty.

596. *Harpy-footed*: Taloned (Harpies were monstrous bird-women).

600. *starve*: Die by freezing.

604. *Lethean sound*: Lethe, river of forgetfulness.

611. *Medusa*: The snake-haired Gorgon whose look turned men to stone.

613. *wight*: Person.

614. *Tantalus*: He was 'tantalized' in Tartarus with water and fruit.

628. *Gorgons*: Snake-haired women. *Hydra* was a nine-headed serpent and *Chimera* a fire-breathing monster.

639. *Ternate and Tidore*: Spice Islands in the Moluccas.

641. *Ethiopian*: Indian Ocean.

642. *Ply stemming*: Make headway against the wind.

647. *impaled*: Surrounded.

652. *Voluminous*: In many coils.

654. *cry*: Pack.

655. *Cerberean*: Cerberus, the many-headed dog of Hell.

660. *Scylla*: A beautiful nymph, monstrously transformed by Circe. Early Christians made her a symbol of sin.

662. *night-hag*: Hecate, goddess of witchcraft.

665. *labouring*: (1) Suffering eclipse; (2) presiding over childbirth.

677. *admired*: Wondered.

688. *goblin*: Evil spirit.

693. *Conjured*: (1) Sworn together; (2) bewitched.

701. *scorpions*: Studded whips.

709. *Ophiucus*: A constellation, the Serpent-Bearer.

710. *hair*: 'Comet' is from the Greek for 'long-haired'. Comets were
     evil omens.

755-8. *Threw forth . . . out of thy head I sprung*: Alludes to the birth
     of Athene from the head of Zeus.

772. *pitch*: Summit.

801. *conscious*: Inwardly guilty.

825. *pretences*: Claims (but the modern sense existed, and here gives
     Satan the lie).

829. *unfounded*: Bottomless.

833. *purlieus*: Outskirts.

836. *surcharged*: Overpopulated.

842. *buxom*: Yielding; *embalmed*: Balmy (with ominous overtones of
     embalming).

883. *Erebus*: Hell.

889. *redounding*: Billowing.

891. *secrets*: (1) Secret places; (2) sexual organs.

900. *embryon atoms*: Atoms as yet unformed in Night's *womb* (911).

904. *Barca or Cyrene*: Cities in the Libyan desert.

905. *Levied*: (1) Lifted up (on the winds); (2) enlisted as troops; *poise*:
     Add weight to.

909. *arbiter*: Arbitrator (with a suggestion of capricious arbitration).

919. *frith*: Firth, estuary.

922. *Bellona*: Roman goddess of war.

927. *vans*: Fans (wings).

933. *pennons*: (1) Wings; (2) ship's streamers (Satan as explorer).

936. *rebuff*: (1) Repelling blast; (2) snub. Even Chaos rejects Satan.

937. *Instinct*: Impelled, inflamed.

939. *boggy Syrtis*: The Syrtes were two large sandbanks off the North
     African coast.

943-7. *As when a gryphon . . . guarded gold*: Gryphons (half eagle,
     half lion) guarded their gold against the one-eyed Arimaspians.

964. *Orcus and Ades*: Names for Pluto (Hades), god of the under-
     world.

965. *Demogorgon*: A mysterious being whom even the infernal gods
     dare not name.

988. *Anarch*: (1) Ruler of anarchy; (2) anti-ruler. Milton's coinage (by analogy with 'monarch').

989. *incomposed*: (1) Agitated; (2) disarranged (as befits Chaos).

1001. *intestine broils*: Civil wars.

1008. *speed*: (1) Hurry up; (2) succeed.

1013. *pyramid of fire*: Playing on the supposed etymology (Greek *pyr*, 'fire').

1017. *Argo*: Jason's ship narrowly escaped the Symplegades (clashing rocks).

1019. *larboard*: Port (opposite of starboard).

1020. *other whirlpool*: Odysseus chose to sail by Scylla's rock rather than risk Charybdis's whirlpool. By placing Scylla in a whirlpool, Milton may be hinting that Satan has no hope.

1024. *amain*: (1) With main force; (2) at full speed.

1044. *shrouds and tackle*: A ship's rigging.

1052. *pendent world*: The whole universe (not just our earth) hanging in space.

BOOK IV

1. *that warning voice*: Rev. 12:12.

11. *wreck*: (1) Wreak vengeance; (2) wreck (himself).

17. *engine*: (1) Cannon; (2) plot.

33. *Look'st*: (1) Surveys; (2) seems to be; *sole*: (1) Unique; (2) Sol, the sun.

36-7. *thy name / O sun*: Satan aggressively puns on 'Son'.

50. *'sdained*: Disdained.

53. *still*: Continually.

56. *owing*: Acknowledging.

87. *abide*: (1) Abide by; (2) abye (pay the penalty for).

122-4. *practised . . . practised*: Plotted . . . become proficient.

123. *couched*: Lying hidden.

134. *champaign head*: Treeless plateau.

136. *grotesque*: Picturesque (from 'grotto').

149. *enamelled*: Bright with various colours.

160. *Hope*: Good Hope (contrasting with Satan's *despair*).

162. *Sabéan*: From Sheba.

163. *Araby the Blest*: Arabia Felix (Yemen).

165. *grateful*: Pleasing.

168-71. *Than Asmodéus . . . Egypt*: Tobias (*Tobit's son*) married Sarah, whose previous seven husbands had been killed on their wedding night by the devil *Asmodeus*. Raphael told Tobias to drive the spirit away by burning fish.

170. *with a vengeance*: (1) With great force; (2) with a curse.

171. *fast bound*: (1) Speedily making his way; (2) securely imprisoned.

186. *hurdled cotes*: Wattled sheep-pens; *secure*: Unsuspecting (with a wry pun on 'safe').

193. *lewd*: (1) Unprincipled; (2) not in holy orders (a paid clergy being no true clergy).

239. *error*: Wandering (the innocent Latin sense).

241. *nice*: Fastidious.

242. *curious knots*: Intricate flower-beds.

250. *Hesperian fables*: The golden apples of Hesperus, guarded by a dragon.

255. *irriguous*: Well watered.

257. *umbrageous*: Shady.

258. *mantling*: Enveloping.

264. *airs*: (1) Breezes; (2) musical airs (notice *attune*).

266. *universal Pan*: The god of all nature ('pan' being Greek for 'all').

267. *Graces . . . Hours*: Goddess of natural beauty and the seasons.

269–72. *Of Enna . . . world*: Pluto (*Dis*) abducted *Proserpine* from the Sicilian meadow of *Enna*. Proserpine ate six pomegranate seeds in Hades, and so had to stay there for six months each year. The story was often related to Eve's Fall.

273. *Daphne*: A laurel grove on the river *Orontes* in Syria. It had a *Castalian spring*, named after that of the Muses on Parnassus.

276. *Cham*: Noah's son Ham, identified with Jupiter-Ammon, who hid his son Bacchus on the island of Nysa (near Tunis).

278. *florid*: Ruddy (Bacchus being god of wine).

281. *Mount Amara*: Where Abyssinian kings raised their sons (*issue*) among secluded gardens.

282. *Ethiop line*: The equator.

293. *severe*: Austere (as in the 'severe' style of sculpture).

300. *front*: Brow.

301. *hyacinthine*: Curled like hyacinth petals.

306. *wanton*: Sportive (here innocent, but proleptic of fallen wantonness).

310. *coy*: Shy (not 'coquettish').

312. *mysterious*: Awe-inspiring, secret (as in a religious rite).

313. *dishonest*: Unchaste.

329. *Zephyr*: The west wind.

332. *Nectarine*: Sweet as nectar.

337. *purpose*: Conversation.
341. *chase*: Unenclosed parkland (with an ominous suggestion of hunting).
343. *ramped*: Stood on his hind legs ('a threatening posture', *OED*).
344. *ounces, pards*: Lynxes and leopards.
348. *Insinuating*: Moving sinuously (not yet sinful, but with proleptic insinuations); *Gordian*: As intricate as the Gordian knot (which Alexander cut).
352. *ruminating*: Chewing the cud.
360. *mould*: Bodily form (suggesting also the earth from which Adam was made).
382. *entertain*: (1) Welcome formally; (2) admit and contain.
404. *purlieu*: Outskirts of a forest.
411. *sole . . . sole*: Only . . . unrivalled.
427. *pronounced*: (1) As legal sentence; (2) as a vocal sound ('Death' is meaningless to Adam).
447. *odds*: Difference, inequality.
460–68. *As I bent down . . . thyself*: Alludes to Ovid's story of Narcissus (*Metamorphoses*, 3, 402f.).
466. *vain*: Futile (with ominous suggestions of personal vanity).
470. *stays*: Awaits.
478. *platan*: Plane tree.
486. *individual*: (1) Inseparable; (2) her individual self.
493. *unreproved*: Irreproachable. This (Latinate) use of the past participle can confuse the modern reader. Cp. 'unvalued' ('On Shakespeare', 11), 'unremoved' (*PL*, IV, 987), and 'unblamed' (*PL*, IX, 5). The point is that Eve is beyond reproach, not merely unblamed for an existing fault.
500. *impregns*: Impregnates.
539. *utmost longitude*: Uttermost west.
557. *thwarts*: Passes across.
567. *described*: Traced with the eye.
592. *prime orb*: The *primum mobile*, outermost sphere in the Ptolemaic system.
594. *Diurnal . . . volúble*: In a day . . . moving quickly on its axis.
600. *accompanied*: (1) Joined the company; (2) played a musical accompaniment.
605. *Hesperus*: Venus, the evening star.
608. *Apparent*: Plainly seen (with a play on 'heir apparent').
628. *manuring*: Gardening (literally 'working with the hands').
640. *seasons*: Times of day.
642. *charm*: Blended singing of many birds.

668. *kindly*: (1) Natural; (2) benign.

669. *foment*: Cherish with heat.

676. *want . . . want*: Lack . . . lack.

685. *rounding*: (1) Walking the rounds; (2) singing 'rounds' (*each to other's note*).

688. *Divide*: (1) Into watches; (2) perform musical 'divisions'.

699. *flourished*: Adorned with flowers.

703. *emblem*: (1) Inlaid ornament; (2) symbolic image.

707–8. *Pan or Sylvanus . . . Faunus*: Fertility gods (half man, half goat).

711. *hymenean*: Wedding hymn (Hymen being god of marriage).

712. *genial*: Presiding over marriage.

714. *Pandora*: Literally 'All gifts': the first woman, made by the gods and given to Epimetheus, brother of Prometheus, who had angered Jove by stealing fire from heaven. She came with a sealed jar containing the world's ills, which were released when either Epimetheus or Pandora (sources vary) opened it.

717. *Japhet*: Noah's son, commonly identified with Iapetos, father of Epimetheus.

719. *authentic*: Original, prototypical.

730. *wants*: Lacks.

743. *Mysterious*: Sacred (marriage as 'a great mystery', Eph. 5: 32).

751. *propriety*: Exclusive possession.

763. *Love*: Cupid, whose golden arrows (*shafts*) kindled love.

769. *starved*: (1) Starved of love; (2) benumbed with cold.

773. *repaired*: Replaced.

776. *shadowy cone*: The earth's shadow. When it is *Half way* between horizon and zenith, the time is 9 p.m.

777. *sublunar*: Beneath the moon.

778. *ivory port*: Ivory gate (the source of false dreams in Homer and Virgil).

791. *secure of*: Unsuspecting.

793. *Who*: One who.

809. *conceits*: Notions. The context (*Blown up, engend'ring*) also suggests sexual conception.

815. *Lights*: (1) Alights; (2) kindles; *nitrous powder*: Gunpowder.

856. *Single*: (1) In single combat; (2) honestly upright.

896. *object*: Put forward as an objection.

899. *durance*: (1) Imprisonment; (2) continuance (a mocking pun on *stay*).

911. *However*: In any way he can.

918. *all Hell broke loose*: Already proverbial.

939. *afflicted powers*: Downcast armies.
945. *distances*: (1) Deferential (from God's throne); (2) cowardly (from battle).
962. *aread . . . avaunt*: Advise . . . begone.
971. *limitary*: (1) Guarding the boundaries; (2) limited in power.
976. *progress*: Royal procession.
980. *ported*: Pointed towards him (not to be confused with the modern 'port arms').
981. *Ceres*: Roman goddess of grain (here, the grain itself).
983. *careful . . . doubting*: Anxious . . . fearing.
985. *alarmed*: Called to arms.
987. *unremoved*: Irremovable (see above, note to IV, 493).
997. *Scales*: Libra. In pagan epics, Zeus weighs the fates of mortal heroes about to fight.
998. *Astraea*: Goddess of justice, stellified as Virgo at the end of the Golden Age.
1001. *ponders*: (1) Weighs; (2) considers.

BOOK IX

2.   *familiar*: (1) On a family footing; (2) as a familiar (guardian) angel.
5.   *Venial*: (1) Permissible; (2) gracious (Latin *venialis*); *unblamed*: Irreproachable. See note to IV, 493.
13.   *argument*: Subject-matter.
14–15. *wrath . . . Achilles*: Homer's subject in the *Iliad* (1.1).
17.   *Turnus*: Made war on the Trojans when Aeneas married Lavinia, Turnus's betrothed.
19.   *Greek*: Odysseus, persecuted (*perplexed*) by Poseidon (*Neptune*) in the *Odyssey*; *Cytherea's son*: Aeneas, son of Venus, persecuted by Juno in the *Aeneid*.
29.   *dissect*: (1) Examine minutely; (2) cut to pieces.
35.   *Impreses quaint, caparisons*: heraldic devices and armour for horses.
36.   *Bases*: Ornamental covering for horses.
38.   *sewers, and seneschals*: Ushers and stewards.
45.   *intended*: (1) Purposed; (2) outstretched (wing).
54.   *improved*: Augmented (in evil).
56.   *maugre*: Despite.
64.   *equinoctial line*: The equator.
66.   *colure*: One of two circles intersecting at right angles at the poles.
77.   *Pontus*: The Black Sea.
78.   *Maeotis*: The Sea of Azov. The *river Ob* is in Siberia.

80. *Orontes*: A river in Syria.

81. *Darien*: The Isthmus of Panama.

89. *imp*: (1) Child of the Devil; (2) grafted scion (implying that evil will grow).

90. *suggestions*: Temptations.

112. *gradual*: Graduated, in steps.

120-21. *siege / Of contraries*: The *Pleasures* besiege Satan's *Torment*, their contrary.

145. *virtue*: Power.

166. *incarnate*: Satan's parody of the Incarnation.

186. *nocent*: Harmful (the opposite of innocent).

191. *close*: (1) Concealed; (2) confined.

197. *grateful*: (1) Pleasing; (2) full of gratitude.

200. *prime*: (1) Best; (2) sunrise; (3) springtime; *airs*: (1) Breezes; (2) melodies.

265. *Or*: Whether.

270. *virgin*: Innocent. Puritans extended the term 'virginity' to marriage.

292. *entire*: Unblemished.

293. *diffident*: Mistrustful.

310. *Access*: Increase.

325. *like*: (1) Equal to Satan's attack; (2) equal to each other.

326. *still*: Always.

328. *affronts*: (1) Insults; (2) faces defiantly (punning with *front*, I, 330, which means 'face').

329. *integrity*: (1) Sinlessness; (2) undivided state (which Eve herself wants to divide).

334. *event*: Outcome.

341. *no Eden*: Literally 'no delight'.

353. *still erect*: (1) Always alert; (2) always upright.

358. *mind . . . mind*: Remind . . . pay heed to.

367. *approve*: Prove.

371. *securer*: Overconfident.

386. *light*: (1) light-footed; (2) fickle, ready of belief.

387. *Oread or Dryad*: Mountain- or wood-nymph; *Delia*: Diana, goddess of hunting.

392. *Guiltless of fire*: Fire was unknown before the Fall (see X, 1070-80). Milton also alludes to Prometheus, who stole fire from heaven (see IV, 715-19).

393. *Pales*: Goddess of flocks and pastures; *Pomona*: Goddess of fruit-trees. Vertumnus seduced her after accosting her in many disguises.

394. *Likeliest*] *1674*; Likest *1667*: Both words mean 'most resembling', but 'likeliest' is enhanced by a number of puns: (1) most seemly; (2) most beautiful; (3) most giving promise of success. All of these senses reflect well on Eve.

405. *event perverse*: Opposite outcome.

413. *Mere*: Entirely.

436. *voluble*: Gliding, undulating (with proleptic suggestions of fluent speech).

439–40. *gardens ... revived Adonis*: Gardens of Adonis were small plots of fast-fading flowers set around his image.

441. *Laertes' son*: Odysseus. He visits the gardens of *Alcinous* in *Odyssey*, 7, 112–35.

442. *mystic ... sapient king*: mythical ... Solomon.

443. *Egyptian spouse*: Solomon married Pharaoh's daughter (I Kings 3: 1).

446. *annoy*: Make noisome.

450. *tedded*: Spread out to dry (as hay); *kine*: Cattle.

465. *Stupidly*: In a stupor.

471. *recollects*: (1) Remembers; (2) summons by effort.

472. *gratulating*: Hailing, greeting (his own *thoughts*).

485. *terrestrial mould*: (1) Bodily form pertaining to this world; (2) earthy clay.

500. *carbuncle*: A mythical gem said to emit a red light in the dark.

501. *erect*: (1) Upright; (2) alert.

502. *spires*: Coils.

503. *redundant*: (1) In waves; (2) copious.

506. *Cadmus*: Legendary founder of Thebes. He and his wife *Hermione* were changed into serpents in their old age.

507. *Epidaurus*: Aesculapius, god of healing, had a temple in Epidaurus from which he travelled in serpent form to end a plague in Rome.

509. *Olympias*: Mother of Alexander the Great. Her husband, Philip II, found her in bed with a snake. The Delphic oracle identified the snake as Zeus-Ammon.

510. *Scipio*: Roman general who defeated Hannibal. Jupiter Capitolinus was said to have fathered him in the form of a serpent.

522. *Circean*: The witch Circe changed men into fawning beasts.

530. *Organic*: Serving as an instrument (of speech); *impulse*: (1) Impelling (of air); (2) suggestion from an evil spirit.

549. *glozed*: Flattered.

558. *demur*: Hesitate about.

580. *Grateful*: Pleasing.

581–3. *sweetest fennel* ... *milk at ev'n*: Snakes were said to be fond of fennel, and of milk sucked from the teat.

601. *Wanted*: Were lacking.

605. *middle*: The air between *heaven* and *earth*.

613. *spirited*: (1) Lively; (2) possessed by an evil spirit.

616. *virtue*: Efficacy.

623. *provision*: What is provided for them.

624. *her bearth*: What she bears.

629. *blowing*: Blooming.

635. *Compact of unctuous vapour*: Composed of oily gas.

637. *agitation*: (1) Friction (of gases); (2) scheming (*OED* 6).

648. *to excess*: (1) In abundance; (2) leading to sinful excess.

668. *Fluctuates*: Moves like a wave.

680. *science*: Knowledge.

687. *To*: (1) In addition to; (2) eventuating in.

694. *virtue*: Courage (which Satan identifies with moral virtue).

695. *denounced*: Threatened.

732. *humane*: (1) Benevolent; (2) human.

771. *author unsuspect*: Trustworthy informant.

776. *cure*: Eve unwittingly puns on Latin *cura*, 'grief'.

792. *knew not eating death*: (1) Did not die while she ate; (2) did not know she was eating death (a Greek construction); (3) did not know death, which devours (Latin *mors edax*).

797. *sapience*: (1) Knowledge; (2) taste (Latin *sapere*, 'to taste,' 'to know').

832. *all deaths*: Eve's plural ominously anticipates damnation, the 'Second Death'.

837. *sciential sap*: Knowledge-producing juice (with another pun on *sapere*).

845. *divine of*: Divining (with a wry pun on the divinity Eve has not got).

846. *falt'ring measure*: (1) Of Adam's heart; (2) of Nature. Early editions spell 'fault'ring'.

854. *apology*: Justification, excuse (not regret).

887. *distemper*: (1) Imbalance of humours; (2) intoxication.

890. *Astonied*: Stunned ('as stone'); *blank*: (1) Speechless; (2) pale.

901. *devote*: Doomed.

928. *fact*: (1) Deed; (2) crime (the commonest seventeenth-century sense).

953. *Certain*: Determined, resolved (Latin *certus*).

980. *oblige*: (1) Morally obligate; (2) make guilty; *fact*: (1) Deed; (2) crime.

984. *event*: Outcome.

994–5. *recompense . . . recompense*: Compensation for loss . . . retribution for crime. Adam will soon cry: 'is this the recompense?' (IX, 1163).

1019. *savour*: (1) Tastiness; (2) perception. Like *sapience, savour* derives from *sapere* (see note to 797).

1021. *purveyed*: Provided foodstuffs.

1027. *play*: Sport amorously, have sex.

1028. *meet*: (1) Appropriate; (2) sexual 'meat'. Contrast Eve as a 'help meet' (Gen. 2:21).

1034. *toy*: Caress.

1050. *unkindly*: Unnatural; *conscious*: Guilty.

1078. *evil store*: Evil in abundance.

1087. *umbrage*: (1) Foliage; (2) protective screen; (3) false show.

1091. *plight*: (1) Peril; (2) sin, offence; (3) clothing.

1094. *obnoxious*: (1) Exposed; (2) objectionable.

1111. *targe*: Shield.

1132. *estranged*: (1) Unlike himself; (2) alienated (from Eve).

1140. *approve*: Prove.

1141. *owe*: (1) Owe; (2) own (and so have no need to prove).

1164. *expressed*: (1) Declared (Eve's love for Adam); (2) manifested in action (Adam's for Eve).

1175. *secure*: Overconfident, careless.

PARADISE REGAINED

Dated 1667–70. *PR* was printed in 1671 in a volume that included *SA*. Milton's nephew, Edward Phillips, records that it 'was begun and finisht and Printed after the other [*PL*] was publisht, and that in a wonderful short space considering the sublimeness of it' (Darbishire (ed.), *Early Lives of Milton*, p. 75). Thomas Ellwood, who was Milton's pupil in the early 1660s, claims to have played some part in the poem's conception (see Introduction, p. xxxii). The plot of *PR* is based upon the Gospels account of Christ's Temptation in the wilderness. Milton follows Luke 4: 1–13 in the order of temptations, but he follows Matt. 4: 1–11 in placing the temptations after Christ's forty-day fast. In Luke, Christ is tempted for forty days.

THE FIRST BOOK

8. *eremite*: Desert-dweller.
14. *full summed*: In full plumage (a term from falconry).
16. *unrecorded*: Unsung (in poetry).
334. *fame*: Rumour.
337. *swain*: Rustic.
363. *unconniving*: Unwinking (Latin *inconivus*). Satan also hints that God connives at his crimes.
369. *Uzzéan*: From Uz.
370. *illústrate*: Render illustrious.
385. *attent*: Attentively.
393. *disposer*: Ruler.
427. *other service*: Satan's deception of Ahab (see 372–6).
447. *president*: Presiding.
452. *parasite*: Including the original Greek sense: 'one admitted to a temple after a sacrifice'.
458. *Delphos*: Delphi, site of Apollo's oracle.
460. *Oracle*: Divine teacher (*OED*), Jesus as Word (from Latin *orare*, 'to speak').
485. *attain*: (1) Attain [Salvation]; (2) detect [Jesus] in an offence (OED 'attain' 3); (3) attaint.
494. *scope*: Aim, purpose.

THE SECOND BOOK

116. *vacant*: At leisure.
120. *Solicitous and blank*: Anxious and nonplussed.
130. *frequence*: Assembly.
131. *tasted*: Made trial of.
151. *Asmodai*: The lecherous devil of the apocryphal book of Tobit. See *PL*, IV, 168–71.
152. *incubus*: A devil that had sex with women while they slept.
168. *magnetic*: Magnet.
178–81. *Before the Flood ... begat a race*: Milton here follows a patristic tradition identifying the lustful sons of God of Genesis 6 with fallen angels.
196. *Pelléan conqueror*: Alexander the Great, from Pella in Macedon.
198. *slightly*: Indifferently.
199. *he surnamed of Africa*: Scipio Africanus.
211. *fond*: (1) Loving; (2) foolish.
214. *zone*: Girdle.

344. *Grisamber*: Ambergris, an intestinal secretion of the sperm whale, used in cooking.

347. *Pontus*: The Black Sea; *Lucrine bay*: A lagoon near Naples, famous for oysters.

348. *cates*: Delicacies.

349. *crude*: (1) Uncooked; (2) sour; *diverted*: (1) Pleased; (2) turned awry.

353. *Ganymede*: The beautiful Trojan boy abducted by Jove to be his cup-bearer. The name was a byword for homosexual love. *Hylas*: A beautiful youth loved by Hercules.

355. *Naiades*: Fresh-water nymphs.

356. *Amalthea's horn*: The horn of plenty.

360. *Logres ... Lyonesse*: Regions of Arthurian Britain.

361. *Lancelot ... Pellenore*: Arthurian knights.

365. *Flora*: Roman goddess of flowers and springtime.

368. *What doubts*: Why fears.

370. *Defends*: Forbids.

THE THIRD BOOK

255. *two rivers*: Tigris and Euphrates.

257. *champaign with less rivers*: Open country (Mesopotamia) with tributaries.

259. *glebe*: Soil.

271. *Araxes*: Aras, a river flowing through Armenia into the Caspian Sea.

274. *drouth*: Desert.

276. *Ninus*: Eponymous founder of Nineveh and King of Assyria.

278. *Salmanassar*: Assyrian king who led the ten tribes of Israel into captivity in 726 BC.

280. *wonder of all tongues*: A pun. Babylon was often identified with Babel.

281. *him*: Nebuchadnezzar, Babylonian king who conquered Jerusalem.

284. *Cyrus*: Founder of the Persian Empire. He conquered Babylon in 538 BC and freed the Jews.

287. *Hecatompylos*: The Parthian capital (Greek, 'hundred gates').

290. *Emathian*: Macedonian.

292. *Ctesiphon*: The winter capital of the Parthian kings.

306. *dread in flight*: Parthian mounted archers would shoot to the rear while feigning retreat.

329. *endorsed*: Carrying on their backs.

338. *Agrican*: Tartar king who leads an army of 2,200,000 in Boiardo's *Orlando Innamorato*.
342. *prowest*: Most valiant.
343. *paynim*: Pagan.
347. *engage*: (1) Exhort; (2) ensnare. The double negative (*not . . . on no*) admits a Satanic ambiguity as to how much protection Satan is really offering.
358. *opposite*: Opposing, resisting.
368. *Maugre*: Despite.

THE FOURTH BOOK

16. *must*: Unfermented wine.
23. *desperate*: Despairing.
31. *Septentrion*: Northern.
40. *parallax*: Apparent change in position of an object.
63. *Praetors*: Magistrates acting as provincial governors.
65. *Lictors*: Attendants who walked before a Roman magistrate, carrying *fasces* (*rods*) as symbols (*ensigns*) of the magistrate's power.
66. *turms*: troops of cavalry, about thirty in number. One turm (Latin *turma*) was the tenth part of a wing.
68. *Appian road*: Rome's principal road to southern Italy.
69. *Aemilian*: Road leading north from Rome.
70. *Syene*: Aswan in Egypt, southern limit of the Roman Empire.
72. *realm of Bocchus*: Ancient Mauretania. Bocchus had been one of its kings.
74. *golden Chersoness*: The Malay peninsula.
76. *Gallia, Gades*: Gaul, Cadiz.
79. *Tauric pool*: Sea of Azov.
90. *Emperor*: Tiberius. He had retired on the isle of Capri in AD 26.
95. *favourite*: Sejanus. He was executed in AD 31 after Tiberius denounced him to the Senate.
115. *citron tables or Atlantic stone*: Citrus wood (famed for its beautiful grain), or stone from the Atlas mountains.
119. *myrrhine*: Chinese porcelain imported from Parthia.
141. *Luxurious*: Voluptuous.
142. *scene*: Theatre.
147-9. *a tree . . . a stone*: Jesus is referring to Nebuchadnezzar's dream, which Christian exegetes interpreted as a prophecy of Christ's Church.
157. *nice*: Fastidious.

201. *Tetrarchs*: Rulers of a fourth part.
226. *Pentateuch*: The first five books of the Bible.
234. *idolisms*: Fallacies.
235. *evinced*: Confuted.
245. *Attic bird*: Nightingale.
251. *who*: Aristotle.
253. *Lyceum*: A grove and gymnasium near Athens, where Aristotle taught; *Stoa*: A colonnade in Athens, where Zeno taught (hence 'Stoic').
262. *iambic*: The metre of dialogue in Greek tragedy.
270. *Shook the Arsenal*: Caused the dockyards to reverberate with *fulmined* (thundered) oratory.
271. *Artaxerxes*: The name borne by several Persian kings hostile to Athens.
293. *the first*: Socrates.
295. *The next*: Plato.
296. *A third sort*: The Sceptics, who held that knowledge was unattainable.
297. *Others*: The Peripatetics, followers of Aristotle.
299. *he*: Epicurus, who was reviled by Stoics and Christians for valuing pleasure.
308. *conviction*: (1) Confutation; (2) consciousness of sin.
321. *An empty cloud*: Alluding to Ixion, who embraced a cloud instead of Juno.
328. *Crude*: Lacking power to digest.
329. *worth a sponge*: (1) Worth very little; (2) worthy of being obliterated.
334. *story*: History.
335. *artful terms*: Artistic figures of speech.
354. *statists*: Statesmen.
377. *Nicely*: Fastidiously.
384. *Voluminous, or single characters*: Satan likens the stars to a large book (*Voluminous*) and single letters (*characters*).
387. *Attends*: Are in store for.
393. *rubric*: Chapter-title (continuing the book metaphor).
400. *mere*: Absolute, entire.
402. *jaunt*: Fatiguing journey.
409. *either tropic*: The northern (Cancer) and southern (Capricorn) skies.
413. *ruin*: (1) Falling; (2) destruction.
419. *shrouded*: Sheltered.
427. *amice*: Hood lined with grey fur.

446. *despite*: Hatred, spite.

454. *flaws*: Squalls.

457. *main*: Universe.

529. *composition*: Truce.

542. *hippogriff*: Fabulous creature (half horse, half griffin) on which Ariosto's heroes fly.

554. *progeny*: Parentage.

565. *Alcides*: Hercules. He killed *Antaeus*, who grew stronger each time he touched the earth, by throttling him in the air. Satan is 'prince of the power of the air' (Eph. 2: 2).

569. *foil*: Including 'throw not resulting in a flat fall' (wrestling term).

572. *Theban monster*: The sphinx. She killed herself when Oedipus answered her riddle.

605. *debel*: Vanquish.

624. *Abaddon*: Hell.

628. *possession*: (1) Military (of *holds*); (2) demonic (of people and swine).

SAMSON AGONISTES

SA appeared in 1671, in the same volume as *PR*. The date of composition is not known, and Milton's nephew Edward Phillips says that it 'cannot certainly be concluded' (Darbishire (ed.), *Early Lives of Milton*, p. 75). The traditional dating is 1666–70, but some critics have argued for the late 1640s or early 1650s. Some parts were almost certainly written after the Restoration, for they have a strong topical relevance (see especially lines 678–704).

Preface: Of that Sort of Dramatic Poem . . .

13–14. *a verse of Euripides*: 'Evil communications corrupt good manners', quoted by St Paul from a fragment anciently attributed to the tragic poet Euripides.

15. *Paraeus*: David Paraeus (1548–1622), German Calvinist.

19. *Dionysius*: Dionysius I of Syracuse (*c.* 430–367 BC, tyrant from 405) wrote a tragedy that was awarded first prize in the Athenian competition.

21. *Augustus*: Suetonius reports that he destroyed his unfinished tragedy *Ajax*.

23. *Seneca*: Milton is correct in his surmise that Seneca the Stoic philosopher (4 BC–AD 65) was the same person as Seneca the tragic poet.

25. *Gregory Nazianzen*: Bishop of Constantinople (329–89), supposed author of *Christ Suffering*.

36. *Martial*: Roman poet (*c.* 40–104) who prefaced several of his *Epigrams* with prose epistles.

45. *apolelymenon*: 'Freed' (from regular stanzaic patterns).

49. *alloeostropha*: Irregular strophes.

54. *explicit*: Simple.

60. *circumscription of time*: Aristotle's 'unity of time', whereby the action of a tragedy is confined to one day. Renaissance theorists hardened this into a *rule*.

The Argument

24. *catastrophe*: The 'overturning' that produces the conclusion of a drama.

25. *by accident*: As a secondary effect (as in Latin *per accidens*). Milton may want to remove the suspicion that Samson committed the sin of suicide.

9. *draught*: Inhaled air.

13. *Dagon*: Chief Philistine god, 'upward man / And downward fish' (*PL*, I, 462–3).

31. *separate*: 'Nazarite' derives from Hebrew *nazar*, 'to separate oneself'.

38. *Promise*: See Judges 13:5: 'he shall begin to deliver Israel'.

55. *secure*: Overconfident.

77. *still*: Invariably.

87. *silent*: 'Of the moon: not shining' (*OED*, first instance 1646).

89. *vacant*: At leisure.

95. *obvious*: Exposed.

106. *obnoxious*: Liable to injury.

118. *diffused*: Sprawled.

131. *forgery*: (1) Forged metal; (2) counterfeit (unlike Samson's authentic strength).

133. *Chalybean*: The Chalybes were a Black Sea tribe of metalworkers.

134. *Adamantean proof*: Armour as strong as adamant (diamond).

136. *insupportably*: Irresistibly.

139. *ramp*: Lions 'ramped' by raising their forepaws in the air (a threatening posture).

144. *foreskins*: Uncircumcised Philistines. Israelites did collect foreskins as military trophies.

147. *Azza*: Gaza. See Judges 16: 3 for Samson's lifting of the gates.

150. *whom*: The Titan Atlas.
163. *visual beam*: Renaissance science held that eyes saw by emitting a beam.
185. *tumours*: 'Swellings' of passion.
190. *superscription*: Stamp on a coin.
209. *transverse*: Off course (continuing the nautical metaphor).
210. *Tax*: Blame.
216. *Philistian women*: Samson's first wife was a Philistine (Judges 14:1). Milton assumes that Dalila was also a Philistine and Samson's wife, but the Bible never says so.
222. *motioned*: Proposed. Compare Samson's 'rousing motions' (1382).
223. *impúlse*: Suggestion from a good (or evil) spirit.
230. *specious*: Deceptively attractive.
235. *peal*: (1) Appeal; (2) guns fired in salute (notice *fort* in 236).
247. *ambition*: Self-advertising, solicitation of applause (Latin *ambitio*).
266. *by this*: By now.
282–9. *Ephraim . . . Shibboleth*: Judges 11 and 12.
291. *mine*: My people.
295. *think not God*: Think there is no God.
299. *doctor*: Teacher, learned divine.
305. *ravel*: (1) Inquire; (2) become entangled.
312. *obstriction*: Obligation (not to marry Gentiles). Milton's coinage (from Latin *obstrictionem*).
327. *careful*: Anxious, troubled.
333. *uncouth*: Unfamiliar.
373. *Appoint*: (1) Find fault with; (2) presume to control.
377. *profaned*: Disclosed (Latin *profanus*, 'outside the temple').
384. *secret*: Samson's riddle of the lion and the honeycomb (Judges 14).
394. *capital*: (1) Most important; (2) fatal; (3) pertaining to the head (Latin *caput*).
405. *over-watched*: (1) Exhausted from staying awake; (2) watched over (by Dalila).
424. *state*: Have an opinion about.
433. *score*: Debt.
454. *diffidence*: Distrust.
466. *connive*: Remain inactive, close his eyes to (Latin *conniveo*).
471. *blank*: Nonplus, 'shut up' (*OED*).
493. *fact*: Evil deed.
496. *front*: Forehead.

526. *instinct*: Prompting, as in 'instincts and strong motions from God' (*OED*, 1633).

528. *sons of Anak*: Giants. See Numbers 13.

533. *venereal trains*: Sexual snares.

538. *wether*: Castrated ram.

541–6. *Desire of wine ... stream*: As a Nazarite, Samson abstained from wine and strong drink.

557. *liquid*: Transparent.

560. *boots*: Avails.

568. *redundant*: (1) Flowing; (2) useless.

571. *craze*: Render decrepit.

574. *draff*: Refuse, pig-swill.

594. *genial spirits*: Vital energy, will to live.

600. *humours black*: Melancholy, black bile.

609. *reins*: Kidneys.

612. *accidents*: Medical symptoms.

622. *mortification*: Gangrene, necrosis.

624. *apprehensive*: Conscious, perceptive.

625. *exulcerate*: Cause ulcers.

639. *nerve*: Strength.

651. *balm*: (1) Ointment for soothing pain; (2) ointment for embalming the dead.

659. *Lenient of*: Soothing to.

678–704. *But such as thou ... both come to evil end*: These lines have often been read as a covert allusion to the treatment of Commonwealth leaders (living and dead) after the Restoration.

700. *crude*: Premature.

714–15. *ship / Of Tarsus*: The common Old Testament phrase 'ships of Tarshish' signifies vanity.

716. *Javan or Gadire*: Aegean isles or Cadiz.

719. *hold them play*: Keep them moving.

720. *amber*: Ambergris (whale dung used as the basis of perfume).

736. *fact*: Evil deed (her betrayal).

737. *perverse event*: Unexpected outcome.

748. *hyena*: Proverbial for deceitfulness.

769. *aggravations*: Exaggerations.

803. *made for me*: (1) Counted with me; (2) worked to my advantage.

812. *fond*: Foolish.

897. *acquit themselves*: Perform the offices of their position.

906. *worried*: Pestered.

913. *sensibly*: Acutely.

926. *grateful*: Pleasing.

932–3. *trains . . . gins . . . toils*: All words for snares.

936. *adder's wisdom*: Deafness. See Psalm 58: 4–5.

950. *To*: Compared to.

989–90. *Jael . . . temples nailed*: Having lured Sisera into her tent, Jael drove a nail through his head (Judges 4: 17–21).

1000. *aggravate*: Make more grievous, add to the weight of.

1012. *inherit*: Possess.

1016. *riddle*: Judges 14: 8–14.

1020. *paranymph*: 'Best man'. In Judges 14: 20 Samson's first wife is 'given to his companion'.

1022. *both*: Both wives.

1030. *affect*: Be drawn to, prefer.

1038. *Intestine*: (1) Domestic; (2) internal (a 'thorn in the side').

1039. *cleaving*: (1) Clinging; (2) separating.

1062. *contracted*: Ended with.

1068. *Harapha*: No such character appears in Judges. The name is Hebrew for 'the giant'.

1075. *fraught*: Cargo of a ship (continuing the nautical metaphor).

1080. *Og or Anak and the Emims*: Biblical giants.

1087. *camp or listed field*: Pitched battle (Latin *campus*) or tournament.

1092. *single*: Challenge to single combat.

1093. *Gyves*: Fetters.

1109. *assassinated*: Wounded by treachery.

1113. *close-banded*: (1) Secretly banded; (2) fighting at close quarters.

1120. *brigandine . . . habergeon*: Body armour . . . chain mail.

1121. *Vant-brace*: Armour for the forearm.

1122. *weaver's beam*: Roller on a loom. Goliath's spear was 'like a weaver's beam' (I Sam. 17: 7).

1138. *ruffled*: (1) Angered; (2) stiffened (quills).

1164. *boist'rous*: Coarse-growing.

1169. *thine*: Thy people.

1195. *politician*: Craftily plotting.

1197. *await*: (1) Wait upon; (2) watch stealthily.

1220. *appellant*: Challenger to single combat.

1237. *baffled*: Disgraced. A knight who had been 'baffled' could never again fight a duel.

1243. *braveries*: Boasts.

1249. *Goliah*: Goliath is son 'of the giant' (Hebrew *ha rapha*) in II Sam. 21: 19–22.

1263. *rid*: (1) Kill; (2) set free.

1287. *patience*: Suffering.

1303. *quaint*: Skilfully made.

1307. *voluble*: Fluent.

1309. *remark him*: Mark him out.

1325. *antics*: Clowns.

1342. *Joined*: Enjoined.

1377. *dispense with me*: Make me exempt from his law.

1382. *motions*: Workings of God in the soul.

1410. *resolution*: Decision (to comply).

1507. *next*: Next of kin (as Danites).

1515. *ruin*: Collapse, fall.

1529. *dole*: (1) Dealing of blows; (2) that which is charitably dealt out.

1538. *baits*: Delays (at an inn, to feed the horses).

1543. *erst*: Just now.

1567. *irruption*: Bursting in.

1574. *windy*: Vain, empty.

1608. *sort*: High rank.

1610. *banks*: Benches.

1619. *cataphracts*: Heavy cavalry.

1659. *vulgar*: The common people. Judges 16: 27–30 places them on and under the roof. Miltan spares them by placing them in an open area (see 1609–10).

1669. *sublime*: Elated.

1692. *dragon*: Large snake.

1693. *perchèd*: Furnished with perches.

1695. *villatic*: Farmyard (adj.).

1699. *self-begotten bird*: The phoenix (reborn from its own ashes).

1700. *embossed*: Hidden in a wood.

1702. *holocaust*: Consumed by fire.

1707. *secular*: Living for ages.

1709. *quit himself*: (1) Borne himself; (2) quit his life.

1713. *Caphtor*: Ancestral home of the Philistines (thought to be Crete).

1737. *legend*: Inscription.

1751. *in place*: Here.

1755. *acquist*: Acquisition.

Index of Titles

Index of First Lines

PENGUIN CLASSICS

DON JUAN
LORD BYRON

'Let us have wine and women's mirth and laughter,
Sermons and soda water the day after'

Byron's exuberant parody involves the adventures of a youth named Don Juan.
His exploits include an adulterous liaison in Spain, an affair on a Greek island
with a pirate's daughter, a stay in a Sultan's harem, a bloody battle in Turkey and
a sojourn in Russia as the lover of Catherine the Great – all described by a
narrator who frequently digresses from his hero in order to converse with his
readers about war, society and convention. A revolutionary experiment in epic,
Don Juan blends high drama with earthy humour, outrageous satire of Byron's
contemporaries (in particular Wordsworth and Southey) and mockery of Western
culture, with England under particular attack.

This edition represents a significant contribution to Byron scholarship and the
editors have drawn on their authoritative edition of the poem published by the
University of Texas Press. Their extensive annotation covers points of interest,
selected variant readings and historical allusions Byron wove into his poem.
This edition also includes an illuminating new introduction by Susan J. Wolfson
and Peter J. Manning, and updated further reading.

Edited by T. G. Steffan, E. Steffan and W. W. Pratt

With a new introduction by Susan J. Wolfson and Peter J. Manning

Penguin Classics

THE COMPLETE POEMS
ANDREW MARVELL

'Thus, though we cannot make our sun
Stand still, yet we will make him run'

Member of Parliament, tutor to Oliver Cromwell's ward, satirist and friend of
John Milton, Andrew Marvell was one of the most significant poets of the
seventeenth century. *The Complete Poems* demonstrates his unique skill and
immense diversity, and includes lyrical love-poetry, religious works and biting
satire. From the passionately erotic 'To his Coy Mistress', to the astutely political
Cromwellian poems and the prescient 'Garden' and 'Mower' poems, which
consider humankind's relationship with the environment, these works are
masterpieces of clarity and metaphysical imagery. Eloquent and compelling, they
remain among the most vital and profound works of the era – works by a figure
who, in the words of T. S. Eliot, 'speaks clearly and unequivocally with the voice
of his literary age'.

This edition of Marvell's complete poems is based on a detailed study of the extant
manuscripts, with modern translations provided for Marvell's Greek and Latin
poems. This edition also includes a chronology, further reading, appendices, notes
and indexes of titles and first lines, with a new introduction by Jonathan Bate.

Edited by Elizabeth Story Donno

With an introduction by Jonathan Bate

PENGUIN CLASSICS

THE NEW PENGUIN BOOK OF ROMANTIC POETRY

'And what if all of animated Nature
Be but organic harps, diversely framed'

The Romanticism that emerged after the American and French revolutions of 1776 and 1789 represented a new flowering of the imagination and the spirit, and a celebration of the soul of humanity with its capacity for love. This extraordinary collection sets the acknowledged genius of poems such as Blake's 'Tyger', Coleridge's 'Khubla Khan' and Shelley's 'Ozymandias' alongside verse from less familiar figures and women poets such as Charlotte Smith and Mary Robinson. We also see familiar poets in an unaccustomed light, as Blake, Wordsworth and Shelley demonstrate their comic skills, while Coleridge, Keats and Clare explore the Gothic and surreal.

This volume is arranged by theme and genre, revealing unexpected connections between the poets. In their introduction Jonathan and Jessica Wordsworth explore Romanticism as a way of responding to the world, and they begin each section with a helpful preface, notes and bibliography.

'An absolutely fascinating selection – notable for its women poets, its intriguing thematic categories and its helpful mini biographies' Richard Holmes

Edited with an introduction by Jonathan and Jessica Wordsworth

THE STORY OF PENGUIN CLASSICS

Before 1946 ... 'Classics' are mainly the domain of academics and students; readable editions for everyone else are almost unheard of. This all changes when a little-known classicist, E. V. Rieu, presents Penguin founder Allen Lane with the translation of Homer's *Odyssey* that he has been working on in his spare time.

1946 Penguin Classics debuts with *The Odyssey*, which promptly sells three million copies. Suddenly, classics are no longer for the privileged few.

1950s Rieu, now series editor, turns to professional writers for the best modern, readable translations, including Dorothy L. Sayers's *Inferno* and Robert Graves's unexpurgated *Twelve Caesars*.

1960s The Classics are given the distinctive black covers that have remained a constant throughout the life of the series. Rieu retires in 1964, hailing the Penguin Classics list as 'the greatest educative force of the twentieth century.'

1970s A new generation of translators swells the Penguin Classics ranks, introducing readers of English to classics of world literature from more than twenty languages. The list grows to encompass more history, philosophy, science, religion and politics.

1980s The Penguin American Library launches with titles such as *Uncle Tom's Cabin*, and joins forces with Penguin Classics to provide the most comprehensive library of world literature available from any paperback publisher.

1990s The launch of Penguin Audiobooks brings the classics to a listening audience for the first time, and in 1999 the worldwide launch of the Penguin Classics website extends their reach to the global online community.

The 21st Century Penguin Classics are completely redesigned for the first time in nearly twenty years. This world-famous series now consists of more than 1300 titles, making the widest range of the best books ever written available to millions – and constantly redefining what makes a 'classic'.

The Odyssey continues ...

The best books ever written

PENGUIN 🐧 CLASSICS

SINCE 1946

Find out more at www.penguinclassics.com